The Inner Journey
Views from the Gurdjieff Work

Series Editor: Ravi Ravindra
Associate Series Editor: Priscilla Murray

Titles in *The Inner Journey* series:
Views from the Buddhist Tradition
Views from the Christian Tradition
Views from the Gurdjieff Work
Views from the Hindu Tradition
Views from the Islamic Tradition
Views from the Jewish Tradition
Myth, Psyche & Spirit
Views from Native Traditions

The Inner Journey
Views from the Gurdjieff Work

Edited by Jacob Needleman

PARABOLA Anthology Series

MORNING LIGHT
P R E S S

MORNING LIGHT
P R E S S

Published by Morning Light Press 2008

Editor: Jacob Needleman
Series Editor: Ravi Ravindra
Associate Series Editor: Priscilla Murray

Copyright © 2008 Morning Light Press
Cover Photo Courtesy of the Gurdjieff Foundation of New York

Morning Light Press
10881 North Boyer Road
Sandpoint, ID 83864
morninglightpress.com
info@mlpress.com

Printed on acid-free paper in Canada.

Philosophy
SAN: 255-3252

Library of Congress Cataloging-in-Publication Data

The Inner Journey: Views from the Gurdjieff Work
Edited by Jacob Needleman.

p. cm. -- (Parabola Anthology Series)
ISBN-13: 978-1-59675-021-0 (alk. paper)
1. Gurdjieff, Georges Ivanovitch, 1872-1949. I. Needleman, Jacob.
BP605.G94G873 2007
197--dc22
2007041730

To the path makers
and the pilgrims on the path

General Introduction to
The Inner Journey: A Parabola Anthology Series

When *Parabola: Myth, Tradition, and the Search for Meaning* was launched in 1976, the founder, D. M. Dooling, wrote in her first editorial:

> *Parabola* has a conviction: that human existence is significant, that life essentially makes sense in spite of our confusions, that man is not here on earth by accident but for a purpose, and that whatever that purpose may be it demands from him the discovery of his own meaning, his own totality and identity. A human being is born to set out on this quest. … Every true teaching, every genuine tradition, has sought to train its disciples to act this part, to become in fact followers of the great quest for one's self.

For over thirty years, *Parabola* has honored the great wisdom traditions of every culture, turning to their past and present masters and practitioners for guidance in this quest. Recognizing that the aim of each tradition is the transformation of human life through practice supported by knowledge and understanding, *Parabola* on behalf of its readers has turned again and again to Buddhist and Christian monks, Sufi and Jewish teachers, Hindu scholars, and Native American and other indigenous peoples, evoking from each of them illumination and insight.

Over the years *Parabola*, in each of its issues, devoted to a central theme of the human condition as it is and as it might be, has gathered remarkable material. "The Call," "Awakening," "Food," "Initiation," "Dreams and Seeing," "Liberation," "The Mask," "Attention": in these and in scores of other issues, a facet of the essential search is explored, always with the aim of casting light on the way.

The purpose of the *Parabola Anthology Series* is to gather the material published in *Parabola* during its first thirty years in order to focus this light and to reflect the inner dimensions of each of these traditions. While every religious tradition has both external and inner aspects, the aim of each is the transformation of the whole being. The insights and understandings that ring true and carry the vibration of an inner meaning can provide guidance and support for our quest, but a mere mechanical repetition of forms which were once charged with great energy can take us away from the heart of the teaching. Every tradition must change and evolve; it has to be reinterpreted and reunderstood by successive generations in order to maintain its relevance and application.

Search carries a connotation of journey; we set out with the hope for new insight and experience. The aim of the spiritual or inner journey is transformation, to become more responsible and more compassionate as understanding and being grow. This demands an active undertaking, and insights from those who have traveled the path can provide a call, bring inspiration, and serve as a reminder of the need to search.

For this series, selections have been made from the material published in *Parabola* relating to each of the major traditions and teachings. Subtle truths are expressed in myths, poetry, stories, parables, and above all in the lives, actions, and expressions of those people who have been immersed in the teaching, have wrestled with it and have been informed and transformed by it. Some of these insights have been elicited through interviews with current practitioners of various teachings. Each of the great traditions is very large, and within each tradition there are distinct schools of thought, as well as many practices, rituals, and ceremonies. None of the volumes in the present series claims to be exhaustive of the whole tradition or to give a complete account of it.

In addition to the material that has been selected from the library of *Parabola* issues, the editor of each volume in the series provides an introduction to the teaching, a reminder of the heart of the tradition in the section, "The Call of the Tradition," as well as a list of books suggested for further study and reflection. It is the hope of the publishers and editors that this new series will surprise, challenge, and support those new to *Parabola* as well as its many readers.

—*Ravi Ravindra*

CONTENTS

The Call of the Tradition

Man's possibilities are very great. You cannot conceive
even a shadow of what man is capable of attaining.
But nothing can be attained in sleep.

In the consciousness of a sleeping man his illusions,
his 'dreams' are mixed with reality.
He lives in a subjective world and he can never escape from it.
And this is why he can never make use of all the powers
he possesses and why he always lives in only a small part of himself.

—Gurdjieff

Remember yourself always and everywhere.

—Gurdjieff

To a man who is searching with all his being,
with all his inner self, comes the unfailing
conviction that to find out how to know in order
to do is possible only by finding a guide
with experience and knowledge,
who will take on his spiritual guidance
and become his teacher.

And it is here that a man's flair is more important
than anywhere else. He chooses a guide for himself.
It is of course an indispensable condition
that he choose as a guide a man who knows,
or else all meaning of choice is lost. Who can tell where
a guide who does not know may lead a man? ...

Go out one clear starlit night to some open space and look up at the sky,
at those millions of worlds over your head.
Remember that perhaps on each of them swarm billions of beings,
similar to you or perhaps superior to you in their organization.
Look at the Milky Way. The earth cannot even
be called a grain of sand in this infinity.
It dissolves and vanishes, and with it, you.
Where are you? And is what you want simply madness?

Before all these worlds ask yourself what are your aims and hopes,
your intentions and means of fulfilling them,
the demands that may be made upon you and
your preparedness to meet them.

A long and difficult journey is before you …
Remember where you are and why you are here.
Do not protect yourselves and remember that no effort is made
in vain. And now you can set out on the way.

—Gurdjieff

Try for a moment to accept the idea that you are not what you
believe yourself to be, that you overestimate yourself,
in fact that you lie to yourself … That this lying rules you
to such an extent that you cannot control it any more …

But you never stop yourself in what you are doing
or in what you are saying because you believe in yourself.
You must stop inwardly and observe. Observe without
preconceptions, accepting for a time this idea of lying.
And if you observe in this way … without self-pity, giving
up all your supposed riches for a moment of reality, perhaps you
will suddenly see something you have never before seen in yourself

*until this day. You will see that you are two. One who is not,
but takes the place and plays the role of the other. And one who is,
yet so weak, so insubstantial, that he no sooner appears
than he immediately disappears. He cannot endure lies,
he is defeated in advance. Learn to look until you have seen
the difference between your two natures, until you have seen the lies,
the deception in yourself. When you have seen your two natures,
that day, in yourself, the truth will be born.*

—Gurdjieff

*Only he will be called and will become the Son of God who
acquires in himself conscience.*

—Gurdjieff

*It is in my essence that I may be reunited
with the one who sees. There, I would be at the source
of something unique and stable,
at the source of that which does not change.*

—Jeanne de Salzmann

The Inner Journey: Introduction

It has been nearly a hundred years since G. I. Gurdjieff first appeared in Moscow in 1912, bringing with him a teaching unlike anything known or heard of in the modern world. And although his ideas have since then been explored in hundreds of books and articles, and now exert a significant influence throughout the Western world, both the teaching and the man himself remain essentially as new and unknown, and as astonishing, as when they first appeared.

Gurdjieff's fundamental aim was to help human beings awaken to the meaning of our existence and to the efforts we must make to realize that meaning in the midst of the life we have been given. As with every messenger of the spirit, Gurdjieff's fundamental intention was ultimately for the sake of others, never only for himself. But when we first encounter the figure of Gurdjieff, this central aspect of his life is often missed. Faced with the depth of his ideas and the inner demands he placed upon himself and upon those who were drawn to him, and becoming aware of the uniquely effective forms of inner work he created, we may initially be struck mainly by the vastness of his knowledge and the strength of his being. But sooner or later what may begin to touch us is the unique quality of selflessness in his actions, the sacrifices he made, both for those who came to him and for all of humanity. We begin to understand that his life was a work of love; and at the same time that word, "love," begins to take on entirely new dimensions of meaning, inconceivable in the state of what Gurdjieff called *waking sleep*.

In most major cities of the Western world men and women are now trying to live his teaching. It is not too soon, therefore, to consider what this teaching has brought or can bring to the world. As human life in our era spirals downward toward dissolution in violence and illusion, one central question rises up before us in the shadow of which all teachings, including the Gurdjieff Work, must now be measured: How can humanity reverse the process leading to its seemingly inevitable self-destruction?

In the face of this question, the heart is restless, but the mind soon falls silent. It is as though the unprecedented crisis of our modern world confounds and all but refutes thousands of years of religious doctrine and centuries of scientific progress. Who now dreams of turning to religion for the answer when it is religion itself that lies so close to the root of war and barbarism? Who dares turn to science for the answer when it is advancing technology, the very fruit of scientific progress, that has so amplified the destructive powers of human egoism? And who imagines that new theories of society, new social programs, new ideologies can do anything more than wrap the falling earth in dreams of flying?

The mind falls silent. But in that silence something within can awaken. In that moment an entirely new kind of hope can appear. The Gurdjieff Work may in part be understood as the practical, painstaking cultivation of that silence and that hope, that state of embodied awakening to the truth of the human condition, in the world and in oneself. The unanswerable question about the fate of humanity and the world is transformed into the question, also unanswerable: What is a human being? Who am I? But it is now a question asked with more of oneself, not with the mind alone—the mind which, with all its explanations, has so little power to resist the forces of violence and brutality; nor with emotion alone, which with all its fervor often ends by making the most sacred of doctrines into instruments of agitation and death. Nor, so the Gurdjieff teaching also shows us, can the question of who and what we are be answered by giving way again and again to the endlessly recurring obsessions of the physical body alone. That is to say, the great question of who and what we are cannot be answered by only one part of the whole of ourselves pretending to be the master. This self-deceptive state of the human being is precisely what Gurdjieff meant by mankind's state of waking sleep. In this sleep, he tells us, we are born, live and die, write books, invent religions, build monuments, commit murders and destroy all that is good.

One thing, and one thing only, is therefore necessary. It is necessary for individual men and women to awaken, to remember Who they are, and then to become Who they really are, to live it in the service of Truth. Without this awakening and this becoming, nothing else can help us.

But it is very difficult. An extraordinary quality of help is needed. To this end, Gurdjieff created what has come to be called *the work*.

Concerning the aim of the present volume, it is instructive to turn to Jeanne de Salzmann's introduction to Gurdjieff's book, *Life Is Real Only Then, When "I Am,"* where, as Gurdjieff's chief pupil, she speaks of the instructions he gave her before he died. In response to the question of whether to publish his writings, he tells her:

> *Publish as and when you are sure that the time has come. ... But the essential thing, the first thing, is to prepare a nucleus of people capable of responding to the demand which will arise.*
>
> *So long as there is no responsible nucleus, the action of the ideas will not go beyond a certain threshold. That will take time ... a lot of time, even ...*

She concludes by saying:

> *The task became clear to me: as soon as the First Series* [Beelzebub's Tales to His Grandson] *had been published, it would be necessary to work without respite to form a nucleus capable, through its level of objectivity, devotion and the demands it would make on itself, of sustaining the current that had been created.*[1]

During the years following Gurdjieff's death in 1949, Madame de Salzmann devoted herself entirely to carrying out this aim until her own death in 1990 at the age of 101. Among those she worked with, many had been direct pupils of Gurdjieff and many of them, living to an advanced age, went on to become the source of direct inner guidance for hundreds of individuals throughout the Western world. Personal interviews with some of these men and women, as well as some of their original writings, comprise the major portion of the Gurdjieff-related material that has been published over the years in *Parabola*.

In relation to the Gurdjieff Work, the *Parabola Anthology Series* therefore offers a rare opportunity to glimpse the human quality of those who were part of this intentional nucleus, and some of their own pupils, working together within the immediate atmosphere and influence of a founding spiritual master—working, moreover, as men and women fully formed and engaged in our present-day world and culture, with all its unique pressures and astounding processes of social change. Obviously, a comparable possibility no longer exists with respect to the great, many-centuries-old spiritual traditions of the world. In these traditions, the immediate circle of the founder's pupils and disciples has long ago been clothed in legend and mystery. Profoundly symbolic legend, perhaps, and sacred mystery, but nevertheless the curtain of time has been irrevocably drawn over the actual flesh-and-blood lineaments of their personal thought and inner search.

Such is not yet the case with what one might cautiously call the Gurdjieff tradition. Here we have the opportunity to hear, as it were, the actual voices of some of the first and second generations of a great source teaching, and to ask these pupils questions that arise in the specific conditions of life and thought that they share with us. They share with us what is existentially our common "native language." They, like us, were born and lived their lives in the world of modern man, "the man of today … someone who no longer knows how to recognize the truth revealed to him in different forms since earliest times."[2] They too have grown up in a civilization which has "wrenched man from the normal conditions in which he should be living."[3] It is this "man of today" that Gurdjieff called to the work of the development of Being, bringing both a language uniquely adapted to the subjectivity of the modern mind and a source of practical methods by means of which he sought to awaken in people an intelligence that could distinguish the real from the illusory.

Who are these men and women who have most fully tried to answer this call? What do they have to offer us? What shall we ask them? And when they speak—as some do in this volume—what shall we listen for in them? What would it mean to hear the being of the person behind the expression of the ideas?—or, more precisely, what would it mean to hear, to sense, the inner struggle, with all its fluctuations and moments of power, love and impartiality, behind the words on the page?

It is the fundamental aim of the Gurdjieff Work to create *people*. The first generation of Gurdjieff's pupils have almost all disappeared, and already many of them, like Gurdjieff himself, are passing behind the curtain of story and legend. But in these talks and interviews, traces still remain of the inner work that these actual men and women tried with all their might to pass on to the next generation and, in this magazine, to the public.

The Gurdjieff Tradition Today

A central focus of the Gurdjieff teaching is the awakening to consciousness and the creation of proper communal and psychological conditions that can support this multi-leveled process. For this, a preparatory work is necessary, as stated by Jeanne de Salzmann:

> *According to Gurdjieff, the truth can be approached only if all the parts which make the human being, the thought, the feeling, and the body, are touched with the same force in a particular way appropriate to each of them—failing which, development will inevitably be one-sided and sooner or later come to a stop. In the absence of an effective understanding of this principle, all work on oneself is certain to deviate from the aim. The essential conditions will be wrongly understood and one will see a mechanical repetition of the forms of effort which never surpass a quite ordinary level.[4]*

Gurdjieff gave the name of "self-remembering" to the central state of conscious attention in which the higher force that is available within the human structure makes contact with the functions of thought, feeling and body. The individual "remembers," as it were, who and what he really is and is meant to be, over and above his ordinary sense of identity. This conscious attention is not a function of the mind but is the active conscious force which all our functions of thought, feeling and movement can begin to obey as the "inner master."

Consistent with the knowledge behind many contemplative traditions of the world, the practice of the Gurdjieff Work places its chief emphasis on preparing our inner world to receive this higher attention, which can open us to an inconceivably finer energy of love and understanding.

The Gurdjieff Work remains above all essentially an oral tradition, transmitted under specially created conditions from person to person, continually unfolding, without fixed doctrinal beliefs or external rites, as a way toward freeing humanity from the waking sleep that holds us in a kind of hypnotic illusion. The moving life of the tradition thus supports the individual search and helps to overcome the seemingly universal impulse of resistance or inertia: the tendency toward attachment, and the gradual fixing on partial aspects, institutionalized forms, dogmatic doctrines, and a habitual reliance on the known rather than facing and entering the unknown. According to the Gurdjieff teaching, the forms exist only to help discover, incarnate, and elaborate a formless energy of awakening, and without this understanding, the forms of the teaching become an end in themselves and lose their meaning.

At present, the general forms of practice in the Gurdjieff tradition may be characterized as follows:

Group meetings: Gurdjieff taught that alone, an individual can do nothing. In group meetings students regularly come together to participate in a collective atmosphere that is meant to function as a principal means for the transformation of the individual state of consciousness. Although, with the help of more advanced pupils, questions are shared and responded to in words, the fundamental support of the group is directed to the individual work of facing oneself and consciously recognizing one's own inner lack, until the appearance of a new quality of energy is possible. The more experienced pupils, helping the group as part of their own search, strive to be sensitive, not so much to the content of the exchange, but to the process of the developing energy and the mutual teaching that can take place under its influence. In their turn, more advanced pupils just as urgently need to work in groups, and in this way a redefinition of the conventional image of the "leader" is inevitable. At each level of inner work, what has been understood needs to be individually and collectively re-examined and verified in the movement of a dynamic, living esoteric school.

The *dances and movements* which Gurdjieff taught were partially a result of his research in the monasteries and schools of Asia, and are of a nature that seems unique in the modern Western world. In certain respects, they are comparable to sacred dances in traditional religious systems (for example, the 'Cham dances of Tibetan Buddhism or the dervish dances of the Sufis). Like them, the Gurdjieff Movements are based on the view that a series of specific postures, gestures, and movements, supported by an intentional use of melody and rhythm and an essential element of right individual effort, can help to evoke an inner condition which is closer to a more conscious existence, or a state of unity, which can allow an opening to the conscious energy of the Self. The Movements are now regularly given at major centers of the work by carefully prepared pupils who emphasize the need for exactitude and a special quality of feeling, without which the Movements cannot provide the help for which they were brought.

The practice of *sitting* is difficult to characterize apart from observing that, in accordance with the overall aim of the work, it is not a "form" in and for itself, but is fundamentally a preparation for the inner search within the midst of life. With or without spoken guidance, the aim is ultimately to help individuals search for an embodied presence that sustains the attempt to enter more deeply into an awareness of all the opposing forces constantly moving within the body. Jeanne de Salzmann gave this special work to her older pupils in the way Gurdjieff had given it at the Prieuré.[5] Later, in the 1960s, when groups had become more advanced, she gradually introduced it more broadly.

Work in life: To be able to work in life in the full sense would be considered a very high achievement. The struggle to be "present" in everyday life constitutes a major aspect of Gurdjieff's teaching, a struggle which leads to a full engagement in the duties and rewards of human life, now and here. In this context, Gurdjieff created conditions to help his pupils experience the fundamental practice of self-observation. Through such experience, a man or woman can begin to come into contact with an ever-deepening sense of inner need which allows an opening to a powerful conscious influence within oneself. According to Gurdjieff, without a relationship to this more central aspect of oneself, everyday life is bound to be an existential prison, in which the individual is held captive not so much by the so-called forces of modernity as by the parts of the self which cannot help but react automatically to the influences of the world. The help offered by the special conditions of the work is therefore understood not as replacing our life in the world, but as enabling us, in the course of time, to live life with authentic understanding and full participation.

Briefly, the movement toward awakening which is meant to be supported by the ideas and these forms of practice becomes in fact an organic process in life and movement, and for that reason dogmatic approaches will inevitably fail. The process of awakening requires not only an understanding of the constituent forces and laws which govern man's psyche and actions, but also a deep sensitivity to and appreciation of individual subjective needs and conditions. In other words, for an effective guidance, the principle of relativity must be recognized in the transmission of the teaching: individuals must be approached according to their respective levels of development and experience. Gurdjieff might have stressed one view to a student at a certain level of understanding and quite another view when that student had reached another level. This might give the appearance of contradiction, but in fact it was consistent in applying only those aspects of the whole teaching truly necessary at a given moment. The same principle applies to the ideas, some of which seemed more accessible at one period while others still remained to be revealed in the unfolding life of the teaching.[6]

For example, the work of "self-observation" acquires a completely new meaning as the developing attention lets go of its effort, joining and willingly submitting to a higher conscious seeing. The action that might take place in this condition—in the quiet of meditation or even in outer action—reflects the simultaneous dual nature of both an impersonal consciousness and a personal attention which has a new capacity to manifest and act in the world. The qualities of both these aspects of consciousness and attention are quite unknown to the ordinary mind. In this new relationship of individual attention and a higher impersonal consciousness, a man or woman can become a vessel, serving another energy which can act through the individual, an energy which at the same time transforms the materiality of the body. This understanding of inner work transmitted by Jeanne de Salzmann can be found today in many of the Gurdjieff Foundation groups worldwide.

The Life of Gurdjieff and the Principal Ideas

Of Gurdjieff's early life we know only what he has revealed in the autobiographical portions of his own writings, mainly *Meetings with Remarkable Men*. Although there is no reason to doubt the accuracy of his account, the fact remains that the principal aim of Gurdjieff's writings was not to provide historical information, but to serve as a call to awakening and as a continuing source of guidance for the inner search that is the *raison d'être* of his teaching. His writings are cast in forms that are directed not only to the intellectual function but also to the emotional and even subconscious sensitivities that, all together, make up the whole of the human psyche. His writings therefore demand and support the search for a finer quality of self-attention on the part of the reader, failing which the thought contained in them is unverifiable at its deeper levels.

Gurdjieff was born, probably in 1866, to a Greek father and an Armenian mother in Alexandropol (now Gumri), Armenia, a region where Eastern and Western cultures mixed and often clashed. The environment of his childhood and early adolescence, while suggesting a near-biblical patriarchal culture, is also marked by elements not usually associated with these cultural traditions. The portrait Gurdjieff draws of his father, a well-known *ashokh*, or bard, suggests some form of participation in an oral tradition stretching back to humanity's distant past. At the same time, Gurdjieff speaks of having been exposed to all the forms of modern knowledge, especially experimental science, which he explored with an impassioned diligence. The influence of his father and certain of his early teachers contrasts very sharply with the forces of modernity that he also experienced as a child. This contrast, however, is not easily describable. The difference is not simply that of ancient versus modern worldviews or patterns of behavior, though it certainly includes that. The impression, rather, is that these "remarkable men" of his early years manifested a certain quality of personal presence or *being*. That the vital difference between human beings is a matter of their level of being became one of the fundamental elements in Gurdjieff's teaching and is not reducible to conventional psychological, behavioral, or cultural typologies.

Meetings with Remarkable Men shows us the youthful Gurdjieff journeying to monasteries and schools of awakening in remote parts of Central Asia and the Middle East, searching for a knowledge that neither traditional religion nor modern science by itself could offer him. The clues to what Gurdjieff actually found, inwardly and outwardly, on these journeys are subtly distributed throughout the narrative, rather than laid out in doctrinal form. Discursive statements of ideas are relatively rare in the book, and where they are given it is with a deceptive simplicity that serves to turn the reader back to the teachings woven into the narrative portions of the text. Repeated readings of *Meetings with Remarkable Men* yield the realization that Gurdjieff meant to draw our attention to the search itself, and that what he intended to bring to the West was not only a new statement of what has been called "the primordial tradition," but the knowledge of how to conduct a search within the conditions of contemporary life. For Gurdjieff, as we shall see, the search itself, when rightly conducted, emerges as the principal spiritualizing force in human life, what one observer has termed "a transforming search," rather than "a search for transformation."

As has been noted, Gurdjieff began his work as a teacher in Russia around 1912, on the eve of the civil war that led to the Russian Revolution. In 1914 he was joined by the philosopher P. D. Ouspensky and soon after by the well-known Russian composer Thomas de Hartmann. Ouspensky was later to produce *In Search of the Miraculous*, by far the best account of Gurdjieff's teaching written by a pupil or (anyone other than Gurdjieff), while de Hartmann, working in a unique collaboration with Gurdjieff, would produce what has come to be called the "Gurdjieff/ de Hartmann music," the qualities of which are discussed by Laurence Rosenthal in the pages of this volume. Soon after, as the Revolution drew near and the coming breakdown of civil order began to announce itself, Gurdjieff and a small band of dedicated pupils, including Thomas and Olga de Hartmann, made perilous journeys to the Crimea and Tiflis (now Tbilisi). There they were joined by Alexandre and Jeanne de Salzmann, the former a well-known artist and theatrical designer and the latter a teacher of the Dalcroze system of rhythmic dance who was later to emerge as Gurdjieff's greatest pupil and the principal guide under whom his teaching continued to be passed on after his death in 1949. It was in Tiflis, in 1919, that Gurdjieff organized the first version of his "Institute for the Harmonious Development of Man."

The account by Ouspensky, and notes by other pupils published in 1973 under the title *Views from the Real World* show that in the Moscow period, before the journey out of Russia, Gurdjieff tirelessly articulated a vast body of ideas about man and the cosmos. It is appropriate here to interrupt the historical narrative in order to summarize some of these formulations, which played an important role in the subsequent development of his teaching, even as Gurdjieff changed the outer forms and certain inner emphases in his direct work with pupils. Also, to a limited extent, these ideas throw light on developments that came later, some of which have given rise to unnecessary confusion in the minds of outside observers. One caveat, however, is necessary. If in his writings Gurdjieff never sought merely to lay out a philosophical system, all the more in his direct work with pupils did he mercilessly resist the role of guru, preacher, or schoolteacher. *In Search of the Miraculous* shows, with considerable force, that Gurdjieff always gave his ideas to his pupils under conditions designed to break through the crust of emotional and intellectual associations which, he taught, shut out the small voice of conscience in man. The often awesome precision with which he was able to break through that crust—ways of behaving with his pupils that were, in turn, shocking, mysterious, frightening, magical, delicately gentle, and clairvoyant—remains one of the principal factors around which both the Gurdjieff legend and the misunderstandings about him have arisen, as well as being the element most written about by those who came in touch with him, and the most imitated in the current age of "new religions."

The Gurdjieff Ideas

It is true enough to say that Gurdjieff's system of ideas is complex and all-encompassing, but one must immediately add that their formulation is designed to point us toward a central and simple power of apprehension which Gurdjieff taught is merely latent within the human mind and which is the only power by which we can actually understand ourselves in relation to the universe. In this sense, the sharp distinction between doctrine and method does not entirely obtain in Gurdjieff's teaching. The formulations of the ideas are themselves meant to have a special action on the sense of self and may therefore be regarded as part of the practical method. This characteristic of Gurdjieff's teaching reflects what Gurdjieff perceived as the center of gravity of the contemporary subjectivity—the fact that modern civilization is lopsidedly oriented around the thinking function. Modern man's illusory feeling of "I" is to a great extent built up around his thoughts and therefore, in accordance with the level of the pupil, the ideas themselves are meant to affect this false sense of self. For Gurdjieff the deeply penetrating influence of scientific thought in modern life was not something merely to be deplored, but to be understood as the channel through which the eternal Truth must first find its way toward the human heart.

Man, Gurdjieff taught, is an unfinished creation. He is not fully Man, in the sense of a cosmically unique being whose intelligence and power of action mirror the energies of the source of life itself. On the contrary, man, as he is, is an automaton. Our thoughts, feelings, and deeds are little more than mechanical reactions to external and internal stimuli. In Gurdjieff's terms, we cannot *do* anything. In and around us, everything "happens" without the participation of an authentic consciousness. But human beings are ignorant of this state of affairs because of the pervasive and deeply internalized influence of culture and education, which engrave in us the illusion of autonomous conscious selves. In short, man is asleep. There is no authentic *I am* in his presence, but only a fractured egoism which masquerades as the authentic self, and whose machinations poorly imitate the normal human functions of thought, feeling, and will.

Many factors reinforce this sleep. Each of the reactions that proceed in one's presence is accompanied by a deceptive sense of I—one of many I's, each imagining itself to be the whole, and each buffered off from awareness of the others. Each of these many I's represents a process whereby the subtle energy of consciousness is absorbed and degraded, a process that Gurdjieff termed "identification." Man identifies—that is, squanders his conscious energy—with every passing thought, impulse, and sensation. This state of affairs takes the form of a continuous self-deception and a continuous procession of egoistic emotions, such as anger, self-pity, sentimentality, and fear, which are of such a pervasively painful nature that we are constantly driven to ameliorate this condition through the endless pursuit of social recognition, sensory pleasure, or the vague and unrealizable goal of "happiness."

According to Gurdjieff, the human condition cannot be understood apart from the purpose of organic life on earth. The human being is constructed to transform energies of a specific nature, and neither our potential inner development nor our present actual predicament is understandable apart from this function. Thus, in the teaching of Gurdjieff, psychology is inextricably connected with cosmology and metaphysics and, in a certain sense, biology. The diagram known as the "Ray of Creation" provides one of the conceptual keys to approaching this interconnection between humanity and the universal order, and as such invites repeated study from a variety of angles and stages of understanding.

The reader is referred to chapters 5, 7, and 9 of *In Search of the Miraculous* for a discussion of this diagram, but the point to be emphasized here is that, at the deepest level, the human mind and heart are enmeshed in a concatenation of causal influences of enormous scale and design. A study of the Ray of Creation makes it clear that the aspects of human nature through which one typically attempts to improve one's lot are without any force whatever within the network of universal influences that act upon man on earth. In this consists our fundamental illusion, an illusion only intensified by the technological achievements of modern science. We are simply unable to draw upon the conscious energies passing through us which, in the cosmic scheme, are those possessing the actual power of causal efficacy. We do not and cannot participate consciously in the great universal order, but instead are tossed about *en masse* for purposes limited to the functions of organic life on earth as a whole. Even in this relatively limited sphere—limited, that is, when compared to man's latent destiny—humanity has become progressively incapable of fulfilling its function, a point that Gurdjieff strongly emphasized in his own writings. This aspect of the Ray of Creation—namely, that the "fate of the earth" is somehow bound up with the possibility of the inner evolution of individual men and women—resonates with our contemporary sense of impending planetary disaster.

How are human beings to change this state of affairs and begin drawing on the universal conscious energies which we are built to absorb but which now pass through us untransformed? How is humanity to assume its proper place in the great chain of being? Gurdjieff's answer to these questions actually circumscribes the central purpose of his teaching—namely, that human life on earth may now stand at a major transitional point, comparable perhaps to the fall of the great civilizations of the past, and that development of the whole *being* (rather than one or another of the separate human functions) is the only thing that can permit us to pass through this transition in a manner worthy of human destiny.

But whereas the descent of humanity takes place en masse, ascent or evolution is possible only within the individual. *In Search of the Miraculous* presents a series of diagrams dealing with the same energies and laws as the Ray of Creation, not only as a cosmic ladder of descent but also in their evolutionary aspect within the individual. In these diagrams, known collectively as the Food Diagram, Ouspensky explains in some detail how Gurdjieff regarded the energy transactions within the individual human organism.

Again, the reader is referred to Ouspensky's book, the point being that humanity can begin to occupy its proper place within the chain of being only through an inner work which within the individual human being may be subsumed under the general term attention. The many levels of attention possible for man, up to and including an attention that in traditional teachings has been termed Spirit, are here ranged along a dynamic, vertical continuum that reaches from the level of biological sustenance, which humans require for their physical bodies, up to the incomparably finer sustenance that we require for the inner growth of the soul. This finer substance is obtained through the digestion of "the food of impressions," a deceptively matter-of-fact phrase that eventually defines the uniquely human cosmic obligation and potentiality of constantly and in everything working for an objective understanding of the Real.

The Ray of Creation and the Food Diagram, extraordinary though they are, are only a small part of the body of ideas contained in *In Search of the Miraculous*. They are cited here as examples of how Gurdjieff not only restated the ancient, perennial teachings in a language adapted to the modern mind, but also brought to these ancient principles something of such colossal originality that those who followed him detected in his teaching the signs of what in Western terminology may be designated a new revelation.

However, as was indicated above, the organic interconnection of the ideas in *In Search of the Miraculous* is communicated not principally through conceptual argument but as a gradual unfolding which Ouspensky experienced to the extent that there arose within him that agency of inner unity which Gurdjieff called "the real I"—the activation of which required of Ouspensky an ego-shattering inner work under the guidance of Gurdjieff and within the general group conditions he created for his pupils. Each of the great ideas in the book leads to the others. The Ray of Creation and the Food Diagram are inseparable from Gurdjieff's teaching about the fundamental law of three forces and the law of the sevenfold development of energy (the Law of Octaves), and the interrelation of these laws as expressed in the symbol of the enneagram.

These ideas are in turn inseparable from Gurdjieff's teaching about the tripartite division of human nature, the three "centers" of mind, feeling, and body. Likewise, the astonishing account of how Gurdjieff structured the conditions of group work is inseparable from the idea of his work as a manifestation of the Fourth Way, the Way of Consciousness, distinct from the familiar traditional paths termed "the way of the fakir," "the way of the monk," and "the way of the yogi."

The notion of the Fourth Way is one of Gurdjieff's ideas that has captured the imagination of contemporary people and has brought quite a new meaning to the idea of esotericism. The meaning of this idea is perhaps best approached by resuming the narrative of Gurdjieff's life, with special attention given to the conditions of work which he created for his pupils.

After a brief period in Constantinople, Gurdjieff and his group of pupils made their way through Europe and finally settled in France where, in 1922, he established his Institute for the Harmonious Development of Man at the Château du Prieuré at Fontainebleau near Avon, just outside Paris. The brief intense period of activity at the Prieuré has been described in numerous books, but even for those familiar with these accounts, the establishment and day-to-day activities of the Prieuré still evoke astonishment. It was during this period that Gurdjieff developed many of the methods and practices of group work that have retained a central place in the work throughout the world today, including many of the Movements or sacred dances. All serious accounts of the conditions Gurdjieff created at the Prieuré give the impression of a community life pulsating with the uncompromising search for truth, engaging all sides of human nature—demanding physical work, intensive emotional interactions, and the study of a vast range of ideas about humanity and the universal world. These accounts invariably speak of the encounter with oneself that these conditions made possible and the experience of the self which accompanied this encounter.

The most active period of the Prieuré lasted less than two years, ending with Gurdjieff's nearly fatal motor accident on July 6, 1924. In order to situate this period properly, it is necessary to look back once again to the year 1909, when Gurdjieff had finished his twenty-one years of traveling throughout Asia, the Middle East, Africa, and

Europe meeting individuals and visiting communities who possessed knowledge unsuspected by most people. By 1909 Gurdjieff had learned secrets of the human psyche and of the universe that he knew to be necessary for the future welfare of humanity, and he set himself the task of transmitting them to those who could use them rightly. After trying to cooperate with existing societies, he decided to create an organization of his own. He started in 1911 in Tashkent, where he had established a reputation as a wonder-worker and an authority on "questions of the Beyond." He moved to Moscow in 1912 and after the revolution of February 1917 there began his remarkable journeys through the war-torn Caucasus region, leading a band of his pupils to Constantinople and finally to France, where he reopened his institute at the Château du Prieuré at Avon. His avowed aim during this period was to set up a worldwide organization for the dissemination of his ideas and the training of helpers. The motor accident of July 1924 occurred at this critical juncture.

When he began to recover from his injuries, Gurdjieff was faced with the sheer impossibility of realizing his plans for the Institute. He was a stranger in Europe, his health was shattered, he had no money, and many of his friends and pupils had left. At that point he made the decision to find a new way of transmitting to posterity what he had learned about human nature and human destiny. This was to be done by writing. His period as an author began in December of 1924 and continued until May 1935. It was during this period that he produced the monumental expression of his thought, *Beelzebub's Tales to His Grandson*; the subtle, crystalline call to inner work, *Meetings with Remarkable Men*; and the profoundly encoded, unfinished *Life Is Real Only Then, When "I Am."* It was also during this period that he culminated his collaboration with the composer Thomas de Hartmann, rounding off the unique corpus of music that now bears both their names.

In fact, although the period of the Prieuré had ended, and although struck by numerous personal blows and tragedies, Gurdjieff by no means limited himself to writing. Quite the contrary. His travels to America, and his seeding of the work there, accelerated and intensified. The creation and development of the Movements continued. And, perhaps above all, assisted by Jeanne de Salzmann, his work with groups and individuals in

Paris not only attracted from Europe and America the men and women who would later carry the work to the cities of the Western world, but at the same time allowed him, within the silence and energy of his Paris apartment, to transmit a portion of his understanding of inner work to many other men and women from many parts of the world.

After his death in Paris in 1949, the work continued under the guidance of Jeanne de Salzmann and now rests largely in the hands of the second generation of pupils in his lineage.

In conclusion, and returning to the idea of the three centers, a succinct statement of this fundamental aspect of what Gurdjieff brought to the modern world as "the Fourth Way" may be cited from the descriptive brochure published at the Prieuré in 1922.

> The civilization of our time, with its unlimited means for extending its influence, has wrenched man from the normal conditions in which he should be living. It is true that civilization has opened up for man new paths in the domain of knowledge, science and economic life, and thereby enlarged his world perception. But, instead of raising him to a higher all-round level of development, civilization has developed only certain sides of his nature to the detriment of other faculties, some of which it has destroyed altogether. ...
>
> Modern man's world perception and his mode of living are not the conscious expression of his being taken as a complete whole. Quite the contrary, they are only the unconscious manifestation of one or another part of him.
>
> From this point of view our psychic life, both as regards our world perception and our expression of it, fails to present a unique and indivisible whole, that is to say, a whole acting both as common repository of all our perceptions and as the source of all our expressions.
>
> On the contrary, it is divided into three separate entities, which have nothing to do with one another, but are distinct both as regards their functions and their constituent substances.
>
> These three entirely separate sources of the intellectual, emotional and physical life of man, each taken in the sense of the whole set of functions proper to them, are called by this teaching the thinking, the emotional, and the moving centers.[7]

It is difficult conceptually, and in a few words, to communicate the meaning of this idea of the three centers, which is one of the central aspects of Gurdjieff's teaching. The modern person simply has no conception of how self-deceptive a life can be that is lived in only one part of oneself. The head, the emotions, and the body each have their own perceptions and actions, and each in itself can live a simulacrum of human life. In the modern era this has gone to an extreme point, and most of the technical and material progress of our culture serves to push the individual further into only one of the centers—one third, as it were, of our real self-nature. The growth of vast areas of scientific knowledge is, according to Gurdjieff, outweighed by the diminution of the conscious space and time within which we live and experience ourselves. With an ever-diminishing "I," we gather an ever-expanding corpus of information about the universe. But to be human—to be a whole self possessed of moral power, will, and intelligence—requires all the centers, and more. This more is communicated above all in Gurdjieff's own writings, in which the levels of spiritual development possible for human beings are connected with a breathtaking vision of the levels of possible service that the developing individual is called on to render to mankind and to the universal source of creation itself.

Thus, the proper relationship of the three centers of cognition in the human being is a necessary precondition for the reception and realization of what in the religions of the world has been variously termed the Holy Spirit, Atman, and the Buddha Nature. The conditions Gurdjieff created for his pupils cannot be understood apart from this fact. "I wished to create around myself," Gurdjieff wrote, "conditions in which a man would be continuously reminded of the sense and aim of his existence by an unavoidable friction between his conscience and the automatic manifestations of his nature."[8] Deeply buried though it is, the awakened conscience is the *something more* which, according to Gurdjieff, is the only force in modern man's nearly-completely-degenerate psyche that can actually bring the parts of his nature together and open him to that energy and unnamable awareness of which all the religions have always spoken as the gift that descends from above, but which in the conditions of modern life is almost impossible to receive without an extraordinary quality of help.

—Jacob Needleman

Acknowledgements

Portions of the Introduction have been drawn from "G. I. Gurdjieff and His School" by Jacob Needleman, originally published in Antoine Faivre and Jacob Needleman (eds.), *Modern Esoteric Spirituality* (New York: Crossroad, 1992) and from "The Gurdjieff Tradition" by Jacob Needleman, originally published as an entry in: Wouter J. Hanegraaff (ed.), *Dictionary of Gnosis and Western Esotericism* (Leiden: Brill NV, 2005).

Notes:

1 G. I. Gurdjieff, *Life Is Real Only Then, When "I Am"* (New York: Dutton, 1982, pp. xiii, xiv).

2 Gurdjieff, *Life Is Real Only Then, When "I Am,"* p. xii.

3 Gurdjieff, See *infra* p. xxxii.

4 Gurdjieff, *Life Is Real Only Then, When "I Am,"* p. xii

5 In 1922 Gurdjieff acquired the Prieuré d'Avon, a large estate and former priory located about 40 miles from Paris where he established intense communal conditions for inner work, especially from 1922 until his automobile accident in 1924.

6 In this light, it is interesting to note that groups that break away at different moments, to work by themselves and on their own, run the risk of clinging dogmatically to certain specific forms and practices.

7 G.I. Gurdjieff's Institute for the Harmonious Development of Man, *Prospectus No. 1* (privately printed, ca. 1922), p. 3.

8 G. I. Gurdjieff, *Meetings with Remarkable Men* (New York: Dutton, 1973) p. 270.

•

CHAPTER ONE

MAN'S POSSIBILITIES ARE VERY GREAT

—In Search of the Miraculous

Parabola
Volume: 19.1
The Call

The Awakening of Thought

Jeanne de Salzmann

Objective thought is a look from Above. A look that is free, that can see. Without this look upon me, seeing me, my life is the life of a blind man who goes his way driven by impulse, not knowing either why or how. Without this look upon me, I cannot know that I exist.

I have the power to rise above myself and to see myself freely ... to be seen. My thought has the power to be free. But for this to take place, it must rid itself of all the associations which hold it captive, passive. It must cut the threads that bind it to the world of images, to the world of forms; it must free itself from the constant pull of the emotions. It must *feel* its power to resist this pull, its objective power to watch over this pull while gradually rising above it. In this movement thought becomes active. It becomes active while purifying itself. Thereby its true aim is revealed, a unique aim: to think *I*, to realize *who I am*, to enter into this mystery.

Otherwise, our thoughts are just illusions, objects which enslave us, snares in which real thought loses its power of objectivity and intentional action. Confused by words, images, forms that attract it, it loses the capacity to see. It loses the sense of *I*. Then nothing remains but an organism adrift. A body deprived of intelligence. Without this inner look, I can only fall back into automatism, under the law of accident.

This look makes me both responsible and free. In the clearest moments of self-awareness, I reach a state where I am known, and where I feel the blessing of this look which comes down to embrace me. I become transparent under its light.

Each time, the first step is the recognition of a lack. I feel the need for real thought. The need for a free thought turned toward myself so that I might become truly aware of my existence. An active thought, whose sole aim and sole object is *I* ... to rediscover *I*.

So my struggle is a struggle against the passivity of my ordinary thought. Without this struggle a greater consciousness will not be born. Through this struggle I can leave behind the illusion of "I" in which I live and approach a more real vision. At the heart of this struggle, order is created out of chaos. A hierarchy is revealed: two levels, two worlds. As long as there is only one level, there can be no vision. Recognition of another level is the awakening of thought.

Without this effort, thought falls back into a sleep filled with words, images, preconceived notions, approximate knowledge, dreams, and perpetual drifting. This is the thought of a man without intelligence. It is terrible to suddenly realize that one has been living without a thought that is independent—a thought of one's own—living without intelligence, without something that sees what is *real*, and therefore without any relation to the world Above.

It is in my essence that I may be reunited with the one who sees. There, I would be at the source of something unique and stable, at the source of that which does not change.

Text dated July 23, 1958, from a notebook of Jeanne de Salzmann. First published in *Georges Ivanovitch Gurdjieff*, Bruno de Panafieu, ed. (Paris: Les Dossiers H., 1992). Reprinted by permission of Michel de Salzmann.

Parabola
Volume: 7.1
Sleep

"Why Sleepest Thou, O Lord?"

Henri Tracol

> *Awake, why sleepest thou, O Lord?*
> *Arise, cast us not off forever.*
> *(Psalm 44:23)*

Indeed, why does He sleep? If the Almighty cannot help sleeping, we may wonder whether it is not for some utterly binding reason—if only for the sake of conforming to the laws of His own Creation. For since the very first day, when He divided the light from the darkness, sleep has been imperative.

Without sleep, no awakening: such is the universal law of alternation which, according to ancient traditions, applies to Creation itself. In going back as far as Vedic India, we find in the laws of Manu: "When that divine one wakes, then this world stirs; when he slumbers tranquilly, then the Universe sinks to sleep."

"The Manvantaras (creation and destruction of the world) are numberless; in sport, as it were, the Creator repeats this again and again." Every time the world is suspended, or reabsorbed, Vishnu peacefully reclines on his cosmic serpent, Ananta, which means "endless."

Why sleepest thou, O Vishnu? A fascinating vision, and so unfathomable that it leaves no room for speculation, for any attempt to reduce it to our scale. And yet endlessly in the secret heart of our own mystery, how can we not wonder?

And if all this were but a dream? When asked by a pupil, "If it is true that the world is God's dream, then what happens when God wakes up?" a Sufi master in the Near East replied: "The world is not God's dream. It is man's dream. And when man wakes, he finds there is only God. Nothing else is real truth (*haq*). The whole world is merely ripples in the Ocean of Truth. Surface stuff. *Look deeper*. Ripples arise; but it is all water, the same water, only water. To awaken is to *see* that."

Am I able to look deeper? And if not, doesn't the question become: Why do I sleep? And do I even know what sleep is?

According to the Upanishads, there are four states of being: the waking state "common to all men" (*jagarita-sthana*) comes first; then the dreaming state (*svapna-sthana*); followed by the deep sleep state (*sushupta-sthana*) and eventually the fourth (superconscious) state (*turiya*), "with which there can be no dealing," the very Self (*Atman*).

Deep sleep: what is this third state, this unknowable "deep sleep"? Is it the one God caused to fall upon Adam in order to create out of one of his ribs "an helpmeet for him"? The Mandukya Upanishad says: "If one asleep desires no desire whatsoever, sees no dream whatsoever, that is deep sleep (*sushupta*)." The Brihad-Aranyaka Upanishad says: "As a falcon or an eagle, having flown around here in space, becomes weary, folds its wings, and is borne down to its nest, just so does this person hasten to that state where, asleep, he desires no desires and sees no dream."

Dreamless sleep appears to be far beyond any definable concept; in the Chandogya Upanishad it is said to be "the ultimate," the "cognitional," and to consist of bliss, eternal Bliss. "Now when one is thus sound asleep, composed, serene, and knows no dream, that is the Self (Atman), that is the immortal, the fearless, that is Brahma."

So that, "having enjoyed himself in that state of deep sleep, having moved about and seen good and evil, he hastens back again as he came to the place of origin, back to sleep." (Brihad-Aranyaka)

Back to sleep as the deepest possible source of full cognition and bliss. No wonder, therefore, that so many Western as well as Eastern "seekers of truth" give it so much value as a propitious ground for their search.

Chuang Tzu wrote: "Everything is one; during sleep the soul, undistracted, is absorbed into this unity; when awake, distracted, it sees the different beings." Some fourteen centuries later, Bernard of Clairvaux praises the *"vitalis vigilque sopor,"* a "sleep alive and watchful," which enlightens the inward senses. And Al-Ghazzali considered sleep the most appropriate, though remote, reflection of what is known as prophetic vision: "A blind man can understand nothing of colors save what he has learned by narration and hearsay. Yet God has brought prophetism near to men in giving them all a state analogous to it in its principal characters. This state is sleep."

We may find an echo of this in the "dark contemplation" of John of the Cross, or in the "innate spirits in man" Paracelsus speaks of ("for it is the Light of Nature which is at work during sleep") or again in Avicenna's dove (soul), which "spies such things as cannot be witnessed by waking eyes."

But here we must be on guard. For is our sleep this deep sleep of vision, and is our waking really waking?

It must be remembered, as the great masters have warned, that there are always traps and false paths in the quest for the unknown. The yearning of the mystics of all religions for another state of being—whether it is called ecstasy, enlightenment, or liberation—must be rigorously examined. These lines from Fray Francisco de Osuna (however enraptured Teresa of Avila may have been when she first read them) require a closer look:

> *Blessed are they who pray before going to sleep and who, on awakening, return promptly to prayer. Like Elias they eat a little, sleep, eat again a little and nestle in the arms of the Lord like children who fall asleep at their mother's breast, having drunk her milk, wake again, suckle and fall asleep again. Thus, with these glorious intervals, their time asleep counts as prayer more than as sleep. ... And although they have slept, they realize on awakening that their soul has slept in the arms of the Beloved.*

These words unavoidably call to mind the *regressus ad uterum*, the yearning to return to the sleep of the maternal womb. This natural reaction has been studied by Professor Alfred Tomatis in his *Liberation d'Oedipe*:

The newborn baby suddenly finds himself flooded in light. Confronted by this sudden and intense brightness, which accompanies the entry into the world of the big people, of the giants, he chooses to escape into sleep as the only way for him to take refuge, forgetting his present condition and remembering the past in which he lived in his previous existence, his fetal existence.

Very few men afterwards ever know how to disengage themselves from this grip of sleep, this very first refusal to face life as it is. The physiological limits of the state of sleep are often largely exceeded by an intention, archaically anchored, to flee the present to the point of not being.

This thoughtful evaluation of sleep requires further pondering, but let us once again scan the four states of being as defined in the Upanishads.

The last and highest one, the superconscious *turiya*, we shall of course keep in sight as our deeply attractive but inaccessible horizon. Closest to it is the deep and dreamless state (*sushupta*) which we have been trying to explore. As for the dreaming state (*svapna*), we could be promptly lost in its utterly polyvalent network of lures, and so we are compelled first of all to consider the lowest one (*jagarita*), the so-called "waking-state."

Awakening gives the appearance of being a sort of victory over sleep, but what if this were only a semblance, another lure, another dream? "Life is a dream; when we sleep we are awake, and when we awake we sleep," says Montaigne. We are familiar with such notions as daydreaming and absent-mindedness, but while we notice these propensities in our fellow men, we hardly ever acknowledge them in ourselves; or when we do, we take it as the exception rather than the rule.

At times, in the course of the day, I come to. As it were, I awake in a flash: "Here I am," more or less intensely. Then, without realizing it, I quickly sink back into that ambiguous state—"paradoxical waking state" we could call it (in contrast with the overused "paradoxical sleep")—in which I am neither fully awake nor fast asleep.

Unavoidably, I mistake these fleeting experiences for my normal state, as if they were going to last, whereas in fact an automatism promptly takes over and deals in a more or less acceptable way with the functional requirements of my day-to-day existence.

If I become partly aware of the bewildering situation, I may acknowledge—with a smile—that it is so and, knowingly, pretend to accept it. But of course this might be just another trap into which, unknowingly, I fall unless, prompted by an enigmatic sense of urgency, I try to stay there and look deeper.

Striving to stay there, aware of my own presence, while everything moves inside me as well as outside, my power of attention, however well trained it may be for other tasks, is at once helplessly swept away from this intimate perception by tidal waves of associations. Over and over again, I may try to take up the challenge and resume this private search for authenticity, which nobody on earth can ever undertake for me. And yet by dint of trying, failing, and trying again, I come to the point where I realize how much I am in need of help.

And help is there. Am I so blind and so deaf as to ignore it? It offers itself in many guises—testimonies of all kinds, sacred books, spiritual ways.

Take, for instance, Buddhist asceticism, the way of the Buddha toward awakening. For "Buddha," from the root *budh*, to awaken, means the "Awakened One." It is thus a designation applied to one who attains spiritual realization, likened to an "arousing" or to an "awakening." He reaches the path, as stated in the Majjhimanikaya, "by the intensity, the constancy and concentration of the will," then "of the energy," then "of the spirit," then "of investigation," and last "of a heroic spirit." "And thus attaining these heroic qualities, he is able, O disciples, to achieve liberation, to achieve awakening."

In my own effort towards concentration, help is also offered by nature itself, life itself—whenever I can remain permeable to the deeply revealing impressions that it never ceases to provide. Therefore, my only concern should be to try and stay attentive to the wordless call from that which is always there, waiting for recognition.

Recognition. This might prove to be the key, not to try to "reach for," but just to come back to what is. "To remember myself," in Gurdjieff's language, means to come back to my *real* self: "Life is real only then, when '*I* am'," which implies that what we call "life" is totally unreal—as well as what we call "I."

The so-called "waking state" is in the way. "A modern man lives in sleep, in sleep he is born and in sleep he dies," writes Ouspensky quoting

Gurdjieff. To awake from this sleep will be the first step toward real being and real life, for "the sleep and waking states are equally subjective. Only by beginning to remember himself does a man really awaken."

How far is it given a man to remember himself? "Theoretically he can, but practically it is almost impossible because as soon as a man awakens for a moment, all the [hypnotic] forces that caused him to fall asleep begin to act upon him with tenfold energy and he immediately falls asleep again, very often *dreaming* that he is awake, or is awakening."

This might help us find a sounder approach to the old perplexing aphorism: "A man may be born, but in order to be born he must first die, and in order to die he must first awake."

"To awake, to die, to be born," which reads now: *to awake* from this so-called "waking state"; *to die* to the misleading reactions that we usually mistake for "life"; and *to be born* again to the higher potentialities of being, evidence of the real intention behind our presence on earth.

If a man proves able to conquer his expectation of reward for his achievements, he might even come to wonder whether life has not been granted him for this very challenge: to accept and play his part in the mystery with his eyes wide open, as man alone can do, through a lifetime of "conscious labors and intentional sufferings."

Hope is there, objective hope: dormant potentialities never vanish. Hidden as they are, they bear witness to the sacred presence, the sleeping god within. And although I forget, over and over again—why sleepest thou, O Lord?—there is a way out of this maze. A very long one indeed. ... It may take a lifetime (and perhaps even more), but it starts here and now.

Parabola
Volume: 21.2
The Soul

THE SECRET DIMENSION

Peter Brook

Although firmly rooted in a very ancient, lost tradition, Gurdjieff's teaching is bitingly contemporary. It analyzes the human predicament with devastating precision. It shows how men and women are conditioned from earliest childhood, how they operate according to deep-rooted programs, living from cause to effect in an unbroken chain of reactions. These in turn produce a stream of sensations and images, which are never the reality they pretend to be; they are mere interpretations of a reality which they are doomed to mask by their constant flow.

Every phenomenon arises from a field of energies: every thought, every feeling, every movement of the body is the manifestation of a specific energy, and in the lopsided human being one energy is constantly swelling up to swamp the other. This endless pitching and tossing between mind, feeling, and body produces a fluctuating series of impulses, each of which deceptively asserts itself as "me": as one desire replaces another, there can be no continuity of intention, no true wish, only the chaotic pattern of contradiction in which we all live, in which the ego has the illusion of willpower and independence. Gurdjieff calls this "the terror of the situation."

His purpose is not to reassure; he is concerned only with an impartial expression of the truth. If we have the courage to listen, he introduces us to a science which is very far from the science we know.

Since the Renaissance, our own science has accurately pinpointed the detailed processes and mechanisms of the universe, from the infinitely large to the infinitely small, but has failed disastrously to introduce into its equations the dimension of living experience. It omits consciousness; it cannot capture the meaning of perception, nor the specific taste of thought. The highly abstract and purely mental system of mathematical symbols has no way of evoking the humanity of artistic experience nor the spirituality of religion. As a result, we have two parallel interpretations of reality which can never meet: the scientific language of definition and the symbolic language of perception. So it seems that we are compelled to take sides, the scientist versus the humanist, and inescapably we are faced with the ancient duality, matter and spirit. For the scientist, the idea that there is a "something" that no one can touch, no one can see, and no instrument can detect is obviously repugnant; for him this can only be "mumbo-jumbo," and we can understand how in his impatience he throws both metaphysics and spirituality into the same trash can of superstition. What he offers in exchange is a seemingly coherent view of the universe in which everything hangs together in a logical sequence of events, leading to the arrival of a lonely accident called man. In this image, the cosmos always ends up as an inexhaustible but senseless dynamo and all energy becomes blind, unfeeling power.

The idea that consciousness is an integral part of energy, and that the level of consciousness is inextricably linked to the frequency of vibration, is nowhere to be found in contemporary science. The profound pertinence of Gurdjieff's work is that it reveals fundamental laws which encompass the "complete field" that both scientists and artists have pursued through the ages. This enables every phenomenon to be situated in its relationship to others, according to the dimension that incorporates human experience: this dimension is perceptible, we recognize it, we speak of it, yet it remains undefined—we call it "quality."

Quality is a word much used and much devalued today—one could even say it has lost its quality—yet all our lives we live according to an intuitive sense of its meaning, and it guides most of our attitudes and decisions. It has become fashionable to mistrust "value judgments," yet we appreciate people, we respond to their presence, we sense their feelings, we admire their skills, we condemn their actions, whether in cooking, politics, art, or love, in terms of unwritten hierarchies of quality.

Nothing illustrates this better than the curious phenomenon called art, which transforms the very nature of our perceptions and opens in us a sense of wonder, even of awe. Certain frequencies of vibrations—colors, shapes, geometric figures, and above all proportions—evoke corresponding frequencies in us, each of which has a specific quality or flavor. There is, for instance, a proportion within the rectangle called the Golden Section that will invariably produce a sensation of harmony, and here as in many other geometrical figures the psychological experience is inseparable from its mathematical description. Architecture has always observed and followed this marriage between feeling and proportion, and on a more intuitive level the painter and the sculptor are tirelessly correcting and refining their work so that its coarse outer crust can give way to the true inner feeling. A poet sifts within his thought pattern, giving attention to subtle intimations of sound and rhythm which are somewhere far behind the tumble of words with which his mind is filled. In this way, he creates a phrase that carries with it a new force, and the reader, in turn, can perceive his own feelings being intensified as their energy is transformed by the impressions he receives from the poem. In each case the difference is one of quality and is the result not of accident but of a unique process.

Most art can be called subjective, because it stems from an individual and private source, but there have been moments in human history when great works have had an "objectivity" that has enabled them to become universal, speaking to all mankind from a level beyond personal experience. What is this level? To understand it, we must examine the source of our creative impulses.

In a confused way today we tend to explain all artistic and religious experiences in terms of psychological and cultural conditioning. To a large extent, this is easy to confirm, but not all of our impulses stem from this subjective conditioning. True quality has objective reality, and it is governed by exact laws: every phenomenon rises and falls, level by level, according to a natural scale of values. This is illustrated very precisely in music, where the passage of a sound from one note to another transforms its quality. What Gurdjieff calls "objective science" uses the musical analogy to depict a universe composed of a chain of energies that stretches from the lowest octave to the highest: each energy is transformed as it rises or falls, taking on a coarser or finer nature according to its place in the scale. At each specific level, an energy corresponds to a degree of intelligence, and it is consciousness itself, fluctuating within a wide range of vibrations, that determines human experience. Gurdjieff does not speak only of energies capable of rising to new levels of intensity; he also affirms the reality of an absolute level of pure quality. From this source, energies descend to meet and interact with the energies we know. When this intermingling of the pure with the gross takes place, it can change the meaning of our actions and the influence they bear on the world.

What we call ordinary life is played out within a field of energies whose limits are strictly circumscribed, and which, using the musical metaphor, rise and fall within a small number of scales. Thus the level of our awareness is low, our power of thought is limited, and these energies produce little vision, little purpose. Gurdjieff demonstrates that there are two exact points in every scale where an evolving movement comes to a stop, where there is an interval that can be bridged only by the introduction of a new vibration of precisely the necessary quality. Otherwise, as nothing in the universe can stay still, the rising energy will inevitably sink again to its starting point. This is an astonishing and radical notion: it implies that all energies, and consequently all human activities, can only rise up to a certain point on their own initiative, like the arrow shot into the sky which must at a certain point exhaust the impulse that launched it, so that it reaches its peak and curves downward toward the earth. However, if the crucial point where the first energy begins to fade can be accurately observed, at this point what Gurdjieff calls a "shock" can occur—which is the conscious introduction of a new impulse that will carry the rising movement across the invisible barrier and permit it to continue in its upward path. This image enables us to understand how it is that without this "shock" lives decay, enterprises and empires pass into decline, calculations are proved false, and heroic revolutions turn back on themselves and betray their great ideals. The same laws show that a certain force exactly applied could have prevented this return to zero, but the basic principle is seldom recognized. So we blame others and ourselves with bitterness and frustration.

If, however, at the crucial moment, the energies that are in action can make contact with energies of a different order, a change of quality takes place. This can lead to intense artistic experiences and to social transformations, but the process does not end here. Intermingling with energies made finer by the intensity of their vibrations, consciousness rises to a higher scale that transcends art; this in turn can lead to spiritual awakening—and eventually to absolute purity, to the sacred—for the sacred can also be understood in terms of energy, but of a quality our instruments are incapable of recording.

In all esoteric traditions, there is a division between a higher level and a lower level, between the spirit and the body. Gurdjieff puts this division in a very different context. Man, he says, is not born with a ready-made soul; he is born incomplete. A soul is material like the body, matter is energy, and each human being can develop finer substances within the body by himself, through conscious efforts. But this is not easy, and neither pious intention nor grim determination is sufficient.

The transformation of a human being only begins when the sources in the body, which Gurdjieff names "centers," from which stem movements, thoughts, and feelings, cease to produce spasmodic and erratic bursts of energy and begin to function harmoniously together.

Then, for the first time, a new quality appears, which Gurdjieff calls "presence." As the intensity of presence rises, the matrix of our reactions and desires, which we call the ego, gradually becomes elastic and transparent, and in the center of our automatic structure of behavior a new space is formed in which a true individuality can arise.

Peter Brook has directed over fifty film and theater productions in London, Paris, and New York. He is the author of *The Empty Space* (Macmillan, 1978) and *The Shifting Point* (Harper Collins, 1987).

From *Gurdjieff: Essays and Reflections on the Man and His Teaching*, edited by Jacob Needleman and George Baker (New York: Continuum, 1996). Used by permission of The Continuum International Publishing Group.

Parabola
Volume: 9.4
Food

THE UNENDING HUNGER

Martha Heyneman

Above all, in things both great and small, the naturalist is rightfully impressed and finally engrossed by the peculiar beauty which is manifested in apparent fitness or "adaptation" —the flower for the bee, the berry for the bird.
                                    —*D'Arcy Wentworth Thompson*

In full summer all I can see out my kitchen window are layers of leaves. I might be living in the trees. The light is green. When the wind blows, green light and leaf shadows stream across the floor. I might be living in the water. I breathe moist air. A purple finch flashes past the window.

I stand up straight. My hands are free to grasp and carry. Through streaming shadows my feet walk over to the vegetable bin. My fingers close around cool potatoes. I count out six. The potatoes smell of earth.

From the refrigerator my hands lift out a package of fish for dinner, lay it on the counter, reach back in and close around two lemons. I lift the lemons to my nose. In my mind's eye I see them hanging, small suns half-hidden, some near, some far, among the leaves. Hands learned to grasp in the trees, closing around branches. I owe my grasp to the lemurs. Color and stereoscopic vision I owe to the monkeys. What had been a flat world took on depth. Such eyes could see what fruit was near, what far. Such hands could close around branch after branch, swinging the body toward the fruit.

I lay the lemons on the counter beside the fish and spread out my hand between white fish and yellow fruit. Before it was a hand it was a fin, not meant for grasping but for balance, guidance, and maneuvering through three dimensions in the water. Jaws did the grasping then. Fins and jaws evolved together. Fins guided the body swiftly toward the target, with quick changes of course and adjustments of roll, pitch, and yaw, if the target was a moving one. Once the jaws had taken hold, fins rolled the body around and around its own axis, twisting off a bite from a whole plant or animal. The jaw, before it was a jaw, supported a gill arch. Old parts change shape and serve new purposes. The bone that attached the fish's jaw to its cranium became the sound-transmitting bone in a reptile's ear. Two bones that articulated the reptile's jaw became the other two. And so now, through articulation of hammer, anvil and stirrup, I hear, through summer air, the call of the finches.

Before there were jaws there was only filter-feeding for the verte-brates, sucking in sea water with muscular mouths (as my babies' mouths sucked milk), filtering out small particles, sending the filtered water on out through slits on either side of the throat. (My babies had such gill slits when they were embryos. So did I. We have all spent time in warm sea water.) Without fins the jawless fishes swam erratically. Nevertheless, they swam. Vertebrates, then as now, were highly motile animals, able to move their bodies to where the food was. Beneath them invertebrates slid slowly along under heavy shells, scraping with rough tongues the film of algae off the rocks; or hid their long, segmented bodies immobile in tubes, each leaving outside a feathery tuft to trap whatever edible something happened by; or stuck fast to the substrate, wafting water weakly toward their mouths with cilia. All the basic invertebrate designs appear at once in the Cambrian rocks of 600 million years ago. Before that only single cells without nuclei have been found—bacteria and blue-green algae, going back as far as three billion years. Vertebrates may have evolved from the free-swimming larvae of one of the sessile invertebrates—something like a sea squirt. If so, it wasn't the only time a kind of failure to grow up has given rise to the wave of the future.

I clench my own jaw now, feeling the force of it. It isn't much, but then it doesn't need to be, what with the rack of knives above the cutting board and the stove beside it, whose oven I now light with a match. I am omnivorous, and so are most other primates, as recent patient, years-long studies of them in the wild reveal, discrediting the rash of books, popular a few years ago, which portrayed us—as if to make excuse for our wars—as the only bloodthirsty apes. Chimpanzees prey on vertebrates with skill and persistence, although they cannot bring down animals larger than themselves, as man can with his weapons. Such books also forgot the role of women in hunting-gathering societies, which are probably the earliest human type. There the everyday diet consists of the roots and tubers the women dig with their pointed sticks, the nuts and the berries they carry home in their baskets. Hunting is an occasion, and the men bring back the kill to camp, dividing it carefully in accordance with traditional rules, so that all have a share.

I have the cutting incisors of a rodent, the grinding molars and pre-molars of a herbivore, the pointed canines of a carnivore. But I cannot crush large bones with the unaided strength of my jaw nor eat the raw bamboo and giant celery that gorillas prefer. I am just as glad, too, because in evolution everything has its price. The finch's ancestors sacrificed the possibility of hands in exchange for wings (and not a bad trade, either). One of our cousins on the hominid bush, *Australopithecus boisei*, sacri-ficed the possibility of a large brain in exchange for a powerful jaw, and became extinct. A massive jaw requires a thick skull, with early-closing sutures, to work against. In such a skull there is no room for the brain to go on growing after birth, as ours does. *Homo habilis* had a brain little larger than *Australopithecus,* but nevertheless had a talent for invention. He could sharpen one stone by banging on it with another and, hitting the sharp stone with the blunt one, could break open bones for their marrow or cut through tough thick stalks or pound them to a pulp. He had no need for a heavy jaw. As for *Homo erectus*, he (or she?) harnessed fire for cooking and devised more and better tools. With the advent of tools, there was no further need to change the shape of the body (or to wait for thousands of years for it to change) to get at a certain type of food. I do not have to wait a thousand years until my hand turns into a pincer or grows stiff bristles. I grasp a potato in my left hand, turn on the water with my right, grasp the handle of a stiff brush and give this potato a thorough scrubbing, then the rest. I put the potatoes in the oven, with silent thanks to *Homo habilis* and *erectus.*

———————

I stand in front of the sink again, pondering with my large brain (no larger than yours). The potatoes will take much longer to cook than the fish. The salad needs only washing, chopping, and dressing. Long since grown up, I go on trying, in intervals between physically necessary jobs of work, to imagine the whole of things, to feel and sense my place in it, to understand what I am supposed to do, in order that I might begin to live consciously and deliberately as well as instinctively. This is all because my ancestors never grew up. We owe our large brains to something called neoteny, where juvenile forms are carried on into sexually mature life.

> *Our embryonic skulls scarcely differ from those of chimpanzees. And we follow the same path of changing form through growth: relative decrease of the cranial vault since brains grow so much more slowly than bodies after birth, and continuous relative increase of the jaw. But while chimps accentuate these changes, producing an adult strikingly different in form from a baby, we proceed much more slowly down the same path and never get nearly so far. (Stephen Jay Gould,* The Panda's Thumb, *p. 106.)*

Some mutation or series of mutations affected out growth rates, so that we spend a long time in the womb, our brains go on growing at fetal rates for four more years after we are born, our childhood is long, leaving plenty of time for our elders to try to transmit the culture to us, the sutures in our skulls do not close completely until well into adulthood, and our lifetime as a whole is longer than that of any other mammal. Scientific theories come and go, and we go on learning.

Although tools make it no longer necessary for me to wait until the shape of my body changes before I can get something to eat, the capacity to use tools has, according to the theory of evolution, taken shape through this groping, trial-and-error process of random genetic mutation and natural selection, a process too slow for the tempo of my brain to imagine without speeding up the film. The call of the finch reminds me that it was the finches of the Galapagos Islands whose images in memory gave Darwin the idea. He does not mention them in the first published edition of his *Journal of the Voyage of the H.M.S. Beagle*. But in the second edition of 1845 he describes "the perfect gradation in the size of the beaks in the different species," and concludes: "Seeing this gradation and diversity of structure in one small, intimately related group of birds, one might really fancy that from an original paucity of birds in this archipelago, one species had been taken and modified for different ends." This was his first public pronouncement on the subject he was to elaborate and generalize into the "one long argument" of *The Origin of Species*.

You can tell what a bird eats by the shape of its beak. Finches generally have broadly conical, strong bills suited for breaking capsules and splitting seeds. Warblers have delicate slender ones suited for dealing with small insects, while hummingbirds have the longest, most delicate, slenderest of all, for probing into flowers to reach the nectar they drink. Woodpeckers have hard and chisel-like beaks, for drilling holes in the bark and wood of trees, and long tongues for probing into the holes to extract the insects. On the Galapagos, Darwin saw birds with beaks of all these shapes, but all of them were finches. David Lack made an exhaustive study of them in 1938 and the years following:

> ... the beak differences between most of the genera and subgenera of Darwin's finches are clearly correlated with differences in feeding methods. This is well borne out by the heavy, finch-like beak of the seed-eating Geospiza, *the long beak of the flower-probing* Cactornis, *the somewhat parrot-like beak of the leaf-, bud-, and fruit-eating* Platyspiza, *the woodpecker-like beak of the woodboring* Cactospiza, *and the warbler-like beaks of the insect-eating* Certhidea *and* Pinaroloxias. (Darwin's Finches, *p. 60*.)

But *Cactospiza* does not have a long tongue like a born woodpecker. Instead, having drilled its hole, "it picks up a cactus spine or twig, one or two inches long, and holding it lengthwise in its beak, pokes it up the crack, dropping the twig to seize the insect as it emerges." (p. 58) *Cactospiza* is almost alone among birds in having figured out how to use a tool.

... the form of an object is a diagram of forces.
                                    —D'Arcy Wentworth Thompson

But how did Darwin's finches feel? Reading about evolution is like watching television with the sound turned off. It might be argued that, being birds of little brain, they felt nothing, but maybe our large brains oblige us to feel for them, consciously. Loren Eiseley thought this human capacity to put oneself in the place of another creature was more important than our capacity to penetrate outer space.

> *... whenever I see a frog's eye low in the water warily ogling the shoreward landscape, I always think inconsequentially of those twiddling mechanical eyes that mankind manipulates nightly from a thousand observatories. ... I stand quite still and try hard not to move or lift a hand since it would only frighten him. And standing thus it finally comes to me that this is the most enormous extension of vision of which life is capable: the projection of itself into other lives. This is the lonely, magnificent power of humanity. (*The Immense Journey, *pp. 45-46)

It must have been that a few (at least two) finches were blown by a great storm, or swept on a raft of vegetation, 600 miles out over the raging ocean west of Ecuador, arriving by luck (how many drowned?) upon these islands. There they found no other land birds. All the ecological niches were vacant. There were no predators. (On this account, the finches are even today not very agile flyers and extremely tame.) Their situation was not unlike that of my great-grandmother (of whom I am reminded by the smell of the potatoes, beginning now to bake). About how she felt, I think I do know something.

> *The real troubles of Ireland ... arose from an increase of population which far outstripped production. ... There were 685,000 farms in all. Of these, 300,000 were under 3 acres in extent; and 250,000 were from 3 to 5 acres. As might be expected, the condition of the vast majority of land workers was miserable.*
> *The potato blight ... reached Europe in 1845. 1846 and 1847—especially the latter—were its worst years. In a few weeks the abundant*

*potato harvest in Ireland became a waste of putrefying vegetation. The total Irish mortality for the five years that ended in 1851 was close upon a million. In the decade that followed 1847 more than 1,500,000 persons emigrated. (*Encyclopedia Britannica, *1947 edition, Vol. 12, p. 612.)*

Tarpey

On October 25, 1852, as Mr. Patrick Tarpey was returning by the Lancashire and Yorkshire Railway to Liverpool, from one of the inland counties, where he had been disposing of several large lots of cattle, purchased at recent fairs in this country, he incautiously stepped from the carriage while in motion, and having missed his footing, fell under the train and was instantaneously crushed to death. Deceased was an extensive cattle dealer residing in the neighborhood of Dunmore, and has left a large family to deplore his loss.   Requiescat in pace.
—Tuam (*Co. Galway, Ireland*) Herald.

In 1855 my great-grandmother, Bridget O'Grady Tarpey, gathered her nine remaining children about her and set sail for America. Her eldest son, Matthew, was already in California. My grandfather, Dominick Patrick, was five years old. Mrs. Tarpey and the children crossed the Isthmus of Panama on muleback and sailed up the west coast to San Francisco.

In 1970 I went to Ireland with my husband and four children. We found the place from which my great-grandmother had set out. Standing there, I felt the ghost of what she must have felt: setting out from the once loved valley where her people had lived, it may be, since prehistoric times; stepping, with her children, into a leaky sailing ship, terror of the monstrous ocean in front of her, tearing sorrow of leaving all she knew behind her, impelled by that inexorable force we call Nature, the will to survive—which is no more personal, no more "I," than a hurricane.

This is the force that drives "natural selection" from behind. We have known that force in ourselves, immediately, with no need for definition in words, if we have ever been drowning or (unlikely for most of us, likely for my great-grandmother) starving to death, or if a child of ours has been threatened with death, or even ridicule. I have been terrified to feel the magnitude of the force with which I struggled, when a great wave knocked me under, to reach the surface, to fill my choking lungs with air; to realize (afterward) the speed with which I ran to snatch my child from in front of oncoming traffic, the murder that arose in my heart if someone picked on him.

In front is the sieve of circumstance, through which most creatures never pass, most dying before they grow up, all suffering, those who make it doing so through accident of birth, luck, or constant vigilance punctuated by bloody battle or swift escape. Most warm-blooded animals have to spend all their time getting food enough to stay alive, to fuel the fires of their fierce metabolism. Even primates have to spend 80 percent of their waking hours in this way. Only human beings have time (and capacity) to ponder, to try to find out where they came from, to imagine how it feels to be someone else, to envision the whole and their place in it, to wonder what they are supposed to do with their large brains and their leisure time.

Sometimes a creature is lucky. The Galapagos were a kind of Golden West of the finches. In California, my great-uncle Matthew bought, in 1859, Rancho Colorado, 4000 acres. His brother Michael established vineyards near Bakersfield and, in 1886, ran for Lieutenant Governor. My grandfather was a miner, an assayer, a railroad land agent, a rancher. He owned the ranch on which the golden spike was driven that united the eastern and western halves of the transcontinental railroad. By the next generation all these ecological niches were filled or had vanished, but that is another story. My grandfather and great-uncles did not develop into new species, but they developed traits they could not have developed in Ireland (supposing they could have survived).

There are moments in Loren Eiseley's *The Immense Journey* when the volume is suddenly turned up and I hear an echo of how much agony lies behind the decorous screen of the theory of evolution. Eiseley is imagining how it was for the freshwater Crossopterygian fish who was the first vertebrate to walk out on dry land, to breathe air, the first to develop the hollow brain without which we would be, like insects, programmed machines with no possibility of ever changing our behavior.

... It began with a strangled gasping for air. The pond was a place of reek and corruption, of fetid smells and of oxygen-starved fish breathing through laboring gills. ... On the oily surface of the pond, from time to time a snout thrust upward, took in air with a queer grunting inspiration, and swirled back to the bottom. The pond was doomed, the water was foul, and the oxygen almost gone, but the creature would not die. It could breathe air direct through a little accessory lung, and it could walk. ... There was dew one dark night and a coolness in the empty streambed. When the sun rose next morning the pond was an empty place of cracked mud, but the Snout did not lie there. He had gone. Down stream there were other ponds. He breathed air for a few hours and hobbled slowly along on the stumps of heavy fins. (The Immense Journey, *pp. 49-51.)*

I fill the sink with water now and begin to wash the lettuce. To stand here in a human body, serenely breathing, with no need for effort on my part, is to stand on top of millions of years of suffering.

Driven from behind, then, by the imperious command to survive, to reproduce (there was a time in my life when I said, like Rachel, "Give me children or else I die"), to see to it that one's offspring survive; through, in front, the sieve of circumstance, whose holes, most of the time, are very fine—at rare moments, unaccountably, large and commodious—we change shape and character, through struggle, suffering, luck, or some combination thereof. But how did the shapes get there in the first place?

––––––––––

Oh! Blessed rage for order, pale Ramon,
The maker's rage to order words of the sea,
Words of the fragrant portals, dimly-starred,
And of ourselves and of our origins,
In ghostlier demarcations, keener sounds.
                    —*Wallace Stevens*

The sun is low now. For a moment the branches part and it flashes through. I am blinded.

In the beginning the sun's radiations were moving on the face of the waters. There was lightning without thunder. There was no air. There were simple inorganic gases—carbon monoxide, hydrogen, methane, ammonia, water vapor. In the 1950s, these conditions were recreated in the lab. After a week, sugars, nucleic acids, and amino acids were found in the moisture. In recently improved laboratory tests, "All five substances that carry the messages of heredity within nucleic acids were spontaneously synthesized." (*New York Times*)

> *... if two particles are put together in an "organized" way, instead of the formula 1 + 1 = 2, we get 1 + 1 > 2, and ... this is the basic equation of biology. Thus if an electron and a nucleus come together in an organized way, a hydrogen atom is born, which is more than an electron and a nucleus. If atoms are built into a molecule, something new is born, which can no longer be described solely in terms of atoms. The same holds true when small molecules are built into macromolecules; macromolecules into organelles; organelles into cells; cells into organs; organs into individuals; and individuals into a society or ecological "associes"...* (The Biology of Nutrition, *Richard N. T-W-Fiennes and others, p. 182.*)

As Sir Peter Medawar points out (*The Art of the Soluble*), information theory is inadequate to explain the kind and degree of organization found in living things (which exist, at least in our solar system, only in the thin film of organic life on earth). We know something of the magnitude of this force of organization by witnessing the magnitude of the force released when it is undone, all at once, as at Hiroshima. All life lives on its energy. In the daisy-shaped molecule of chlorophyll in green leaves, photons of sunlight raise electrons to less probable, higher-energy levels in the organization of atoms. The high-energy electrons are then stored in chemical bonds or passed on stepwise through the metabolic reactions of life—in plant, herbivore, and carnivore—until they reach their lowest energy level in water, whence they are raised up again by sunlight in the leaves. Into the descending stream we are all plugged, like the factories that used to be built along New England rivers, harnessing their energy with every sort of contraption—water wheels, driving belts, turning spools, banging looms—as the water descended from mountain springs down to the sea.

*Men talk much of matter and energy, of the struggle for existence that molds that shape of life. These things exist, it is true; but more delicate, elusive, quicker than the fins in water, is that mysterious principle known as "organization," which leaves all other mysteries concerned with life stale and insignificant by comparison. For that without organization life does not persist is obvious. Yet this organization itself is not strictly the product of life, nor of selection. Like some dark and passing shadow within matter, it cups out the eyes' small windows or spaces the notes of a meadowlark's song in the interior of a mottled egg. That principle—I am beginning to suspect—was there before the living in the deeps of water. (*The Immense Journey, *p. 26.)*

I have some immediate experience of this force too—as you do, if you have ever "made" anything (that is, have been the medium through which a multiplicity of unrelated items strive to combine into a harmonious whole, an organized unity). Every morning I look and see it is not yet right, and again the next day it is not yet right, and so on, through a peculiar kind of suffering, until either time is up or further work begins to make it worse instead of better.

Now I finish "making" dinner: mix golden oil pressed from olives that grew in Italy, wine vinegar, garlic, spices from all over the world; put the fish in the broiler, squeeze the juice of the lemon over it. The family gathers. A daughter sets the table. We serve the plates, add parsley and paprika, slices of lemon, a pat of golden butter to melt and mingle with the mealy white flesh of the split potato. A dim striving impels us to try to make a harmony of colors, textures, flavors, nutrients on each round plate. We call the others and carry the plates into the dining room.

Daylight is pearl-grey now. We light the candles. I sit down, heave a sigh and look around at my family, this unity in multiplicity, these variations on a theme. There they are with their large brains, their thoughtful faces in the rippling candlelight betraying the presence of inner lives I cannot know.

We too live at the edge of the sea, like Rachel Carson's snails and mussels, barnacles, sea urchins and starfish. But the thin strip of shore we inhabit lies not between continent and ocean, between dry land and water, but between the outer and the inner worlds. Our attention lives now in one, now in the other. First one, then the other, is real to us. For four hundred years now the center of gravity of attention in the West has been in the outer world. Scientific facts, observations, and theories are piled up like shells and pebbles, loosely intertwined with seaweed, scattered along the shore. Now the tide turns. We have got ourselves in trouble, into an evolutionary impasse. Attention begins to turn toward the inner, and we find that various sciences of the inner have already long ago reached high levels of development in the East and in the medieval West. Some cast their Western-educated brains behind them, plunge in, and drown.

The next phase of evolution could be outer. The force of organization could take hold of societies, until my children and grandchildren become, like ants and termites, cells in an elaborate structure of imposed functions and interconnections. Or the next phase could be inner and individual, radiations of the inner sun moving on the face of our inner waters, organizing our inner earth, which is now a chaos, without form, and void.

I have to acknowledge that about my own face in the mirror and about these loved faces in the candlelight there is something unformed, soft, unannealed. Our faces do not show the iron determination I see in the portrait of my great-grandmother. They have not the aching emotional intelligence I see in the faces of the statues at Chartres, refined in the fires of moral suffering. Is this softness a sign of degeneration or another case of the "never growing up" which prepares a wave of the future, a drawing back *pour mieux sauter*? We have not been forced to struggle much, by external circumstances or externally imposed doctrine. For the moment, we do not need to struggle for food. Supermarkets stand like horns of plenty on every street corner. The air is not yet too polluted to breathe. These children of mine, descendants of frontiersmen, would not take well to the external imposition of doctrine. We are not likely to engage in moral struggle until we know what for. It has to be on our own initiative, on the basis of our own understanding of what we owe, where we have come from, what our purpose is.

I received in the mail not long ago an invitation to a conference, on a Mediterranean island, whose purpose was to devise a myth for the post-Newtonian age. Indeed it is a myth we need, an imagined whole we could digest, a framework within which the bewildering multiplicity of unrelated impressions accumulated over a life-time might begin to take on meaning, find their place in a living, growing organism. But when a myth is alive, people do not think of it as myth but as the truth, the way things are. We already have half our myth in science, our story of the creation of the world and the evolution of man. But it is in a form indigestible for most of us. Scientific facts, theories, and observations are as numberless as the grasses of the original Great Plains. Fortunately, there are a few herbivores—Loren Eiseley, Rachel Carson, Lewis Thomas, a few others—who are able to graze upon these fields, to imagine, feel, and sense what they know and to communicate it to us in digestible language. What we need now are carnivorous poets—who will feed upon such writings and who also have practical experience in the sciences of the inner world—to imagine the whole and digest it into one body.

It is a pity the creationists and evolutionists can't get together. Whether we think of the species of living things as created all at once or developing painfully one from the other over three billion years is a matter of how, at the moment, we are experiencing time. To God, all time is present at once; and we know, from Dante, Christian saints, Hindu holy men, Zen masters, that human beings also have the possibility of this level of consciousness. "Does the wind move or does the grass move?" ask the pupils. "Your mind moves," answers the Zen master.

> *Time is but the stream I go a-fishing in. I drink at it; but while I drink I see the sandy bottom and detect how shallow it is. Its thin current slides away, but eternity remains.*
> *—Henry David Thoreau*

"Take the understanding of the East and the knowledge of the West—and then seek," said G. I. Gurdjieff. And bring us back a myth that contains the whole horizontal expanse of outer science, the whole vertical height and depth of the possible qualities of man's inner world. And do not cram it down our throats, but let each one eat in his own time, digest at his own organic tempo, then rise and do, on his own volition, on the basis of his own understanding, the work that only he, as "a particle of a part of the great whole," with his particular capacities, in his particular circumstances, was born to do.

Parabola
Volume: 23.2
Ecstasy

Beyond Words

William Segal

How, indeed, could it be possible for man, who is limited on six sides—by east, west, south, north, deep, and sky—to understand a matter which is above the skies, which is beneath the deep, which stretches beyond the north and south, and which is present in every place, and fills all vacuity?
    —St. Gregory the Wonderworker (c. 213–268)

The moment I die to myself, the moment I throw myself away, joy—even ecstasy—bursts through me. At this moment, I can say yes to everything I affirm as my existence. All the world is fine just as it is.

Ecstasy is an experience that is beyond verbal and intellectual comprehension, a glimpse of another existence and completely different from ordinary attitudes and viewpoints. The onset of the ecstatic moment does not depend on, nor does it come from, outside oneself. It is a call from the "purity in oneself," in St. Gregory's words; it is present everywhere and fills all vacuity. It is the same force which animates one's instinctive drives, one's associative thoughts. But it is a force which now takes another form.

How can one experience ecstasy without transcending oneself, without freeing oneself from the incessant domination of one's instinctive life? To go out of oneself, to be in touch with one's essential reality, is to hold in abeyance those forces which dominate one's existence.

Sometimes a sudden shock will bring a cessation of the associative processes, will intervene to free one from imprisonment by oneself. But too often man is unable to disengage himself from himself. He is unable to move outside of the two-dimensional bondage of this twenty-four hour conditioning by society into the free world of joy and ecstasy. From the moment of his birth, an ersatz culture has chipped away at whatever spiritual dimension he may have possessed.

Nirvana is where the two-fold passions have subsided and the two-fold hindrances are cleared away.
—Lankavatara Sutra

From *Opening: Collected Writings of William Segal, 1985-1997*, published by Continuum.

Parabola
Volume: 9.4
Food

A QUESTION OF BALANCE

An Interview with Henri Tracol

The system taught by Gurdjieff includes within it a complex elaboration of the place of food on cosmological and psychological levels. In 1984 Parabola *sought out Mr. Tracol in his summer retreat in the south of France to speak with him about these ideas in the light of his own long experience. He greeted us in his shaded courtyard where among the trees, herbs, and flowers were several of his large stone sculptures— massive forms smoothed out of a local white stone. His latest work,* Ganesha, *awaited final polishing in an open-air studio adjoining the main house.*

Once inside the cool, high-ceilinged living room, we sat together at a large, old wooden table. Mr. Tracol responded to our questions with great interest and intensity. Gentle, unpretentious, direct, full of quick humor, he seemed somehow to accompany his words. As we spoke, the exchange became not only a discussion of abstract ideas but a kind of nourishment in itself.

—Lorraine Kisly

Parabola: *We might start out by speaking about physical food. In the United States now, perhaps in Europe as well, there is a great interest in experimentation—in macrobiotics—in vegetarianism, in organically grown foods, and it becomes almost a moral issue what sort of food we eat. But in the*

Gospels Christ says, "For what goes into your mouth, that will not defile you, but that which issues from your mouth—it is that which will defile you." Does it make a difference what sort of food we eat?

Henri Tracol: It certainly does. Now, what is the point of view from which we could evaluate this first food, physical food? Of course, we cannot be without a certain discrimination about what is good or bad from an ordinary point of view. But what is more important? First, this question can be understood only in relationship to the whole. You have to be attentive to your food, and not only the first food, but to the others. Whether you know it or not, you depend very much on what you eat, and breathe, and so on. It is not only necessary for the physical body, but also for the whole of your being. Food is needed not just to sustain our physical existence, it's also for other purposes. It is not to be belittled. Now, of course, you can eat the best food, drink the best drinks, and if you do not understand what it is for, it is lost—very largely, lost. What is absorbed and what feeds you really is a very small proportion of what is given. A small part sustains the outer existence, but most of it is wasted. Now I think of something that has been very striking for me. Perhaps you know a book by Viktor Frankl, *Man's Search for Meaning*. He speaks about the way people who were doomed to death in concentration camps could survive. What they ate was very, very little, very insignificant. But for them there was something much more important. There was a wish to be. Even though they did not fully realize the importance of it, they perceived that something was necessary, and was far more important than their comfort, their despair and so on. They knew that something was offered them, and they wanted to live. And on that basis, they could survive in conditions that were impossible—medically impossible.

So this is what is really important, to understand that the question of food is not just an outer, mechanical process, it is also something of significance. Insofar as you are able to be attentive to this perspective, it is really of value that you do not treat this food as something insignificant.

I would also say, in another field, that there was something that Mr. Gurdjieff never accepted—a completely stupid disregard for the body, or any kind of scorning of the body. He evoked a respect for the body. In the same perspective, what is really important there is not only that which we ordinarily call the body, with its pleasure, or fear of pain and so on, but the body itself as a place where something can be born again, and develop. So it has to be respected, and its needs, its real needs, met. There are many misinterpretations of what he said or wrote about the necessity to compel the body to obey higher imperatives. It is not *against* the body, it is *for* the body. And the body knows it, too!

P: *Mr. Gurdjieff has written that it is necessary to strive to have everything indispensable and satisfying for the physical body. This surprises me—not only everything necessary, but satisfying. When is it possible to have both?*

HT: This question implies the need for a degree of understanding. If we were to draw up a list of what is necessary and what is satisfying it would, of course, be futile.

It is a question of balance, mostly. And it means a balance with other needs as well. Otherwise, something can be quite satisfactory for the body itself, as separate from the rest, but it creates a lack of balance. What is necessary and what is really satisfactory is a balance between all the different needs of the being—physical, psychological, and spiritual.

P: *So the body needs this balance in order to be truly satisfied.*

HT: Yes.

P: *How do you see the point of the dietary restrictions that occur in so many traditions—Islam, Judaism, Buddhism? So many traditions set out very clear rules about what to eat, and when, and how much. What is the point of such rules?*

HT: Mr. Gurdjieff has spoken of such rules, and how they are always linked with other rules. They form part of a whole, and if something is missing in the other rules, then it is pointless. You forget what the reason is. At certain times it may be necessary to refrain from certain foods, and at other times not. In any case that is not the real point. We have to adapt ourselves to outer conditions, of course, but to inner conditions as well. Otherwise we make fools of ourselves in trying to stick to something as though it had to be followed at any cost.

P: *Did Mr. Gurdjieff subscribe to any particular rules about eating?*

HT: In *Meetings with Remarkable Men,* he speaks of his encounter with an old Persian dervish at a time when he, as a young man, was very keen to follow certain rules; for example, in regard to the thorough chewing of food. Asked by the dervish why he was so scrupulously practicing such a demanding method of eating, the young Gurdjieff explained at length why this was highly recommended by certain schools of Indian yogis. To which the old man shook his head and said, "May God kill him who does not know and yet presumes to show others the way to the doors of His Kingdom." After explaining to his young visitor that it was imperative at his age, not to deprive his stomach of the opportunity to exercise itself in its natural work, the old man concluded by hinting that those who recommended such mastication had, as is said, "heard a bell without knowing where the sound had come from."

As a matter of fact, Mr. Gurdjieff trained us to eat all sorts of things that were not particularly recommended! He would insist that you at times had to eat all sorts of greasy, fatty foods, all sorts of extremely spicy ingredients which, from an ordinary medical point of view were totally unacceptable. Of course there were those who needed to be on a special diet, and he was resilient enough to exempt them. But otherwise, you *had* to eat what was served. He would go to the market and choose the ingredients and prepare the food early in the morning for the evening. He would allow very few people to help him. He had his own ways of doing things. And when we were eating with him, he was very attentive to how we ate our food. It was very important for him. When he saw someone who was preoccupied with a question he perhaps wanted to ask, and was eating without realizing he was eating, he would frown, and sometimes scold the person. So there was a respect for food, no matter *what* it was!

P: *This respect for food that you mention seems to have almost completely disappeared from our lives—perhaps because most of us live so far away from the cultivation and production of food, we no longer know what it has cost before it arrives at our table.*

HT: It is true. It is not easy to count the cost. But, you see, when we speak of food, we are speaking of one category, forgetting or neglecting the others, and I think that is misleading. In fact, there are all sorts of foods—foods which concern the whole being. It is said that there are three kinds of food: ordinary food, air, and impressions. We can go on existing for days without ordinary food. We can survive if we do not breathe for a few minutes perhaps, not very long. But we cannot exist for one second without impressions. This is an extraordinary idea. One can hear it, perhaps be surprised by it and say, "That is very interesting." But it is immediately forgotten because it has not been received in the proper way. Perhaps it demands a lifetime to understand what it means. The food of impressions is taken in constantly. We need this third kind of food in order to really absorb the first kind. We also need it in order to breathe. What is essential there is mostly neglected, ignored. It is fantasy for us. Of course it is closely related to another idea which very largely escapes us, according to which only the higher centers can really receive the food of impressions. Higher centers—and it is said that higher centers are fully developed in a human being—function perfectly well; what is missing is the proper link with the lower centers. In *Beelzebub's Tales,* Mr. Gurdjieff speaks of what happens to this finer food of impressions. Most of it is lost. But a part of it is always maintained and perceived and absorbed for the development of the higher components of a being, so that, without our knowing—and especially when we are asleep—something is taking place.

P: *These impressions are being received all the time, so it is a question of digestion?*

HT: Yes. In fact, something is digested without our knowing it. Regardless of what becomes of our lower centers, the higher centers need to go on existing. It is also said that accidentally—but it is no mere accident, it is for higher purposes—we receive the necessary help for the digestion of these finer impressions. I do not claim to understand that, of course, but it is true that something echoes in me. So we are made use of for the sake of the higher centers, and even though we feel ourselves to be cut off from them, they are there.

P: *It really does seem that it is impossible to speak of one food at a time, as if we eat at one moment, breathe at another, and then receive an impression.*

HT: We are enslaved by the notion of time, of course.

These questions also evoke the mystery of what is called "conscious attention." Ordinarily speaking, what we call conscious attention is our instant translation of our experience into ordinary terms. "This is that": we give a definition. But in fact, this sort of attention is marginal, it remains at the surface. It is an automatism that goes on endlessly. The machine is very good. It functions very well, outerly. But for the whole being, including the higher parts, this attention is almost negligible. It deals with the outer part of our existence, that's all; for the essential is not there. That is why it is so important to take into account what happens in very special conditions, as in the case of the prisoners Frankl speaks of. Ordinary conditions of existence are important, of course; they have to be taken into account, but the real meaning does not lie there.

P: *It has been said that every creature is designed for a certain kind of food, and can be defined in relationship to what it eats. Each creature can be seen as a kind of specialist in eating certain foods. It seems that there might be here a kind of definition of the difference between human beings and all other beings in this question of impressions. Are there certain kinds of impressions that only human beings can receive? Are we, in some way, specialists having the possibility of receiving a certain kind of food?*

HT: Undoubtedly. But is it for our ordinary mind to try to understand what that means? It is very dangerous, because most of the time we translate it into inadequate terms, into words which do not correspond. Ordinary thinking cannot grasp this at all. Is there, then, something that we could call "higher mind"? Do we know something about it, or is it just the projection of an image? Is it once again a wrong functioning of ordinary thought which tries to define what "higher mind" should be?   No. I think we need to keep a kind of respect for what is given us at certain moments to perceive—not as the result of some mental construct but as something which is offered and offered and offered … and that *for once* we perceive. Does this perception depend on me, or is this something which is granted to me? I think that even if it depends partly on me, it is mostly granted; and it has to be perceived as granted, as a gift.

P: *Several times now you have said that the energy we draw from all the different kinds of food is largely wasted. What, then, is wasted?*

HT: One cannot help thinking of everything that is wasted in nature. All the seeds which seem to be completely lost—but they are not lost; they serve for something, so nothing is lost, nothing is wasted completely. But we cannot remain indifferent when we see what is *partly* wasted and which, planted, would have grown into a magnificent tree. We are sensitive to this difference. It calls to something in us. There is something there which could be fully developed and that is what evokes our real interest. And it applies to man as well. He could, of course, be a very splendid animal for the Olympic Games, or an outstanding artist. But something is missing from the plenitude, the full stature of the being—I do not mean someone who could do everything; no, that is not the question. I mean that we have been born with a certain balance of capacities which go far beyond what our ordinary imagination could conceive.

But there is first of all a sense of balance, of right balance, and there is a certain balance at the moment when a man awakens to his own destiny. He is able to join what is in him, what is there as a seed in him, and find the corresponding attitude and functioning to bear witness to the presence of this capacity. It may not correspond to what could perhaps be expected from someone else, but it corresponds to what *he* is. I think that this is a real source of commitment, by which I mean not to dream of an impossible realization, but to be receptive to a call; capacities are there waiting to be recognized, waiting to be actualized.

P: *Whatever awareness is (again, a word probably misunderstood), it seems that one can sense that the quality of physical food, of air, of impressions would completely change if there was the light of awareness on the process which takes place in the dark, and somehow unrelated. This was what Mr. Gurdjieff seemed to be calling for all the time.*

HT: Oh, yes, he knew that what was usually meant there was most of the time a far distant approach—something that did not correspond really to what he was calling for. If you are not "one," whole, there will always be something missing. Of course, a person who dreams of understanding the Whole makes a fool of himself. It is simply impossible. He is just dreaming. What you can try is to open to what corresponds to you, and to you only. I would say—jokingly—that in a certain way you can understand something that God cannot understand. God cannot become so small! The idea of specificity, of what is possible for each person, evokes a completely different interest than a claim to understand more and more and still more, up to the Whole. That is simply stupid. It is not what is demanded. What is offered and demanded is to approach what corresponds to you and to no one else. It also means that you must share with others. There are many things to share with others, but there is something specific to *you* and to no one else on earth. In century after century you are the only one who can understand in that way, that way so very particular and special to you alone.

And this is very appealing—a real call which helps us to understand that something is expected of me.

P: *Mr. Gurdjieff speaks a very great deal about self-remembering. In reference to an earlier question, is the impression of oneself unique to human beings? Does it constitute a kind of food only humans can receive?*

HT: Another mystery. To remember oneself ... to awake. If we think in our ordinary terms, what does it mean to awake? Do I decide at a certain time to awake? And who decides? There is no answer to that, except to realize that I am awakened by something. It is not that I decide to awaken and I awake: that is quite simply impossible. But maybe "I" reminds me, calls me back. The sense of my being: that is not something I invent, or that I think about. It is. And it calls me back. It is once more rejoined. And that is self-remembering. Most of the time it is enjoyed by someone in me who claims to be the owner: "Oh yes! I know that." That is a betrayal. I have been given to see something, to understand something, and I try to join with it. But if I let in this claim to be the *one who* ... it is spoiled. Does it mean that I have to keep passive about it? Not at all. In order to stay awake, something is demanded of me, demanded of the whole of me, of all my faculties and capacities, including my ordinary attention, my possibilities to establish connections, useful associations.

In the name of what has been given me, what is being given me now, I do not allow myself to be passive. There is something behind. Something —there is no question of reaching for anything. It is not to be reached; it is there. This gives an objective meaning to my attempt at joining what is offered me. If I keep that, if my ordinary, outer self keeps that, is faithful to this recognition, then it is given me over and over again to discover what is proposed and proposed and proposed. Of course, it cannot last very long, but for a moment it can last. I can experience it and it leaves a trace. A vivid memory is left in me which I can find again later.

This memory is given. To remember myself is memory, isn't it? But who will remember? It is given me to remember and awake again to *the sense* of this hidden presence.

So ... Food. Food of impressions, impressions of myself. You know, when a journalist comes to interview, say, a potter, and asks him, "Well, could you explain to me how you do that?" If the potter begins to say, "Well, first you do this, and then you do that ... " and so on, what does it convey? But if the potter goes on with his pot, the answer is there without explanation—without reducing it to an explanation. It can be perceived. And then the journalist, if he is a really good journalist, would *also* try with *his* tools to translate what had been perceived into something which could be read. He has *seen* the work of the potter. But most of the time one reads nothing but stupidities. I don't know what objective art is, but at least I know that those who pretend to explain are neither artists nor objective witnesses! Very often we *think* we understand, and very often it is a misappropriation. "Oh yes, I understand." It is given me to understand at the moment when I am sensitive to what is offered me. But as soon as I take hold of it, it is finished.

Isn't it marvellous? You know—the person who always understands everything, who has an explanation for everything ... he is dead!

P: *Is there for you, at another level, a relationship between the idea of reciprocal feeding on a cosmic scale and the idea of the three foods?*

HT: Part of it is certainly the question of scale. It cannot be approached without keeping the sense of relativity. In the representation of a human being, for example, it is said that the human mind is thirty thousand times slower than the body. Do you understand what that means? "Oh, yes, of course I do!" But you don't. It is out of scale with our ordinary way of thinking. We can talk about it, but we do not understand it. Sometimes we can perceive a correspondence, but it is always late, only comes afterwards. It's a reflection of a reflection, dimmer and dimmer, so slow, and so much has happened in the meantime. So once again we are in front of this mystery that is far beyond our ability to understand anything about it. Nevertheless, these questions have a value, provided of course we do not attempt to answer them. But they may help to enlarge the scale of our interrogation. What we are given to perceive in our ordinary surroundings is a reflection of a reflection of a reflection of something much bigger and much greater. It is really of value to understand that what is taking place here is insignificant in a way, and at the same time it is extremely significant for me if I see it from another viewpoint. I am a small piece of life, which is invisible on this larger scale. So, if I begin to *think* about it and to draw conclusions … then I need to keep a sense of mystery. When I quote an objective thought from a great thinker and just quote it, I spoil it. But if I capture the sense of wonder I know that I don't understand, but I do know that it opens an understanding, opens it more and more. Then I feel closer to what was offered. I am thinking of certain formulations that, even if I live for another twenty years, I am sure I will still not be able to understand. There are things which are unfathomable, but each time they are so powerfully evoked in me that each time it is a discovery. I don't understand why sometimes we try so hard to "understand." It could destroy something in me. Once again, the sense of mystery is so much greater.

P: *There seems to be an appetite of the mind, a kind of greed it has when it is working alone and isolated, which wants its own satisfaction without any regard to the rest of the being.*

HT: There is certainly a greed for impressions, but this greed prevents a real reception. It is true that the mind has this avidity. However, there is always the possibility of referring to something which goes further. I am thinking of attitudes which are manifested outwardly by tensions (*he leans forward, banging the table*).

"What do you mean?" For me that means that it is finished; it makes it impossible for other impressions to come and awake corresponding spheres of interest in my mind, in my body, and in my feeling. But these awaken only insofar as I am able to remember the amplitude of the gift which is offered me again and again. If I succumb to my ordinary pretense and greed I lose something; but if I try to remain open to what I know is there, whether I am aware of it or not—it is there. Then there is a natural attempt at remaining open—I remain open. I know that something is offered me over and over again, and I try not to be far away from it.

P: *So there is a kind of fasting which is possible for the mind, a not allowing the greed of the mind, the greed of the feeling, the greed of the body to overtake this openness?*

HT: Yes, fasting. Remaining available for what cannot satisfy my ordinary greed. Memory is also there to help me—a certain kind of memory. Memories, most of the time, are obstacles, but there is memory in depth that we can try to open ourselves to again and again. We lack the corresponding words—in the same breath we speak of memory and memory, real memory and false memory. But *it is there.*

Parabola
Volume: 12.2
Addiction

On Love

Freely adapted from the Tibetan

A. R. Orage

You must learn to distinguish among at least three kinds of love (though there are seven in all): instinctive love, emotional love, and conscious love. There is not much fear that you cannot learn the first two, but the third is rare and depends upon effort as well as intelligence. Instinctive love has chemistry as its base. All biology is chemistry, or perhaps we should say alchemistry; and the affinities of instinctive love, manifesting in the attractions, repulsions, mechanical and chemical combinations we call love, courtship, marriage, children and family, are only the human equivalents of a chemist's laboratory. But who is the chemist here? We call it Nature. But who is Nature? As little do we suspect as the camphor which is married to the banyan suspects a gardener. Yet there is a gardener. Instinctive love, being chemical, is as strong, and lasts as long, as the substances and qualities of which it is the manifestation. These can be known and measured only by one who understands the alchemical progression we call heredity. Many have remarked that happy or unhappy marriages are hereditary. So, too, are the number of children, their sex, longevity, etc. The so-called science of astrology is only the science (when it is) of heredity over long periods.

Emotional love is not rooted in biology. It is, in fact, as often anti-biological in its character and direction. Instinctive love obeys the laws of biology, that is to say, chemistry, and proceeds by affinities. But emotional love is often the mutual attraction of disaffinities and biological incongruities. Emotional love, when not accompanied by instinctive love (as it seldom is), rarely results in offspring; and when it does, biology is not served. Strange creatures arise from the embraces of emotional love: mermen and mermaids, Bluebeards and *les belles dames sans merci*. Emotional love is not only short-lived, but it evokes its slayer. Such love creates hate in its object, if hatred is not already there. The emotional lover soon becomes an object of indifference and quickly thereafter of hatred. These are the tragedies of love emotional.

Conscious love rarely obtains between humans; but it can be illustrated in the relations of man to his favorites in the animal and vegetable kingdoms. The development of the horse and the dog from their original state of nature, the cultivation of flowers and fruit—these are examples of a *primitive* form of conscious love, primitive because the motive is still egoistic and utilitarian. In short, man has a personal use for the domesticated horse and the cultivated fruit, and his labor upon them cannot be said to be for love alone. The conscious love motive, in its developed state, is the wish that the object should arrive at its own native perfection, regardless of the consequences to the lover. "So she become perfectly herself, what matter I?" says the conscious lover. "I will go to hell if only she may go to heaven." And the paradox of the attitude is that such love always evokes a similar attitude in its object. Conscious love begets conscious love. It is rare among humans because, in the first place, the vast majority are children who look to be loved but not to love; secondly, because perfection is seldom conceived as the proper end of human love—though it alone distinguishes adult human from infantile and animal love; thirdly, because humans do not know, even if they wish, what is good for those they love; and fourthly, because it never occurs by chance, but must be the subject of resolve, effort, self-conscious choice. As little as Bushido or the Order of Chivalry grew up accidentally does conscious love arise by nature. As these were works of art, so must conscious love be a work of art. Such a lover enrolls himself, goes through his apprenticeship, and perhaps one day attains to mastery. He perfects himself in order that he may purely wish and aid the perfection of his beloved.

Would one enroll in this service of conscious love? Let him forswear personal desire and preconception. He contemplates his beloved. What manner of woman (or man) is she (or he)? A mystery is here: a scent of perfection the nascent air of which is adorable. How may this perfection be actualized—to the glory of the beloved and of God her Creator? Let him think, is he fit? He can only conclude that he is not. Who cannot cultivate flowers, or properly treat dogs and horses, how shall he learn to reveal the perfection still seedling in the beloved? Humility is necessary, and then deliberate tolerance. If I am not sure what is proper to her perfection, let her at least have free way to follow her own bent. Meanwhile to study—what she is and may become; what she needs, what her soul craves and cannot find a name, still less a thing, for. To anticipate today her needs of tomorrow. And without a thought all the while of what her needs may mean to me. You will see, sons and daughters, what self-discipline and self-education are demanded here. Enter these enchanted woods, ye who dare. The gods love each other consciously. Conscious lovers become gods.

Without shame people will boast that they have loved, do love or hope to love. As if love were enough, or could cover any multitude of sins. But love, as we have seen, when it is not conscious love—that is to say, love that aims to be both wise and able in the service of its object—is either an affinity or a disaffinity, and in both cases equally unconscious, that is, uncontrolled. To be in such a state of love is to be dangerous either to oneself or to the other or to both. We are then polarized to a natural force (which has its own objects to serve regardless of ours) and charged with its force; and events are fortunate if we do not damage somebody in consequence of carrying dynamite carelessly. Love without knowledge and power is demonic. Without knowledge it may destroy the beloved. Who has not seen many a beloved made wretched and ill by her or his "lover"? Without power the lover must become wretched, since he cannot do for his beloved what he wishes and knows to be for her delight. Men should pray to be spared the experiences of love without wisdom and strength. Or, finding themselves in love, they should pray for knowledge and power to guide their love. Love is *not* enough.

"I love you," said the man. "Strange that I feel none the better for it," said the woman.

The truth about love is shown in the order in which religion has been introduced into the world. First came the religion of Power, then came the religion of Knowledge, and last came the religion of Love. Why this order? Because Love without the former qualities is dangerous. But this is not to say that the succession has been anything more than discretion: since Power alone, like Knowledge alone, is only less dangerous than Love alone. Perfection demands simultaneity in place of succession. The order is only evidence that, since succession was imperative (man being subject to the dimension of Time, which is succession), it was better to begin with the less dangerous dictators and leave Love to the last. A certain prudent man, when he felt himself to be in love, hung a little bell around his neck to caution women that he was dangerous. Unfortunately for themselves they took too much notice of it, and he suffered accordingly.

Until you have wisdom and power equal to your love, be ashamed, my sons and daughters, to avow that you are in love. Or, since you cannot conceal it, love humbly and study to be wise and strong. Aim to be worthy to be in love.

All true lovers are invulnerable to everybody but their beloved. This comes about not by wish or effort but by the fact of true—i.e., whole—love alone. Temptation has not to be overcome; it is not experienced. The invulnerability is magical. Moreover, it occurs more often than is usually supposed. Because "unfaithfulness" is manifested, the conclusion is drawn that invulnerability does not exist. But "infidelity" is not necessarily due to temptation, but possibly and often to indifference; and there is no Fall where there is no Temptation. Men should learn to discriminate in themselves and in women real and assumed invulnerability. The latter, however eloquent, is due to fear. Only the former is the fruit of love. Another prudent man, desiring, as all men and women do in their hearts, invulnerability in himself and in the woman he loved, set about it in the following way. He tasted of many women and urged his beloved to taste of many men. After a few years he was satisfied that nothing now could tempt him. She, on the other hand, had had no doubt of herself from the beginning. She had been born invulnerable; he had attained it.

The state of being in love is not always defined in relation to one object. One person has the talisman of raising another to the plane of love (that is, of polarizing him or her with the natural energy of love); but he or she may not be then either the sole beloved or, indeed, the beloved at all. There are, among people as among chemical substances, agents of catalysis which make possible interchanges and combinations into which the catalysts themselves do not enter. Frequently they are unrecognized by the parties affected, and usually by themselves as well. In the village of Bor-na, not far from Lhassa, there once lived a man who was such a catalyst. People who spoke to him instantly fell in love, but not with him, or indeed, immediately, with anybody in particular. All that they were aware of was that they had, after conversation with him, an active spirit of love which was ready to pour itself into loving service. The European troubadours were perhaps such people.

There is no necessary relation between love and children, but there is a necessary relation between love and creation. Love is for creation; and if creation is not possible, then for procreation; and if even that is not possible, then for creations of which, perhaps fortunately, we are unconscious. Take it, however, as the fundamental truth about love: that it always creates. Love created the world—and not all its works are beautiful! The procreation of children is the particular function of instinctive love; that is its plane. But above and below this plane, other kinds of love have other functions. Emotional love is usually instinctive love out of place; and its procreations are in consequence misfits in the world. The high forms of love, on the other hand, either exclude procreation, not artificially but naturally, or include it only as a by-product. Neither the purpose nor the function of conscious love is children, unless we take the word in the mystic sense of becoming as little children. For, briefly, the aim of conscious love is to bring about rebirth, or spiritual childhood. Everybody with perceptions beyond those of male and female must be aware of the change that comes over the man or woman, however old in years, who loves. It is usually instinctive; yet it symbolizes the still more marvelous change occurring when a man or woman loves consciously or is aware of being consciously loved. The youth in such cases has all the air of eternity; and it is, indeed, the divine youth. The creations of such a spiritual child in each of the two lovers is the peculiar function of conscious love, and it depends neither upon marriage nor upon children. There are other creations proper to still higher degrees of love; but they must remain veiled until we have become as little children.

We are not one but three in one, and the fact is represented in our physiological make-up. The three main systems, cerebral, nervous, and instinctive, exist side by side, sometimes appearing to cooperate, but more often failing, and usually at cross-purposes. In relation to the external world, it depends upon the system in charge of the organism at the moment what the response to any given stimulus will be. If the cerebral system is on duty—that is, temporarily in charge of the organism—the response will be one. If the nervous or instinctive system is alone awake, the replies will be different. Three quite different people, each with his own ideas of how his organism should act, exist in us at once—and usually they refuse to cooperate with each other, and, in fact, get in each other's way. Now imagine such an organism, tenanted by three squabbling persons, to "fall in love." *What* has fallen in love; or, rather, which of the three? It seldom happens that all three are in love at the same time or with the same object. One is in love, the others are not; and either they resist, or, when the lover is off guard, make his organism unfaithful (driving the poor lover to lies and deceit or self-reproach); or they are forced into submission, battered into acquiescence. In such circumstances, which every candid reader will recognize, what is a lover?

You imagine that you are continent because you have refrained from sex-relations; but continence is of the senses as well as of the organs, and of the eyes chiefly. From each of the senses there streams energy—energy as various as the man himself. It is not only possible but it is certain that we can expend ourselves intellectually, emotionally or sexually through any one of the senses. To look with lust is much more than simply to look: it is to expend one of the finer substances of which complete sex-energy is composed; something passes in the action of vision which is irrecoverable; and for the want of it the subsequent sex-life is incomplete. It is the same with the other senses, though less easily realized. In short, it is possible to become completely impotent by means of the senses alone—yes, by the eyes alone—while remaining continent in the ordinary meaning of the word.

The chastity of the senses is natural in a few people; but by the many it must be acquired if it is to become common. Under the greatest civilization human history has yet known, the capital of which was the city whose poor remains are Baghdad, the chastity of the senses was taught from early childhood. Each sense was carefully trained, and exercises were devised to enable pupils to discriminate the different emanations arriving from the sense perceptions intellectually, emotionally, instinctively, or erotically motivated. From this education people acquired the power of directing their senses, with the result that chastity was at least possible, since it was under control. Eroticism thereby became an art, in the highest form the world has seen. Its faint echoes are to be found in Persian and Sufi literature today.

Bluebeard and La Belle Dame are the male and female types, respectively, of the same psychology—inspirers of hopeless because unrequitable passion. The decapitated ladies who hung about Bluebeard's chamber were really about his neck, and they had only to let go to be free. Similarly the pale warriors and princes in the cave of La Belle Dame were there by choice, if an irresistible attraction can be called choice. The legends present Bluebeard and La Belle Dame from the point of view of their escaped victims, that is to say, as monsters delighting in erotic sacrifice. But both were as much victims as their titular victims; and both suffered as much, if not more. In such cases of uncontrolled attraction, power passes through the medium, who thus becomes formidably magnetic; and men and women in the sympathetic relation are drawn towards him or her like filings toward a magnet. At first, no doubt, the experiences of a Bluebeard or La Belle Dame are pleasant and fortifying to self-pride and self-vanity. The other sex is at their feet. But when, having realized that the power is neither their own nor under their control: they discover that they too are victims; the early satisfaction is dearly paid for. The cure for all parties is difficult. It consists in the re-education of the body and the senses.

Love without divination is elementary. To be in love demands that the lover shall divine the wishes of the beloved long before they have come into the beloved's own consciousness. He knows her better than she knows herself, and loves her more than she loves herself, so that she becomes her perfect self without her own conscious effort. *Her* conscious effort, when the love is mutual, is for him. Thus each delightfully works perfection in the other.

But this state is not ordinarily attained in nature; it is the fruit of art, of self-training. All people desire it, even the most cynical; but since it seldom occurs by chance, and nobody has published the key to its creation, the vast majority doubt even its possibility. Nevertheless it is possible, provided that the parties can learn and teach humbly. How to begin? Let the lover, when he is about to see his beloved, think what he should take, do, or say so as to give her a delightful surprise. At first it will probably be a surprise that is not a complete surprise; that is to say, she will have been aware of her wish, and only delighted that her lover had guessed it. Later the delightful surprise may really surprise her, and her remark will be: "How did you know I should be pleased, since I should never have guessed it myself?" Constant efforts to anticipate the nascent wishes of the beloved while they are still unconscious are the means to conscious love.

Take hold tightly; let go lightly. This is one of the great secrets of felicity in love. For every Romeo and Juliet tragedy arising from the external circumstances of the two parties, a thousand tragedies arise from the circumstances created by the lovers themselves. As they seldom know the moment or the way to "take hold" of each other, so they even more rarely know the way or the moment to let go. The ravines of Mount Meru (i.e., Venusberg) are filled with lovers who cannot leave each other. Each wishes to let go, but the other will not permit it. There are various explanations of this unhappy state of affairs. In most instances the approach has been wrong: that is to say, the parties have leapt into union without thought of the way out. Often the first five minutes of the lovers' *first* meeting are decisive of the whole future of the relations. In some instances the original relation has been responsible for the subsequent difficulty of "letting go"; it should never have been, or not have been in the precise circumstances of its occurrence. Mistimed relations always cause trouble. In other cases the difficulty is due to difference in age, education, or "past." One is afraid to "let go" because it appears to be the last hope, or because too much time has already been spent on it, or because it has been the best up to date; or because his "ideal," created by education, demands eternal fidelity even where it is not possible, because it is not desired by both; or because one is oversensitive from past experience and cannot face another failure; or because the flesh being willing, the spirit is weak, i.e., neither party can use a knife; or because circumstances are unfavorable, that is, both parties must continue to see each other; or because of imagination, as when one or the other pictures the happiness of the other without him or her. There are a thousand explanations, and every one of them, while sufficient as a cause, is quite inadequate as a reason, the fact being that when one of the parties desires to separate, the other's love-duty is to "let go." Great love can both let go and take hold.

Jealousy is the dragon in paradise, the hell of heaven, and the most bitter of emotions because associated with the sweetest. There is a specific against jealousy, namely, conscious love; but this remedy is harder to find than the disease is to endure. But there are palliatives of which the first therapeutic condition is the recognition of the disease and the second the wish to cure oneself. In these circumstances let the sufferer deliberately experiment. Much may be forgiven him or her during this process. He may, for instance, try to forward the new plans of his former beloved—but this is difficult without obvious hypocrisy. Or he may plunge into a new society. Or he may engage himself in a new work that demands all his energy. Or he may cast a spell on his memory and regard his former beloved as dead, or as having become his sister, or as having gone away on a long journey, or as having become enchanted. Best, however, if he "let go" completely with no lingering hope of ever meeting her again.

Be comforted. Our life is but one day of our Life. If not today, tomorrow! Let go!

Parabola
Volume: 10.3
The Body

THE MYSTERY OF REBIRTH

Henri Tracol

This essay was translated and adapted by D. M. Dooling from "Homme, ciel, terre," which first appeared in L'Age Nouveau, *No. 112. A talk with Henri Tracol follows the article.*

"At the moment of creation," says the Zohar, "the four cardinal points united with the four constituent elements of the world here below: fire, water, earth, and air. It was by mixing these four elements that the Holy One, blessed be He, created a body in the image of that above. The body is thus composed of the elements of both worlds, those of the world below and those of the world above."

Two worlds: Heaven and Earth. And between these two worlds, there is a ladder, each rung representing an intermediary world, a level of realization, a degree of participation in the total Being. In the mysteries of Mithra, each corresponds to one of the seven planetary spheres that the initiate traverses, one after another, before attaining the highest Heaven. This is the ladder of Seth, whose posts were supported by the four sons of Horus to allow the dead Pharaoh to enter Heaven. It is the ladder of light which was to lead Mahomet from the ruins of the temple of Jerusalem to the foot of the divine Throne. It is Jacob's ladder, of which St. John was to say: "Henceforth ye shall see Heaven open, and the angels of God ascending and descending *upon the Son of Man.*"

But any attempt to push the analogy too far is bound to fail if too much weight is put on surface resemblances. The only way to avoid useless correlations, and to penetrate closer to the source of the common essence of traditional wisdom, is with a more open interest, a freer inner movement. This means putting oneself in a state of *resonance* to the vibration of the true analogy; this is the key to that universal symbolic language which we lost the use of so long ago. For even within a single tradition, there may be differing views; numbers and terms often disagree. Brahmanic thought holds to the division of the Tribhuvana: Heaven, Atmosphere, Earth. However, according to the Upanishads, the being who, after the death of his physical body, is reintegrated into the primordial unity by the *deva-yana*, passes first through the Kingdom of Fire, whose ruler is Agni, then through the various domains of the Rulers of the day, that of the bright half of the lunar month, those of the months of the Sun's ascension, and finally that of the year.[1]

Israel, like Islam, distinguishes seven earths under the seven firmaments, some gloomy or arid, others fertile and drenched with light, peopled according to their level of being by the degenerate descendants of Adam and of Cain.

The Chinese, for their part, count nine heavens, but here again we find the idea of the Axis of the World—in the *Kien-Mou*, an erect piece of wood analogous to the sacrificial stake of the Brahman, or to the shaman's birch tree, cut into seven, nine, or sixteen notches—"by which the Sovereigns ascend and descend."

In the course of these ascensions the spiritual "space traveler" is often called upon to rid himself gradually of his various "garments," so that he can put on the "tunic of light" which becomes a sort of reflection of his own transformed being. The garments are the different "bodies," the temporary supports of an inner process of becoming.

But what misapprehensions we weave into these bodies! Since there is nothing within or outside of us that remains motionless, it is a little absurd to try to enclose the moving aspects of our being in summary concepts. Besides, the multiplicity of the systems proposed and their differences of opinion soon put a stop to this sort of self-limitation. The points of view are so different that there is no use in trying to establish an exact correspondence, for instance, between the four bodies of Christianity—the carnal, natural, spiritual, and divine—and the five envelopes (*koshas*) described by the Vedanta, in their relation with the three *shariras*—principal or causal form, subtle form, gross or corporeal form. It is the general movement that we need to understand, and the meaning of the relationships established between the elements of each doctrine as a whole.

On the other hand, this ascension has for an accompanying theme (though in an opposite sense) the "fall" of the soul into forms which are increasingly material and gross. The very idea of the liberation of the imprisoned soul by its escape from the accursed body plunges us directly into Manicheism—whereas man's true destiny on earth is linked to his effort to bring about the laborious fusion of the opposing tendencies in himself.

"One cannot move the soul without the body, nor the body without the soul," writes Plato,[2] and St. Thomas Aquinas speaks of a "natural inclination" of the soul to unite with the body; "considered as the height of human perfection, the soul is not able to live separated from the body."[3]

For a human being also, the mystery of incarnation exists. How can he approach it? For it is not enough to awaken to the evidence of a more inner, more subtle presence. It is necessary to have an exchange in which he takes part as a whole being. He must acquaint his body and its members with what his head and his heart have welcomed.

It is at this point that Jacob's ladder is set up in him, with angels bearing messages ascending and descending. Between these two poles of his presence, between his Heaven and his Earth, a new life circulates, in which he is now beginning to believe.

"I am a doubting Thomas," say the skeptics. And the orthodox look at them scornfully—or rather, through them, at St. Thomas himself. Both would do well to take another look. Judas betrayed, Peter denied. Thomas doubted—how easy it is to say this!

Thomas—one of the twelve men whom Christ himself chose and appointed, and who remained close to him even after the "hard sayings" of Capernaum, who followed his Master everywhere, shared his trials, was present at his miracles. He was there when Jesus went into the house of Jairus, whose daughter had just died, and he took her by the hand and bade her rise; when the son of the widow of Nain sat up in his coffin and began to speak; he was there when Lazarus arose from his sepulcher at his Lord's command. He needed no conviction of Jesus' divinity. He believed in it, not with a sanctimonious and bigoted belief but with all the force of an inner certainty which was to lead him, in spite of taunts and threats, even to the Mount of Olives. After the "It is finished," he was still there, one of the eleven who remained united in their faith.

What did he still need to see? What new proof was necessary for this believer? What was the nature of the doubt that arose in him? He was an apostle. He had fully accepted his mission. He felt himself pledged, "committed," as we would say today. And this is precisely why he doubted—not Christ, certainly, nor the others, but himself. What was in question for him was not so much Mary Magdalene's testimony, nor that of the other ten; it was his own belief.

There was something that he had not yet been able to understand. Why was it that Jesus, the son of God, needed once more to assume the human condition? Son of David, are you never to be delivered? Has not everything then been fulfilled? And yet, to deny the resurrection would be to deny the divine utterance, to deny the Word.

Thus Thomas awoke to himself and knew that he was two. His soul had not ceased to believe, but it had left his body in the shadows. And inasmuch as his flesh hesitated, as his senses did not know or refused, he trembled before his destiny as an apostle; he felt helpless to bear witness in full. So evidently it was his body that he had to convince before he could go any further. "Except I shall see in his hands the print of the nails, and put my finger into the print of the nails, and thrust my hand into his side, *I will not believe.*"

Thomas, the Didymus—twin of Jesus, as the Gnostics were to call him—did he not feel Christ in himself as his divine brother? In order to realize this presence fully, he needed to experience this mystery in himself, to know for himself the return of Jesus of Nazareth into his body, allowing his faith to become incarnate through the communion of sense and spirit. And at this instant, the apostle Thomas was reborn. "My Lord and my God." He was transfigured by the overflowing joy of a new encounter; for at that moment, he met Christ, both in his spirit and in his body.

Jesus had said to Mary Magdalene, "Touch me not." She had been the first to see him, but she "knew not that it was Jesus." Then his disciples from Emmaus had met him. He walked beside them, he spoke to them; "but their eyes were holden that they should not know him." A little later, Jesus appeared and "stood in the midst" of the disciples; "but they were terrified and affrighted, and supposed that they had seen a spirit." And he said to them: "Behold my hands and feet, that it is I myself. Handle me, and see; for a spirit hath not flesh and bones, as ye see me have." Finally, he appeared to them again on the shores of the Sea of Tiberias. There again they failed to recognize him. A miraculous haul of fish was necessary to convince them.

What they saw, and what filled them with amazement, was clearly the *body* of the Son of Man. But it was his resurrected body, his body from now on incorruptible, his "radiant body." It was he and it was not he. The great mystery was accomplished.

But there he was among them. He broke bread. He ate with them. Surely this transcends human experience. And yet it is to this rebirth that we are called, even before death. It can be given to us to experience this in our lifetime—by analogy.

But as Karl von Eckharthausen writes: "So that this deification and transformation of earth into heaven can come about, there must be a change, a conversion of our being. This change of being, this conversion, is called rebirth.

"The rebirth is threefold: firstly, the rebirth of our *reason*. Secondly, the rebirth of our *heart* or *will*. And finally, the rebirth of our whole being.

"The first and second are *spiritual rebirths*; and the third, *corporeal rebirth*.

"Many serious men in their search for God have been reborn in intelligence and will, but few have known this rebirth of the body."

Parabola: *"Corporeal rebirth."* ... *There are so many things which are really the body which we call something else. I think most people think of the body as something very separate from the mind and the feelings.*

Henri Tracol: Separate, yes, and even alien. Alien and despicable. I must confess I always feel distressed when I am confronted with this tendency to look down on the body. Looking down on it, and ignoring the essential part it has to play in the awakening to reality.

P: *Isn't it a question of levels?*

HT: Indeed, but on which scale? I can think of the body as the lower part that has to be hidden and left behind, but I may also rediscover it as something that evokes a very different approach to the experience of life.

P: *But here is the problem: it* does *have to be left behind. If there is anything of more duration in us, it is going to have to get along without the body, the body as we know it. What is the real relation, then, between what we might call the body and what we might call the soul? If this evident body is going to be discarded, what will take its place? Perhaps that is what I'm asking. What is this possible "corporeal rebirth," as von Eckharthausen puts it?*

HT: Maybe it has something to do with recurrence.

P: *Recurrence? What do you really mean by that?*

HT: Beyond the lure of time in succession, we have been given the idea that endlessly we come back, and come back, and come back, that we are born again and again. So, we have a sense of recurring time which can be perceived even in a very simple way through breathing in air and breathing out, through waking again and again to the alternation of day and night, the round of the seasons, and so on. Of course, there is decay and there is death, but what is my experience of rebirth? I cannot just sweep this idea away. To be born again is something I am invited to welcome. I have been absent for hours and all of a sudden I wake up: I am born again. Where am I born again? In this body.

P: *I think my question has to do with the necessity for understanding incarnation. In a piece you wrote you said that the "body and its members need to participate in the knowledge which the heart and head have welcomed." Right away, one agrees and knows that it is so. At the same time one recognizes the difficulty, the resistance, and the sort of darkness which the body at times can represent. Yet one knows that without that organic understanding all knowledge is empty and without any force. I suppose I'm asking: what is the contribution of the body in understanding?*

HT: I would say that when one is granted this awakening to a deeper reality, the body does indeed take part in it. I cannot but appreciate the resonance of it in my body. There is something which responds quite naturally to it—something neither invented nor imposed. It is there of its own accord. Why should I blame the body for any resistance? In fact, is it not the mind that resists?

P: *When we speak of human experience, do we speak of the physical body alone?*

HT: The physical body alone—what does it mean? It means a man crippled in some way. There is no communication, no coming together. Maybe most human beings are like that—these millions of seeds that disappear for lack of the ferment of life. But insofar as a man is sensitive to what he is offered as a means to awaken and be part of something which gives him a new meaning, the distinction between mind, body, and feeling becomes meaningless. We are much more concerned by the *relationship* between mind and body, feeling and body, and by the presence of that which bears witness to their unity. And here again, despising the body has no relevance.

P: *I wonder if I understand the idea of two opposing forces and the reconciliation of those forces. Perhaps there isn't a split between the mind and body so much as a distance between them. And yet every tradition recognizes two opposing forces that do not automatically tend toward unity. In this article, too, you speak of the "laborious fusion" of opposing tendencies in oneself. But is the body at one end of the pole and the mind at the other? And if it is, isn't it necessary? Can there be any movement without that initial separation?*

HT: I think this is a source of many misunderstandings. There is no doubt that there is an opposition, which may be applied to mind and body; its origin, its source, however, is not mind itself, or body itself. It seems that the mind has a natural tendency to feel independent from the body. And the body is rather passive there. Now, the necessary opposition between "yes" and "no" takes advantage of this division. And we also know that it is possible not to refuse this contradiction, but to make use of it in order to go further, and to reconcile "yes" and "no"—which is not at all what we do when we look down on the body.

P: *So would you say that it is a false idea that the source of the "no" is the body and the source of the "yes" is the mind?*

HT: It's mainly a delusion—the pretense of the mind to be superior. Both are meant to take part in a process which brings them together—a reconciliation. Otherwise, there is only an endless opposition between yes and no, yes and no.

P: *This is where the mystery is, in the relation between the two—there is a mystery in the relation between yes and no, in the relation between any two opposing forces. I was thinking of the physical body as the ground in which something can appear. And yet if I put a stone into the earth, nothing is going to appear; but if I plant a seed—what is this something in the ground and something in the seed through which the shell of the seed breaks and life appears? This is where the mystery is, isn't it? In the relation. A yes and no can oppose each other forever without bringing about a result.*

HT: That's exactly the way I look at it. It is a mystery and I seem to ignore it when I stick to this opposition of yes and no, or body and mind, or whatever contradiction. It's a mystery which I have to respect and I have to bow to its evidence. How to awake to it? I think there is room for opening to the great miracle of nature itself. If I am moved by the vision and perception of nature—looking at the sky, looking at a tree, or any natural phenomenon—I can look at the body with the same awe and gratefulness. Then, I am given to perceive something which in itself is so great: it is a call, and I hear it.

P: *Yes, but it only becomes marvelous and worthy of respect when one knows that by itself the body is nothing. And even the soul by itself is nothing. Isn't it so? It's only in the name of what it makes possible that it has value.*

HT: Yes; and we may be helped by seeing how objective art makes use of the body as a subject. It is not naturalistic with emphasis on all sorts of awful and wonderful details; the body itself is an intermediary. It bears witness to that which is far beyond our ordinary perceptions. I see how so often my mind interferes and tries to analyze. But in certain statues of the Buddha, let's say, there is a sense of oneness. Not "Where is the body? Where is the mind?" It is *one*. There is a sense of unity, of oneness.

I would say that when I try to come back and awake again, when I hear the call and try to answer it, I feel invited to experience *myself here, now*. I could be in China—"here" is not China—"here" is my body. And "*now*": neither yesterday, nor tomorrow. Right now, here and now … this is when and where mind and body come together, and I am left with the impression that there is no longer any opposition. That's what touched me so deeply in this text of von Eckharthausen, this third possibility, to welcome the rebirth *of our whole being*.

The first tendency is to discard the body. Yet at times, more subtle forces coming from an independent source, and not from the mind alone, the feeling or the body alone, can bring about their reintegration. Obviously, there is a recurring temptation of, I would say, dream and disincarnation, a dream of being free from all this. And then arises the possibility of reincarnation, with the acknowledgement of the reality of what is offered me through the perception of my body, transformed as it is by these subtle forces.

Of course, I cannot claim to "understand" what is meant by this reincarnation, but neither can I deny it. Sometimes, I come closer to a recognition of the process of creation; I feel worked on, and permeated by an impression of being born again. I'm not the master, I'm not the one who directs this—but it is granted me, I am here to receive it, and I do receive it—not passively, but by taking part in it as actively as possible. It does require my participation, otherwise it passes through me but it leaves practically no trace.

P: *When you spoke before about the possibility of reincarnation, somehow you gave me the idea of a connection between that and the Christian idea of the divine incarnation.*

HT: One can try to think about this extraordinary sacrifice of God: accepting to be reincarnated into a human body. That I cannot understand, but it calls for a deep wish to come closer to it. Christ accepted and assumed this incarnation, and moreover, after his death—the death of his provisional body—he even decided to come back to it. ... This is far beyond our capacity of thinking, except by analogy; I mean there are moments when I am lifted towards another sense of my own reality, another way of being, through very subtle thoughts and feelings that seem to have nothing to do with my body—until all of a sudden it opens itself to a real wish to join and take part in this experience; it reminds me of its existence and calls me back. As far as I am able to awake, and keep awake, to this call as to a genuinely objective demand, I may feel a little bit—a very little bit—closer to Christ's situation when he does come back.

P: *What can you say about the real relationship between my ordinary body—my ordinary self in this body—and its relationship with this possible subtle body that it seems to recognize at moments? What is the relation?*

HT: It cannot be understood from outside. It is like asking a craftsman: "How do you do it?" He cannot explain. He can only say: "Just try and you will see for yourself." It is not something to be spoken about; it is something to experience.

P: *It seems the more open one is, the more possible this is. The difficulty is that we live most of our lives completely closed, and we start from a closed place and want to figure out how to be open—in words. How can we begin to find an approach to the body through an idea? In* Parabola *10.1, on* Wholeness, *Kobori Roshi said that the instinctual functioning needs to be free, and a question for me is: what is a free body free from? What is it free to do—what place can it take? What is it free for?*

HT: There is no easy answer to that. We could go deeper into the question. I am thinking of the familiar experience of looking at a landscape with somebody. I am interested in everything I see, until the other person says, "Have you noticed this or that?" No! "But look." And all of a sudden, it appears. In fact, I had seen it, but without realizing that I had. It is there as if it were not there, but it is there. And this applies to myself as well. There are times when I come back to myself, here, now. Then something else emerges, which we call memory. It's amazing, isn't it? What is there to remind me of myself when I have been swept away? The memory is there. I see there is a purpose, an intention. It is not mine; it works through me. I am reminded of what I have been granted to experience—for a purpose.

Notes:

1. See René Guenon, *Man and His Becoming According to the Vedanta*.

2. *Timaeus*.

3. *Summa Theologica*.

Parabola
Volume: 15.3
Liberation

THE FREEDOM OF CHILDREN

*An Interview with Henry Barnes
and Margaret Flinsch*

*Both Margaret Flinsch and Henry Barnes have spent over
fifty years teaching and working with children. They share—
without a trace of romanticism or sentimentality—an abid-
ing respect for the child as a whole person.*

*In 1929, Margaret Flinsch founded the Princeton Nurs-
ery School, which is still in existence today. She is also the
founder and guiding spirit of The Blue Rock School in West
Nyack, New York. She remembers her childhood vividly and
has a remarkable ability to enter into a child's world, meeting him or her directly without fear or any form of falseness
or hypocrisy. Her approach is intuitive and inspired, and she
confesses to a somewhat harrowing method of teacher training: "I pretty much leave them free, and come down hard
when they do something wrong."*

*Henry Barnes is the president of the Rudolph Steiner
Educational and Farming Association in Harlemville, New
York, an organization that encompasses the Hawthorne Val-
ley Farm, a full-scale diversified farm operated in accordance
with the bio-dynamic method of agriculture, and the Haw-
thorne Valley School. The school is one of the 400 autonomous
Waldorf schools worldwide based on the principles given by
Rudolph Steiner, founder of the Anthroposophical movement*

and a thinker whose contributions extend across fields as diverse as medicine, agriculture, education, philosophy, and the arts and sciences. Henry Barnes began teaching in 1940 in what was then the only Waldorf school in the United States. A warm and thoughtful man, he is known for his exceptional dedication to his students—both to the young people in his thirty-seven years of teaching and to the teachers he trains today.
                              —Lorraine Kisly

Lorraine Kisly: *I would like you both to begin by telling me what you think an unfortunate educational experience is for a child, and why it is unfortunate. I think this might lead us to something more positive later.*

Henry Barnes: Any education that divorces a child from reality is a misfortune. But of course reality takes many forms. Nature is one reality, human society is another, their own self, their own interior being is yet another reality. And wherever a separation comes about—which is so often caused by an intellectuality which is not really grounded in experience—we find one of the root causes of misfortune in education. There are the obvious conditions of social and economic deprivation in the inner city, for instance, that work against any real education. But there are other conditions not limited to the inner city, by any means, because there is a pervasive abstraction which I think has really wreaked havoc with our education. I think the theme of liberation is very much to the point here. There are so many children today who grow up with great economic and social advantages and who have brilliant intellectual capacities, but who find themselves really very alienated from society.

LK: *Unprepared in another way.*

HB: Right.

Margaret Flinsch: I agree very much with what Mr. Barnes has been saying. I think that the typical education aims to teach children, to impose answers on them, depriving them of the freedom of discovery. They are even deprived of the struggle to find out, because answers are given to them. While everything is supposedly being done for the child, the child is deprived of that marvelous search, which every child has within him—to grow, to discover, and to question. It is such an intricate process because the children need to learn, and also need people who are accomplices in that learning process—not by teaching them, but by allowing them, and seeing what the next step is for them without imposing the next step, giving them the opportunity to come to that, each one in his or her own time. I feel that it is one of the great sins of mass education that all children are supposed to reach a certain level at a certain time. Some need to go quickly and some need to go much slower. It's a very interesting thing; there are even certain organic signs that show when a child is ready for something—when a child's teeth come the child is ready to begin to eat solid food, he no longer needs just milk. Everything is indicated, and yet we don't seem to observe this. Now there is this tremendous push to force a mental training on children before they are ready, and to prevent the full flowering of that imaginative period which is so strong in children, their time of needing to learn through play, which would go on much longer than is allowed in the great majority of schools.

LK: *My next question is about what it is that is educated in a child. What are you educating?*

HB: That is quite a challenging question. I have often felt, and even sometimes said to quite young children, "My responsibility is not just to you or to your parents, but there is a man or a woman standing behind you that I am looking at—the person you will be when you are forty or fifty. If I now ask you to do something that you may not enjoy or you may not like, I am asking it because of that invisible man or woman who is standing behind you; because I know that he or she will need that."

As a parent, but particularly as an educator, I see my responsibility as preparing the instruments which that invisible and as yet not fully present human being will need—physical instruments of temperament, of intelligence, of feeling. My task is to try to help those instruments be as permeable, as flexible, as clear and transparent, as usable, as possible.

LK: *As free as possible.*

HB: Yes. Because I have known that the real education will begin when I'm finished, which is the education that the individual takes on for herself or for himself as an adult. All I can do is to prepare the way, and to clear some of the underbrush, and let them find those threads that they will be following in later life.

MF: Again, I come back to the teacher. You ask, "What does one educate in the child?" and I say, "What does one educate in the teacher?" If the teacher is not really searching and learning there is very little chance that he or she will have the sensitivity required to see what needs to be maintained. The conscience that is in every small child, for example, is completely wordless. It becomes covered over by so many "dos" and "don'ts." The child is told "no," and this "no" is then transferred to the forbidden object, and there is no understanding in the child. It's just a "no." So if the mother or father—the early educators—or if the teachers later don't have the sensitivity to see more than one side of things, to give the child freedom and a kind of choice, the child's capacities remain undeveloped. I'll give you an example: If a small child is prevented from touching a hot stove, he never has that experience. If the teacher or parent has the courage to allow them to go close to something dangerous— not really go far enough to endanger the child, but to give the child that experience—then they are given a freedom to explore.

LK: *You started talking about the child's conscience here. I think that most people feel that it's in this series of "nos" that a child's conscience is developed.*

MF: It's in the "yes" *and* the "no" that a child's conscience is developed— only when there is a choice. I don't think it's a question of development, I think it's allowing conscience to be there. It's there, and then it gets covered over.

LK: *Do you feel that the child's conscience is there?*

HB: At an unconscious level, yes. But I think that conscience is something that sits really very deep in the human being, and if that deep sensitivity, that deep awareness, has been suppressed or overlaid or distorted, then as the human being matures, it either goes to sleep, or it rebels, or it takes on some distorted form.

MF: It remains usually in the subconscious.

HB: Right. That is why I feel that conscience is not an intellectual thing. Conscience is something much deeper than that. That is why it seems to me that one of our fundamental errors as educators, in this century particularly, has been that we have limited the whole concept of intelligence. And of course economics has played enormously into that, and also political controls. In order to quantify, you have to quantify intelligence, and so much of education today in this country is geared to quantifiable results. So you have the whole battery of testing that has become, in the massive bureaucratic system which we have in our state schools, the measure of success or failure. The teacher is placed in a situation where he or she has no choice except to teach to these quantifiable norms—and at the sacrifice of real education, and often to the deep frustration of the real teachers.

I believe that the revolution of our time or of the next century should be very similar to the revolution that took place in the seventeenth century, where religion was emancipated from political control. I feel that education also needs to be emancipated from political control. We must be willing to look at this root question of where education belongs. Is it really a function of the state to administer? I think that this is one of the fundamental questions that, as a society, we have yet to face. I think that the state's role in education is a very different role. The state's role is to see to it that every child has a fair opportunity, but not to control the educational process. That is a form of liberation that you probably are not prepared for!

LK: *The state's idea of results inevitably is completely intellectual.*

HB: Quantifiable ones, and usually geared to an economic result.

MF: We are discovering, however, that the quantitative approach is not even useful for business, because schools are turning out students who are not able to read, write, or add. So it doesn't work for business, either.

LK: *Every tradition says that the soul is not of this world, that its home is elsewhere. If it is totally embedded in the material things of this world, if its attention is taken only by those things, then this soul will turn in on itself, even destroy itself. It's as if the soul needs to have light from another source, from another level. Does this view hold true for children, or are they more at home in the world? Do they have to be fed?*

HB: I would agree wholeheartedly that the child comes from another world, as Wordsworth said, "trailing clouds of glory." There is no question about it. But the function of education is to help the child to find him or herself in *this world*. For the very small child, the elements of nature are much more than just physical material. There is a life, there is a soul, in nature itself that speaks to the child directly, so to speak "soul to soul." I think the whole of education is to help that invisible, intangible element in the child, over which we really have no control. It is not up to me as either a parent or a teacher to determine who or what this individual ought to be. I can only try to read who this individual in front of me is, and try to help that individual find his or her way into this world into which they have been born and really wanted to be born. We don't come here for nothing, we come here for a purpose. There is a deep motivation: human beings enter life today with an unconscious expectation, and they find that the world doesn't live up to that expectation. In a deep, unconscious disappointment, they turn away. They go to drugs, or they go to one or another alternative, or just give up.

I feel that to educate is an artistic process, and that it is the task of the educator as an artist to try to meet the inner expectation of the child, at whatever level of conscious development the child has reached, in such a way that the child can find answers, can find the experiences for him- or herself. There are also great developmental processes that are based in the organism, and if one can read that organic development, one also has the keys to what it is inwardly that the child is expecting.

MF: For me, it is the question of the development of the individual. Each child is trying to be himself or herself, from the very beginning. It is this process that we need to allow. Is that a freeing process? I agree that the children come from a freedom, in a sense. So it's a question of keeping something open, of allowing the freedom to search and to make efforts, to try, to struggle towards something. We come into the world with a struggle, and now even that is being interfered with, because of an over-use of Caesarean operations. We prevent the child from tasting struggle, tasting what it means to enter into a process of growth, of development. This struggle is what is necessary for the development of an individual, which can be for his life in this world, but also for producing a soul.

LK: *I am thinking of the very clichéd image of the butterfly. The butterfly's transformation, however, is aided by natural law. The human being's potential can easily be crushed by life. Is it due to our abnormal society, or is it one of the lawful factors of struggle in life?*

HB: I would say that it is both. I think we have lost sight of the fundamental developmental processes. Mrs. Flinsch mentioned the fact that until you have teeth you can't chew solid food—that's an obvious natural phenomenon. And there are other organic milestones. For instance, if I really want a child to understand the inner relationship between a cause and an effect, I have to recognize that they need also to have passed through a certain moment of organic development when the muscles and tendons take a new hold on the skeleton. Because it is in the actual exercise or movement of the skeleton that we experience the laws of mechanical cause and effect. So, for instance in the teaching of history, I would keep my teaching of history in the early years in a much more pictorial, imaginative, biographical, dramatic, narrative form, until such a time as this new capacity to relate historical cause and effect is actually physiologically available to the child.

LK: *From the outside, for someone with no experience in education, it seems to me that the feeling about freedom for the child has been completely forgotten. I hear that nine-year-olds are getting courses in money management, and television is coming into the kindergarten. Do you feel that somewhere there is a little gem of hope for a new sensitivity towards children, or can't there be, on a mass scale?*

HB: I'm afraid that disaster is going to be our best educator in that sense. Mrs. Flinsch mentioned the experience of the business community. They know now the failure of mass education. They don't have the simplest tools.

LK: *And a true discriminatory intelligence has many more elements.*

HB: That is an intelligence that develops over a long period of time. It starts in the very young child at a deeply unconscious but tremendously active level of experience. The four- or five-year-old who engages herself or himself in intense, concentrative imitative play is practicing this potential discriminatory intelligence.

LK: *I wonder if people really appreciate this. They notice that children imitate, but beyond that I wonder if they appreciate what is happening in the child.*

HB: I think that is one of the disaster areas. To substitute a mechanical device, let's say a computer, in the kindergarten, because it always gives the child the same answer to the same question—which is one of the arguments that is used, that it is absolutely reliable—to me this goes against the nature of the child. There is in a healthy small child, a three- to six-year-old, a tremendous ability to lose themselves in the experience of the world around; that's what imitation is. You slip out of yourself into the gesture, the tone, the action of the world around you. And if you present just a mechanical image, they slip into that also. But that doesn't nurture the child.

MF: It in fact limits him, enormously. That's the action of non-liberation.

LK: *Children not only imitate externally, but they seem to grasp the situation wholly.*

MF: Because they are much more connected, in the sense of the body and the mind. Their minds have many fewer associations in it than ours, and that part of the mind is related to the body much more correctly. Not consciously so, but it is related, and therefore they are much more whole. When you are in the presence of a very small child, you don't feel that he is divided. So in a way this idea of liberation doesn't apply, because actually, children are more liberated, more whole, to start with. What we are really doing in education is to try to allow that freedom to be there, in spite of all the dividing elements that come in, usually through this forcing of the mental process.

Children are related to their experience. But when one tries to indoctrinate them from very early childhood by telling them what to say and do, one is teaching them to imitate a completely mechanical process, rather than allowing them to discover and work for what they receive. Only then will there be something independent in the child. They need this nourishment for their different parts that comes through their own effort.

LK: *I'm looking at the adult behind the child. He comes into the world with an enormous imitative capacity. But, as he imitates everything around him, he is also losing himself, isn't he? Isn't that an inevitable process of life? For the real liberation, the great awakening which we are also talking about here, all the great traditions say, "you are born, you sleep, and you have to awaken." But perhaps the child has to have material so that when the time comes to make another struggle—*

MF: He will have the material, yes. But if he or she has been given material that is already completed, it can't be worked on.

HB: The very small child absorbs his environment primarily through his sense perceptions. But that sense perception perceives much more than just the physical. It also perceives the moral environment. And that all works through the powerful faculty of imitation, which goes directly back into his physical organism. The kindergarten teachers tell me we are beginning to see children who do not come into the kindergarten with the ability to imitate—that has already been lost—and the teachers are having to help the children to rediscover this ability, which is a fundamental learning capacity.

LK: *What do you attribute this to?*

HB: To many things. In a certain way, sensory bombardment, sensory stimuli, have been so powerful that they have really knocked the child back into, or out of, him- or herself.

MF: I think television is absolutely lethal.

HB: Yes, I don't think there is any question about that. It's not the content, primarily, it's the actual medium itself. The content is bad enough—for a small child to experience violence for I don't know how many hours a day is, of course, destructive. But children need also to have the opportunity to develop all of their senses. What does television do? It is primarily the sense of sight.

MF: And sense of sight in a most abnormal way, because it's constricted to the screen, and there's no possibility of other impressions coming from the outside. So they are funneled into this, with absolutely no other associations to compare with them. It is all an extraordinary attack on the sensory system.

In the Waldorf school system, I understand that you only accept parents who will agree not to have television in the home.

HB: We are not able to eliminate it, but we do our utmost. The younger the children are, the more we try to explain to the parents how destructive the effect of television is.

LK: *Could you say more about why? People are told that television is not good for children, but I think it is really important to understand as clearly as possible why.*

HB: Mrs. Flinsch mentioned that a child needs something that they can work on. What comes through the television screen is finished image, it's complete, there is nothing more that the child can do with it. He takes it in, as a finished product, into his imagination, and it has a killing effect on the child's imagination. Whereas if a child is "deprived," as we would say, and has nothing but nature to play with, mud and sticks and stones, think what they can do with that! There their imagination is active—they have to make something of what is available. What about the tactile sense? What about the sounds that come through the television? What does that do to the physical organism? What is the flickering image doing to the child's eyes? It works right into the organism as well as the whole inner psychic configuration.

LK: *And what state is their attention in while they are watching television?*

MF: Utterly passive, hypnotized. It is a drug we are giving our young children. It is the most horrible thing. And yet so many parents cannot be convinced that television is a poison for their child.

LK: *And you feel that this is true especially in that imitative young period?*

MF: Particularly.

HB: I would say that even through the elementary years I would do everything I could to at least limit television. I'm so happy when a family will say, "no television during the week."

LK: *In the later part of the last century and the early part of this century, there was a great interest in handwork in the schools. One educator said that the main reason they wanted children to work with clay was to help them develop what they called a "willed attention," an attention that would be able to follow things through. He felt that the body was involved, in three dimensions, and that this was critical. Is that why you have handwork here?*

HB: Absolutely. I think of a ninth grader—you know how all over the place a ninth grader can be; they're fourteen going on fifteen—they have just come into adolescence, puberty. But if they work with a forge, and they are working with hot iron, that's a very dangerous process. But the concentration, the self-discipline, the attention, that is developed when you are working at a forge, is incomparable. To get that same attention to work with an equation—the consequences are not nearly as immediate as if you take hold of a hot iron.

LK: *And yet that attention is what can be transferred later, to any subject.*

HB: What we as adults need are the muscles of imagination, the muscles of emotional response, the muscles of intellectual response. It's the muscles that are needed. We don't know in detail what those children are going to face thirty or forty years later. But we know that they are going to need certain capacities, certain muscles.

LK: *What is the one quality that you are happiest to see in a child?*

MF: What really brings joy is to see the whole attention engaged. That brings the greatest joy. If, for instance, one is telling a story to a group of children, there is a kind of absorption that they have, which is not the absorption they have in front of a TV. It is active and not passive. That relationship is what binds the teacher with the class. In that kind of ambience of active attention, it is possible for the children to grow. That is when the questions come, and that's when the teacher has to be so enormously sensitive, not to impose at that moment, not to tell them. I once asked an adolescent boy, "What is it that bothers you the most about grown-ups?" And he said, "They always tell me things." They wish to be able to find out for themselves. They want to be able to ask you—that's different—but not to have the adult impose it first. Isn't it something like that?

HB: That's right. Of course that is the art of teaching. There is a concept that has to be communicated, but the art lies in whether you can communicate it in such a way that the student feels that he or she has discovered it.

LK: *Do either of you think that there was at any time a sort of golden age in the raising of the young?*

HB: The relationship with the child has been so different in different ages. I don't think we could set up an Egyptian schoolroom in the twenty-first century. But we have to find what is the golden age for today, in the midst of our complex, technological world. But I do think that the environment is teaching us a great deal, because ecological thinking is a thinking that sees things as a whole. And this is a faculty of imagination which was excluded from the I.Q. of the multiple choice.

LK: *We can appreciate that quality only when we begin to see people who don't have it. I was talking to a college professor who said that books are opaque to the students who are coming to him. They can read the words, but no images come to them. Maybe the ways of the earth will lead to another way.*

HB: I think so. We are waking up. There is a tremendous awakening. But of course there is so much that is built in and that has become a vested interest which has to be overcome. Mrs. Flinsch spoke of telling a story to a group of children. If the teacher tells a real story, let's say, the story of Perseus, and with the conviction that he is communicating human experience, then the children are actually in the story itself. When Perseus goes to slay the Medusa with Athena's shield, the children are there in that moment, they are just hanging on the question, will he forget and will he look around and be turned into stone? Will he really only look into that shield? And this is an exercise of muscles, these are muscles of learning, muscles of imagination. That is why the great literature of the past needs to be brought alive in the teacher; the teacher has to love it, has to know it. And then that communicates to the children. That feeds, that nourishes. And then when they come to college, they don't just read the words, because the words have been embedded in a whole experience.

LK: *This speaks to a question I had about what makes a good teacher, a great teacher.*

HB: I think you have to love children. You have to care about them, not in a sentimental way, but you have to care about the human being I mentioned before.

MF: There are many adults, maybe most adults, I don't know, who have forgotten what it was to be a child. One puts oneself back at their age, in a certain way. It's a kind of a double thing. One is there as an adult, and yet one is feeling the way the children are responding. I feel that one of the big difficulties is to find teachers who feel that education of the children is important.

LK: *I've felt that the teacher means something special to the child.*

MF: "My teacher," a child will say. It means the step that he is taking out into the next phase of his life, away from that close relationship of father and mother. "My teacher" is the next one. Children wish that more than anything, they wish to grow; then they wish to grow more, then they wish to grow still more. The teacher is their stepping stone to that. And it's a step not only into the world, but also into the possibility of being allowed to search further.

HB: You talk about liberation. The teacher needs to be liberated, as well as the child. And one way that the teacher can be liberated is really to be given the possibility of administering the school, his or her school, with his or her colleagues, and not have it administered by bureaucracy.

As I was thinking about this question of liberation, I realized that in every situation in life, whether it's a child who is developing toward adulthood or whether it's an adult of whatever age, there is always the possibility of a divergence towards a formalism, a form that then becomes really hardened and restricted and unfree, which leads eventually to a death in form, a rigidity that allows no growth. Or one is in the situation where all restraints are removed, outwardly, and where one just loses oneself in a kind of escape from reality. Real liberation, it seems to me, lies in the education of the capacity to keep this inner dynamic balance. One needs the element of form, one needs the element of freedom. It's rhythmic—fundamentally, all life is rhythmic. This ability to live with a rhythmic movement, inner rhythms as well as biological ones, is one of the fundamental goals of education. Rhythm involves an element which I think is overlooked, and that is the ability to let go. This is essential to all creative action. A creative act is always a risk, I always have to let go of what I have had or what I have been in order to go toward the next step. And rhythm requires that. If I keep contracting, I'll die. If I keep expanding, I'll die. I have to contract and at a certain point I have to let go, and risk that it is going to swing back. When I expand, I have to let go of that expansion, which may be blissful, in order to come back. That rhythmic element is fundamental to all life. Every organism exists through the grace of rhythm.

LK: *I remember that Rabbi Adin Steinsaltz once said, "In order to move, I have to become unstable." If I sit still, I am stable. If I begin to walk I'm already becoming a little unstable. If I begin to run, I become even more unstable. Any movement requires that. I think the question of freedom and liberation begins to make much more sense now in terms of education than it did at the beginning, because you can see how a certain kind of education will make a child rigid at a very young age, never mind rigid at forty or rigid at sixty or rigid at seventy-five, but rigid at six or at ten.*

MF: Not only rigid, but also only partially developed. There is a lack of equilibrium because nothing is educated except the head. So to say, the head is stuffed with information. It would be better, in my opinion, to have no education at all than to have the kind of public education we have at the present time.

HB: There is also the question of death.

LK: *It's exactly what I was thinking of when you were talking about the concept of the need to let go and expand—it doesn't stop. It goes on through old age, the demand is even greater, and the greatest demand, maybe, is at the end.*

HB: I don't think that we will really be able to answer the questions of education of children today until we can also answer some of the questions about death. If death is the end, then it's no liberation. Our eleventh grade goes down for a week to a wonderful old people's home in Spring Valley in Rockland County. It is such an experience for these sixteen-year-olds; when they come back and tell us about their experience; even after just a week, their whole perspective on life has changed. They realize then that the other end of life has dimensions that are entirely different from any most of them have ever experienced. The family today no longer includes the elder generation, usually. This is really such a vital part of education, that the little child should also experience both ends of life. In our American culture, we live in fear of death. Our whole idea is "Stay young, stay healthy, stay physically fit."

MF: And we put the old people away. I had a three-year-old come up to me, and say: "You're very old, aren't you?" And I said, "Yes, I'm very old." He said, "How did you get that way?"

HB: What did you say?

MF: I said, "Well you know, I've been through Christmas, and another Christmas, and another Christmas, until finally, I got that way."

HB: That's a wonderful answer. A wise answer, perfect for a child.

•

CHAPTER TWO

REMEMBER YOURSELF
ALWAYS AND EVERYWHERE

—Views from the Real World

Parabola
Volume: 7.1
Sleep

THE LIFE OF SLEEPING MEN

P. D. Ouspensky

At one of the following lectures G. I. Gurdjieff returned
to the question of consciousness. ...

"In order to understand what the difference between
states of consciousness is, let us return to the first state
of consciousness, which is sleep. This is an entirely subjective state of consciousness. A man is immersed in
dreams, whether he remembers them or not does not
matter. Even if some real impressions reach him, such
as sounds, voices, warmth, cold, the sensation of his own
body, they arouse in him only fantastic subjective images.
Then a man wakes up. At first glance this is a quite different state of consciousness. He can move, he can talk with
other people, he can make calculations ahead, he can see
danger and avoid it, and so on. It stands to reason that
he is in a better position than when he was asleep. But if
we go a little more deeply into things, if we take a look
into his inner world, into his thoughts, into the causes
of his actions, we shall see that he is in almost the same
state as when he is asleep. And it is even worse, because
in sleep he is passive, that is, he cannot do anything. In
the waking state, however, he can do something all the
time and the results of all his actions will be reflected
upon him or upon those around him. *And yet he does not
remember himself.* He is a machine, everything with him
happens. He cannot stop the flow of his thoughts, he

cannot control his imagination, his emotions, his attention. He lives in a subjective world of 'I love,' 'I do not love,' 'I like,' 'I do not like,' 'I want,' 'I do not want,' that is, of what he thinks he likes, of what he thinks he does not like, of what he thinks he wants, of what he thinks he does not want. He does not see the real world. The real world is hidden from him by the wall of imagination. *He lives in sleep.* He is asleep. What is called 'clear consciousness' is sleep and a far more dangerous sleep than sleep at night in bed.

"Let us take some event in the life of humanity. For instance, war. There is a war going on at the present moment. What does it signify? It signifies that several millions of sleeping people are trying to destroy several millions of other sleeping people. They would not do this, of course, if they were to wake up. Everything that takes place is owing to this sleep.

"Both states of consciousness, sleep and the waking state, are equally subjective. Only by beginning to *remember himself* does a man really awaken. And then all surrounding life acquires for him a different aspect and a different meaning. He sees that it is *the life of sleeping people*, a life in sleep. All that men say, all that they do, they say and do in sleep. All this can have no value whatever. Only awakening and what leads to awakening has a value in reality.

"How many times have I been asked here whether wars can be stopped? Certainly they can. For this it is only necessary that people should awaken. It seems a small thing. It is, however, the most difficult thing there can be because this sleep is induced and maintained by the whole of surrounding life, by all surrounding conditions.

"How can one awaken? How can one escape this sleep? These questions are the most important, the most vital that can ever confront a man. But before this it is necessary to be convinced of the very fact of sleep. But it is possible to be convinced of this only by trying to awaken. When a man understands that he does not remember himself and that to remember himself means to awaken to some extent, and when at the same time he sees by experience how difficult it is to remember himself, he will understand that he cannot awaken simply by having the desire to do so. It can be said still more precisely that a man cannot awaken *by himself.* But if, let us say, twenty people make an agreement that whoever of them awakens first shall wake the rest, they already have some chance. Even this, however, is insufficient because all the twenty can go to sleep at the same time and dream that they are waking up. Therefore more still is necessary. They must be looked after by a man who is not asleep or who does not fall asleep as easily as they do, or who goes to sleep consciously when this is possible, when it will do no harm either to himself or to others. They must find such a man *and hire him* to wake them and not allow them to fall asleep again. Without this it is impossible to awaken. This is what must be understood.

"It is possible to think for a thousand years; it is possible to write whole libraries of books, to create theories by the million, and all this in sleep, without any possibility of awakening. On the contrary, these books and these theories, written and created in sleep, will merely send other people to sleep, and so on.

"There is nothing new in the idea of sleep. People have been told almost since the creation of the world that they are asleep and that they must awaken. How many times is this said in the Gospels, for instance? 'Awake,' 'watch,' 'sleep not.' Christ's disciples even slept when he was praying in the Garden of Gethsemane for the last time. It is all there. But do men understand it? Men take it simply as a form of speech, as an expression, as a metaphor. They completely fail to understand that it must be taken literally. And again it is easy to understand why. In order to understand this literally it is necessary to awaken a little, or at least to try to awaken. I tell you seriously that I have been asked several times why nothing is said about sleep in the Gospels. Although it is there spoken of almost on every page. This simply shows that people read the Gospels in sleep. So long as a man sleeps profoundly and wholly immersed in dreams he cannot even think about the fact that he is asleep. If he were to think that he was asleep, he would wake up. So everything goes on. And men have not the slightest idea what they are losing because of this sleep. As I have already said, as he is organized, that is, being such as nature has created him, man can be a self-conscious being. Such he is created and such he is born. But he is born among sleeping people, and, of course, he falls asleep among them just at the very time when he should have begun to be conscious of himself. Everything has a hand in this: the involuntary imitation of older people on the part of the child, voluntary and involuntary suggestion, and what is called 'education.' Every attempt to awaken on the child's part is instantly stopped. This is inevitable. And a great many efforts and a great deal of help are necessary in order to awaken later when thousands of sleep-compelling habits have been accumulated. And this very seldom happens. In most cases, a man when still a child already loses the possibility of awakening; he lives in sleep all his life and he dies in sleep ...

"There are a thousand things which prevent a man from awakening, which keep him in the power of his dreams. In order to act consciously with the intention of awakening, it is necessary to know the nature of the forces which keep man in a state of sleep.

"First of all it must be realized that the sleep in which man exists is not normal but hypnotic sleep. Man is hypnotized and this hypnotic state is continually maintained and strengthened in him. One would think that there are forces for whom it is useful and profitable to keep man in a hypnotic state and prevent him from seeing the truth and understanding his position.

"There is an Eastern tale which speaks about a very rich magician who had a great many sheep. But at the same time this magician was very mean. He did not want to hire shepherds, nor did he want to erect a fence about the pasture where his sheep were grazing. The sheep consequently often wandered into the forest, fell into ravines, and so on, and above all they ran away, for they knew that the magician wanted their flesh and skins and this they did not like.

"At last the magician found a remedy. He *hypnotized* his sheep and suggested to them first of all that they were immortal and that no harm was being done to them when they were skinned, that, on the contrary, it would be very good for them and even pleasant; secondly he suggested that the magician was a *good master* who loved his flock so much that he was ready to do anything in the world for them; and in the third place he suggested to them that if anything at all were going to happen to them it was not going to happen just then, at any rate not that day, and *therefore* they had no need to think about it. Further the magician suggested to his sheep that they were not sheep at all; to some of them he suggested that they were *lions*, to others that they were *eagles*, to others that they were *men*, and to others that they were *magicians*.

"And after all this his cares and worries about the sheep came to an end. They never ran away again but quietly awaited the time when the magician would require their flesh and skins.

"This tale is a very good illustration of man's position."

Note: All selections in the present volume that cite the authorship of P. D. Ouspensky have been excerpted from *In Search of the Miraculous*, Ouspensky's unrivalled record of Gurdjieff's teaching as it was given from 1915 to 1923. Through a prodigious effort of memory and intuition, Ouspensky was able not only to faithfully recall and frame the words of Gurdjieff, but to allow them to be perceived within a clear representation of the lived spiritual process within which they were spoken. It is fair to say, therefore, that the author of all these selections is Gurdjieff himself.

Parabola
Volume: 15.1
Time and Presence

Living Time

Maurice Nicoll

There is something in everyone which, if he acts from it, gives an entirely different quality to all he does. ... One real moment, one real thought, one real feeling, one real sensation—a single moment of self-existence—is worth all the rest. There is a certain kind of action, a certain experience of oneself, that is the beginning of "eternal" life. Without it, whatever we do, is "natural," i.e., *reaction*. The object is to emancipate ourselves from the power of the momentary *I*, the event of the moment.

The realization of what passing-time is can have the same effect, i.e., we live in the world of becoming where nothing ever *is*. This need not only produce sadness, but, by separating us from the effect of passing-time, it can bring us ever closer to another level of consciousness, with its accompanying different feeling of *I*. This is shown in the following passage about a female pupil and her Buddhist teacher: "There arose in her heart the insight into truth clear and stainless which perceives that whatsoever has a beginning has the inherent quality of passing away" (*The Questions of King Milinda*). Note that *insight* is said. It is not merely thinking about passing-time or thinking things are ephemeral or hopeless. It is a stage beyond that, whereby she is free from illusion and has become detached from a thousand things, seeing her relation to the visible world as

•

from within. Nothing ever *is* in passing-time. That is what we do not see. The perception may bring us to *now*.

No reveries, no conversations, no tracing out of the meaning of fantasies, contain this *now*, which belongs to a higher order of consciousness. This *time-man* in us does not know *now*. He is always preparing something in the future, or busy with what happened in the past. He is always wondering what to do, what to say, what to wear, what to eat, etc. He anticipates; and we, following him, come to the expected moment, and lo, he is already elsewhere, planning further ahead. This is *becoming*— where nothing ever *is*. We must come to our senses to begin to feel *now*. We can only feel *now* by checking this time-man, who thinks of existence in his own way. *Now* enters us with a sense of something greater than passing-time. *Now* contains all time, all the life, and the aeon of the life. *Now* is the sense of higher space. It is not the decisions of the man in time that count here, for they do not spring from *now*. All decisions that belong to the life in time, to success, to business, comfort, are about "tomorrow." All decisions about the right thing to do, about how to act, are about tomorrow. It is only what is done in *now* that counts, and this is a decision always about *oneself* and *with* oneself, even although its effect may touch other people's lives "tomorrow." *Now* is spiritual. It is a state of the spirit, when it is above the stream of time-associations. Spiritual values have nothing to do with time. They are not in time, and their growth is not a matter of time. To retain the impress of their truth we must fight with time, with every notion that they belong to time, and that the passage of days will increase them. For then it will be easy for us to think it is *too late*, to make the favorite excuse of passing-time.

The feeling of *now* is the feeling of certainty. In *now* passing-time halts. And in this halting of time one's understanding has power over one. One knows, sees, feels in oneself, apart from all outer things; and above all, one *is*. This is the state of faith, as I believe was originally meant—the certain knowledge of something above passing-time. Faith is *now*. What the time-man understands about faith is something quite different. Faith has to do with that which is alone in oneself and unknown to anyone else. "Every visible state, every temporal, every pragmatic approach to faith, is, in the end, the negation of faith" (Karl Barth). All insight, all revelation, all illumination, all love, all that is genuine, all that is real, lies in *now*— and in the attempt to create *now* we approach the inner precincts, the holiest part of life. For in time all things are seeking completion, but in *now* all things are complete.

So we must understand that what we call the present moment is not *now*, for the present moment is on the horizontal line of time, and now is vertical to this and incommensurable with it. So Barth points out that the true, living life of a man does not lie in historical time, nor is faith something that begins at a certain point in time and grows along time. He is really talking about another level of consciousness—another dimension. It is the Moment that "qualifies and transforms time," and all else, all that is taken as faith, belongs to the "unqualified time of sleep." For Barth truly observes that without this Moment, this *now*, all "men are asleep, even the Apostle, even the saint, even the lover," and in this state of sleep "men are sold under time, its property. They lie like pebbles in the stream of time." Did we but awake, he says, did we but realize that we stand at every moment on the frontier of time, we should know that all we seek and all that some connect with the *future* life, has nothing to do with historical time or with visible history. The future world is not in the future of time. "What delays its coming is not the Parousia but our awakening."

If we could awaken, if we could ascend in the scale of reality concealed within us, we would understand the meaning of the "future" world. *Our future world is our own growth in now, not in the tomorrow of passing-time.*

Something must be brought into every moment, the cumulative effect of which is to create *now*. *Now* is not given. While living our ordinary life we must always be doing *something else*—internally. Consider the exercise of self-knowledge in this respect. Whatever we understand by self-knowledge, one thing we certainly do not understand, that it has to do with *now*. The time-man in us does not understand this. Eckhart says: "Mark how to know yourself. To know himself a man must ever be on the watch over himself, holding his outer faculties. This discipline must be continued until he reaches a state of consciousness." The object is to reach *now*, where one is present to oneself. "What I say unto you I say unto all, *be awake*." The translation *watch* is insufficient. Is not this idea about self-knowledge absolutely different from the moral significance we usually give it? Can we understand the New Testament at all unless we understand that it is constantly dealing with a higher level of consciousness possible to man? Is not this the treasure hidden in us, that a man can find if he seeks? "The highest wisdom consists in this, for man to know himself, because in him God has placed his eternal word." What is this *word* (*logos*)? "In the beginning is the word." Is it not this, the interior expression of the universe itself as potentiality, beginning with the highest meaning and existing as a scale of reality within?

If we could penetrate to the eternal reality of our own being we would find the one and only solution for every situation—in the right sense of our own existence—primarily *in itself.* The "cause" of our existence would then be internal. This I call the *aeon* of our lives—that which is behind all manifestation of the life in time, and is summed up in the growth of the feeling of *now* into which all the life enters. This is the *eternal creation of man*, having no source in time whatsoever.

Excerpted from Maurice Nicoll, *Living Time* (London: Stuart & Watkins, 1952). Reprinted by permission.

Parabola
Volume: 10.1
Wholeness

THE SEARCH FOR BEING

An Interview with Pauline de Dampierre

Much has been written about a certain spot in Paris where a kind of inner fire was kept burning throughout the dark days and nights of the German occupation. In a small and crowded apartment in the rue des Colonels Renard, a strangely assorted group of people met nightly to listen with absorbed attention to Gurdjieff, to eat the amazing meals he cooked for them, and to hear read aloud Beelzebub's Tales to His Grandson.

Pauline de Dampierre was one of the circle. She was a young attorney who turned journalist after the war was over; but like many another of the gifted young, she was not destined to follow either of the careers she had originally chosen for herself. Her meeting with Gurdjieff was definitive. After it, her professional work continued only as a practical necessity and as a ground for self-study. After Gurdjieff's death in 1949 she continued, in company with others of that same circle, the process of work on his teaching, for herself, and with the many new people who came asking to know more about the enigmatic Master and the ideas he expressed.
—*D. M. Dooling*

D. M. Dooling: *I understand that Gurdjieff had a complete cosmological system, so in relation to our subject of wholeness, there would be interesting aspects of his teaching on a cosmic scale. But we would rather ask you about it in relation to the human being: what did Gurdjieff consider a whole man, a fully developed person? And by the way, I'd like to make clear from the start that when we talk about "whole man" or "real man," we use the word man in the generic sense of human being, not as man differentiated from woman. I suppose Gurdjieff also meant that?*

Pauline de Dampierre: Of course. He said very specifically that men and women have equal possibilities of inner development. He insisted on the difference in their types of natural energy, and the roles to be played in outer life in order to be in tune with them. But the work on oneself is the same for all; there is no difference.

DMD: *I have been very much interested in the definition at the end of the introduction to his book,* Meetings with Remarkable Men. *He says, "He can be called a remarkable man who stands out from those around him by the resourcefulness of his mind, and who knows how to be restrained in the manifestations which proceed from his nature, at the same time conducting himself justly and tolerantly towards the weaknesses of others."*

PD: Yes. He can be *just* in front of the weakness of the other, because by having learned to contain his own manifestations, he knows what he is; and he knows what the difficulty is. There is a Zen story that I think illustrates this very well. A blind man was listening to a conversation going on near him, and suddenly he cried out: "Oh, what an extraordinary man! I have never heard anything like it!" When he was asked what he had heard that was so remarkable, he explained: "You know that blind people always develop a very fine sense of hearing. Now, in my entire life, I have never heard someone congratulate another for some good fortune without hearing in his voice at the same time a note of jealousy; and I have never heard anyone sympathize with a misfortune without hearing in his voice a shade of superiority or of satisfaction because he himself was spared. But in the voice of this man who just spoke, when he spoke of happiness I heard only happiness, and when he expressed sorrow, I heard nothing but sorrow ..."

The man he had listened to was in fact a monk, a great Buddhist saint. Maybe you could say he was a "whole man."

DMD: *It's a very striking story.*

PD: But I don't mean by this to say that only people who reach this degree should be called "real"; because between the fully realized man who has attained the greatest development possible, and the ordinary contemporary man—"a slave entirely at the disposal of tendencies which have nothing to do with his true individuality"—there is room for another category of mankind: those who search for a way toward truth. In other words, one might say that these are people who have discovered a truth in the words of the blind man that goes far beyond a mere clever observation, which concerns them very deeply. They have seen that these almost unconscious states of feeling into which they let themselves fall are just one aspect of a much more serious problem—a fundamental problem basic to their whole life. So they have decided to put everything they have into confronting it.

DMD: *You mean that this fundamental problem has to do with the slavery you spoke of?*

PD: Yes—it has to do with slavery, and its opposite: that is, one's possible liberation.

But to come to the definition of a "whole man," or as one could say, a "real man," one who has turned toward what is real in himself—two definitions could be given. On one hand, there is the developed man, as he has appeared at exceptional moments in humanity's history: the man described by Gurdjieff as having acquired his own "I" with all its attributes of conscience, of objective thought and feeling; and on a more modest level, there are people such as the "remarkable men" that Gurdjieff speaks of in his book, who are on the way. These are people of very diverse backgrounds; you find among them a priest, a Russian prince, a street vendor, an archeologist, an alcoholic, a young musician. Some of them enter monasteries, others remain lay people, but what they have in common is that they are all moved, with the same ardor and the same determination, by the conviction expressed at the end of the book by one of them, old professor Skridlov, that "apart from the vanities of life, there exists a 'something else' which must be the aim and ideal of every more or less thinking man, and that it is only this 'something else' which may make a man really happy and give him real values, instead of the illusory 'goods' with which in ordinary life he is always and in everything full."

Of course, this "something else" is what is presented as fundamental and unique by all the great traditions and religions which have appeared in the course of human history. And Gurdjieff brings to it a new vision, which conforms to the changes and the possibilities of understanding peculiar to our time: a vision of extraordinary force and extraordinary scope, because while it enters into the smallest details of our modern situation, it also extends into the cosmic plane, into the very process of the creation of the world. Yet it has to do with something simple. This "something else" which should be the aim of every thinking man, and which is the only thing that can make a man happy, is "*being*," the real being of a person, which has been placed in him as a seed and which is called upon to grow and to play a role in the universe. But contemporary man has degenerated; he has lost contact with his real essence, his consciousness of himself; he "*is not.*" His thought, his feeling, and his organism have developed in a kind of anarchy, full of contradictions, continually wasting his energies without any connection with his true individuality. He is only an automaton; Gurdjieff insisted very much on the automatism of our life, the human mechanicalness which makes us obedient to an illusory scale of values, and makes us incapable of fulfilling what he called our "being-duty."

DMD: *Now you come to an idea that I think is very hard to grasp. You speak of "being" and "being-duty." Can you explain what he meant by these terms?*

PD: I would have to explain it from two different points of view. The first is theoretical. Man's nature is double; in a sense, he was created for two different purposes. For one, he is animated by nature exactly in the same way as plants and animals, and even his ordinary thoughts and ideas are only a supplementary development of this kind of creation that exists for a certain purpose. One sees very well that plants and animals serve a certain chain of existence, and perhaps mankind also serves such a chain, but this is a natural creation that doesn't really concern his own *being*, a life to which he responds. But in contradistinction to the plants and animals, which can only be exactly what they are, the human being has received another possibility, to develop and acquire a real individuality.

To explain in a more practical way, the difficulty in understanding what our being really is is that we experience it only mixed with something else; we know ourselves thinking, or in an emotion, or in movement; but these thoughts and emotions and movements are all transitory, temporary. The question is, does man have something in him that is really *himself*, that exists in himself, not attached to something changing, which doesn't come from something outside his control? Can he be present, have the feeling, the consciousness of his being, of a being that is independent of all these surrounding conditions? A person who is on the road to truth is one who has begun to open his eyes to his situation, to feel that he is always pulled out of himself, to see his poverty, his weakness. And after having struggled, been sincere, worked on himself, tried to remember himself and be present to himself, then he begins to enter into contact with his true nature, and he discovers the greatness of the potential that has been given him. At the same time, he sees how strong the automatisms are that continually turn him away from this potential, and finds that with his ordinary means he is powerless. In order to open to his being, he needs to open to these higher influences from which he has been cut off until now.

Then he understands better this ideal that Professor Skridlov talks about, that every thinking man should have: to become a conscious, responsible being, capable of doing—which means to act from one's own initiative, an initiative that doesn't come from the suggestions and appetites of ordinary life, but from his being: a being which calls him to allow these influences from a higher level to operate in him. This is what his "being-duty" is; and it concerns not only himself, but the whole world, because if a man doesn't recognize these influences and open to them, they can have no action in the world.

DMD: *I think it's hard for many people to believe that they are in such a bad way as Gurdjieff says—to accept, for instance, that they can't "act of their own initiative"—or indeed that there is any other way to be than the way they are.*

PD: We think in that way until we begin to see how we live our lives. Gurdjieff spoke of the necessity to know oneself; we do not know ourselves. But in order to know oneself, he said, one must first study oneself, and we cannot even do that until we begin to observe ourselves. He was very insistent on this point with all his pupils; he told them just to watch, to catch themselves—as it were, take snapshots of themselves.

In *Beelzebub's Tales* there is a vivid description of what such a series of snapshots can show. Gurdjieff chose as an example a clever, respected, successful man whose willpower and self–control would seem to be enviable. This man gets up one morning in a bad mood. While he is brushing his hair he makes an awkward move and drops his hairbrush; he picks it up even more clumsily and it flies out of his hand and breaks the mirror. This puts him into an even worse temper and he is cross with his servant who hasn't brought him the paper with his morning coffee. In a very irritated state, he leaves the house to go to a business appointment. It is a beautiful day, really lovely, and outdoors he feels better. He sees a street accident, but his thoughts hurry on because a face in the crowd reminds him of something—a birthday party where he ate a delicious meringue. He is just passing a café where he often goes; why not stop and finish his breakfast? He sits down; there is a woman at a nearby table, a charming woman, who looks at him with evident interest. They enter into conversation, and his mood changes as if by magic. Suddenly he remembers the appointment he was supposed to be going to, and he decides to telephone; several times in succession he gets the wrong number. Once again his irritation appears. ...

The description ends, but it could have gone on indefinitely. These insignificant things have taken over the day for this "free" man, without his even being aware of it; he has been completely enslaved by them.

The story illustrates an idea that Gurdjieff emphasized: that of different "I's." A person is constantly saying "I"—but this "I" doesn't represent what he really is. He is always the prey of the partial, superficial, changing "I's" to which he gives in, instead of having a stable "I" in which he could recognize his whole self.

As for the notion that our situation cannot be changed—Gurdjieff says very emphatically that, such as he is, a man is absolutely incapable of changing anything; he is completely enslaved by all his impulses and all his associations, unless he begins to awaken to what he is—that is, to become aware of the way in which he is continually dragged along by his impulses, which are formed in spite of him so that he doesn't even know when he is taken by them; and in the action of returning to himself, of presence to himself, he begins to find the possibility of developing his being.

DMD: *You said that there were three categories of people: the completely unconscious, ordinary man whose vagaries are described in your story; then the one who is awake to the facts and begins to try to change; but what about the accomplished man, the real man? Is there actually such a thing?*

PD: You see, there are also degrees even within these categories. Gurdjieff spoke of the real man as one who has gone to the end of his possible development. Naturally, from the point of view of a man on the way, it can never really be said if a man has reached the end or not; there is no measure for that. But I knew Gurdjieff, and I can say that it is he who comes closest in my experience to what I can call a *real man*. So in the light of this experience with him, I can describe to you how I conceive of the real, whole man.

One of the first characteristics is a natural authority, which has a kind of grandeur and power; and at the same time it is associated with a physical presence that is human and free to manifest itself on every plane, even the most down-to-earth. In the "whole man" the harmonious development of his nature keeps pace with the interior development. He must have the power to make "the wolf and the sheep" (this was an expression Gurdjieff used) live together in him, each keeping its proper place. It is on this condition that his freedom depends. So he can show himself open and friendly, or formidable—but always, beyond all conventions. And each person feels himself measured in relation to that presence—for each one, it is the measure of his limits and his most hidden weaknesses. The exchange between the "whole man" and an ordinary one may quite well remain on this life-plane: it is like a lesson in life, like a game between someone of great force and great development and someone with less—almost a contest. For some people, this is hard or even impossible to accept; in others, it arouses gratitude and affection. But when this authority, this grandeur, makes itself felt, it is a kind of event. People who witness it receive an unforgettable impression—partly because it is accompanied by something very human, a kindness, which restores the role of father to its rightful place.

DMD: *That's interesting; because I don't think the usual image of Gurdjieff is one of fatherliness, or benevolence; in fact, his teaching has been accused of being "harsh" and "without love." How did this kindness you speak of show itself in him?*

PD: I think to show that, and to show also how there can be such misunderstandings of the nature of his teaching, I have to speak first of another characteristic of the "real man," which is an immense knowledge—a detailed knowledge, reaching back into the darkness of time; it would be truer to say, into the *light* of time, to those remote epochs in which true knowledge appeared, knowledge of what Tradition calls the Law, which is the formation of the universe, with man's place in it. This law speaks of the meaning of man's life, the weight of his heritage, and the hope which is always open to him of the place he might occupy.

So I would say that behind the alert look, attentive to every detail, with which the "real man" regards the world around him, there is this knowledge: a lived knowledge, because the "real man" is the place where this law operates, and at every moment it is passing through him. His kindness is impregnated with this knowledge of what is in people and what is necessary for them; and this kindness takes on many different aspects also. With Gurdjieff, for instance, contrary to many things that have been said about him, it didn't at all exclude charity to the poor; quite the contrary. Certain people were surprised to discover how much he did for others—this was during the war, and there were many people in real need whom he took care of; but this was always done secretly, not in the open. In other cases, his generosity took the form of a transmission. An exercise that he gave might help in understanding that. It was an exercise accompanied by slow, rhythmic movements, and in doing it, the pupil had to represent to himself the presence of his father on his right, and that of his son on his left. And as the exercise went on, he would begin to feel that he was simply an intermediary through whom passed an existence that came from elsewhere—his father—and went toward someone else—his son; a transitory existence.

DMD: *What do you think is the place, the function in life of the "real man"? Is he necessarily a teacher?*

PD: He is not necessarily a teacher, a Master, but he is inevitably a *trans-mitter*, a transmitter of this higher influence. He plays the role of *man*, which it has been said before is to be open to energies, influences, that come from a higher level, and which need to have the human being open to them, someone through whom they can be known, in order to have their action on the world. Even in the desert, he is a transmitter. He doesn't necessarily play the role of teacher, in this sense, but by the fact that he has been open to these influences and has allowed them to pass through him, by his conscious effort, and to have an action by which other people have benefited—in a way, one can say he is a "father." But sometimes he takes on himself in a more direct way the task of helping others so that they also may play this part. In this moment, he takes on the role of teacher.

DMD: *Then, what does that imply? What must he do?*

PD: Help them understand the truth; support them where he feels that they are weak; guide them, even perhaps undertake to live with them, because by his presence they will learn certain things that they couldn't understand without a living example. But his action has a limit: he can-not do anything *in the pupil's place*; he cannot make his effort for him. In that sense, he depends on them.

It sometimes happens that with his help the pupil reaches a certain level of inner work; and the experience is so precious that nothing else in life seems to equal it. I remember during the war the acrobatics each of us had to perform, in the midst of our professional and private obliga-tions, in order never to miss such an event, and to arrive on time at Gur-djieff's apartment. It was the strict rule never to be late; but for several weeks I was in a situation so truly impossible and so painful for me that, as a great exception, I had received permission to arrive in the middle of the meeting. After pedaling halfway across Paris on my bicycle as fast as I possibly could, I entered the room which I knew so well, where the meeting was being held, like all the others I had attended. ...The impression was arresting: I felt literally at the doorway of something whose atmosphere was so special it had a light and a force which could not be penetrated—the feeling and thinking of the people in the room had been so kindled during the three-quarters of an hour of exchange which I had missed. So when I heard Gurdjieff say to me, "Too late!" I never considered reminding him that he had given me permission—it was so clear that what he said was true.

In order to put the pupil in front of the reality of what he has, what he can expect, what is possible for him, the obstacles, and so forth, the teacher will use all sorts of means. He may be very demanding; perhaps he will show himself as severe, hard, perhaps he will provoke public scenes. And many people will not understand that, but the teacher knows the price that has to be paid, he knows what the pupil has to go through in order to understand; and if one can see through this apparent hardness, there is always a "maybe" to soften the outburst and help him endure it. Or the relation may take the form of a private conversation, and in spite of the importance of the situation, it may be quite down-to-earth, familiar. The pupil may feel himself completely recognized and accepted, even chosen, by the teacher. And there is a reason for that, because he is taking part in a relation he has never known before: a relation of being to being, although the teacher has had to hide himself behind a language that the pupil can understand. Really no one knows what the teacher has to demand of himself so that the pupil will understand something. An anecdote which Kathryn Hulme tells, in her book, *Undiscovered Country*, may give some idea:

> *We were aware how often his seemingly jocose remarks lifted suddenly to another level of understanding and listened attentively to his tale of a brand new car he might be able to get with no down payment whatsoever—a deal so unique that he thought he should have some help to see it through. He asked if any of us had a special saint to whom he might burn a candle, looking first to Miss Gordon, our senior, for a suggestion. She named a saint noted for granting requests, but the master shook his head. He knew all about that one. "No," he said, "It must be a saint who would be indulgent for one of us." One of us in the Work ... you, me ... Canary, Thin One ... his eyes searched our blank faces, then he shrugged.*
>
> *"If you cannot suggest such a one," he said, "I could just as well take my own saint—Saint George. But he is a very expensive saint. He is not interested in money, or in merchandise like candles. He wishes* suffering *for merchandise, an inner-world thing. He is interested*

only when I make something *for my inner world; he* always *knows.*
But … such suffering is expensive …"[1]

DMD: *That seems a wonderful example of what I have often heard about the indirect way in which Gurdjieff was able to show something to a pupil. I suppose, though, that he sometimes did speak very directly, and I wonder if he gave any clear definitions of what he considered a "real man."*

PD: In *Beelzebub's Tales* he gives one very clear definition, which is that "a man is a being who can do, and 'to do' means to act consciously and by one's own initiative." And on almost every page, he evokes the huge difference between the real man and what he calls the pseudo-man, the man in quotation marks. Although he makes it clear that both are slaves of Great Nature, the first, taking a conscious attitude toward his slavery, has accomplished the task given to him to work for the development of his being, of his conscience, and of his objective feeling and thought. He has acquired "imperishable being." The other, who refuses to open his eyes and who remains the prisoner of his illusions, remains for the whole of his life merely "a thing." He has allowed his possibilities to "beat their wings in vain."

DMD: *What more can you say about those who have seen something, heard a call, and tried to follow the way a teacher gives them? What sort of people are they, and how must they show themselves?*

PD: That is such a big question and includes so many different aspects and degrees that it would be impossible to answer it in a few words. But I think an essential element of the answer is to be found in a passage of *Beelzebub's Tales* which is at the end of the book. He says that it must be everyone's aim to become a *master*, not because of his power or his riches, but because he "acquires in himself that *something*" which makes him recognized and respected by those about him.

This passage takes us back again to the words of Professor Skridlov that I quoted at the beginning of our talk, to this "something" which is the only thing that can bring real happiness instead of the illusory values which life provides.

DMD: *What is at the beginning of a search for this "something" which you defined as real being?*

PD: On talking with people who have a real inner search, it seems that most often what was at the beginning of it was a decisive encounter with someone, and that what touched them more than the ideas or doctrines they were told about was "something" they felt in this person—something tangible, something alive, something they could trust, and which they hadn't met with before in the ordinary course of life. And this "something" they felt in the person speaking with them came from the contact which had begun to be established in him with his real being—the beginning of the ability to *be* which he had acquired, and which, whatever his faults and weaknesses, acted on him as a guide and a source of harmony between his body, his feeling, and his thought.

Of all the qualities which Gurdjieff fostered in people, there was one to which he attached a special importance, and he returned to it constantly. It is the counterbalance to this habitual world of illusions with all their accompanying vanities and boasts and pretentions. It is an "active being–thought"—*active* because it is always awake, *being* because it is independent of all suggestion and relies entirely on conscience. So the "real man" has an objective judgment, an objective aim, and the strength to struggle in himself against what could turn him away from them.

DMD: *You speak of conscience; I would be very much interested to hear what was Gurdjieff's teaching about that.*

PD: The idea of conscience is a central one in Gurdjieff's teaching. In *Beelzebub's Tales*, he explains that for what could awaken man to his reality, it's no longer possible to lean on the great theological virtues of faith, hope, and love; they have degenerated too much in contemporary man. However, one quality has remained intact in him: his conscience. And what must he understand by that? As always, Gurdjieff presents this idea in several ways and with each, he wishes to touch a different facet of the person he is addressing. In *Beelzebub's Tales*, he presents it in its highest, theological aspect: speaking of the highest degree of consciousness, "objective conscience," he calls it a "divine impulse" which must be served by the struggle between the functioning of the physical body and that of the being, which strives to perfect and develop itself.

Elsewhere, he speaks of it as a person's grasp of an immediate and total awareness of everything that he is; and as each part has a contradictory feeling, and these feelings range from a deep impression of powerlessness, or even nothingness, to the most high-flown notions of oneself, to feel all that simultaneously would be unbearable. That is why conscience is always covered up in the ordinary person. It's only gradually, and to the degree that a person can make contact with his real being and have a relation with an inner life, that at the same time conscience begins to open and one begins to recognize what it is in which hope and confidence can really be placed. So it is only by a gradual process that Gurdjieff tries to make a person come little by little to feel his contradictions and the need to change. We've already spoken of the series of snapshots taken in the course of the day which show these insignificant "I's" which succeed each other in us, without leaving behind the faintest memory of the real I which can exist and which would represent us more fully.

DMD: *One often hears the idea of man's plurality—"man is legion," and so on—but there is not so often a clarity about his possibility of wholeness, of unity; of bringing these many "I's" into some sort of organization, under some kind of government.*

PD: In order to explain the action of these limited, powerless "I's" and this possibility of a better organization that you speak of, Gurdjieff made use of an ancient allegory. Man is represented by an equipage in which the coachman corresponds to thought, the carriage to the body, and the horse to feeling. At first sight the whole thing looks very fine. The coachman wears a superb top hat, and the carriage has a brand new body with a famous trademark. But you shouldn't look too closely. The rest of the coachman's get-up is in a pitiable condition, and he himself is a nobody; he is lazy, greedy for cheap pleasures, and he takes no interest in the rest of the equipage—he is only a hired driver. As for the carriage, under the new body, the wheels and undercarriage are dirty and worn out almost beyond repair. It has become completely unfit for the use it was really made for. And last and above all, there is the horse—the poor horse, who suffers because nobody pays attention to him. No one has thought about educating him, or providing him with the kind of food he needs. He's deprived of all interest or incentive; he lives in a sort of limbo, neglected, like an orphan, closed in on himself, ready to let himself be seduced by anyone who shows any interest in him.

The equipage is in this state because it has no master. It is a hackney cab, at the disposition of chance passengers—these authoritarian "I's" who appear and are soon replaced by others just as dictatorial and as changeable.

This allegory needs to be expanded on at length to be thoroughly understood, and there isn't time for that now. At first sight, the image may seem exaggerated. But that's because we usually know only the most obvious of all our thoughts, feelings, and bodily movements—our capacity to reflect, to conduct our affairs successfully, make physical efforts, be fond of certain people. But behind this facade, we know nothing of these unstable "I's" and their continually shifting movements—the dreams, the preconceived judgments, the organic rigidity which closes us into our automatism, this skin-deep sensibility which in fact—unless a central, essential aspiration touches our consciousness—determines the orientation of our whole lives.

DMD: *It sounds like rather a hopeless picture. ...*

PD: No, it's not hopeless—on the contrary; because, in fact, the real Master is not far off. He is in the carriage, but helpless—like a prisoner. He has no way of making himself heard, but he is there, within. And in his heart, the coachman knows that quite well, because when a difficulty or a danger arises and the carriage goes into a ditch, he turns toward the Master and calls him. As soon as the problem is solved, he forgets again. But it's not impossible to talk to the coachman and persuade him to shake off his dream and listen for that voice. What the Master has to communicate comes from very high, and it is bound to have an action on him and on the rest of the equipage. The coachman is capable of understanding, of making efforts, of centering his attention, of looking toward the future, and of seeing through those who want to impose on him.

To put this image into another form, it could be said that there are several states, several degrees, of consciousness. The one we ordinarily live in has been called a state of sleep. Between this sleep and that highest possible degree of consciousness we have spoken of, there are intermediate stages, and these we need to know. They are accessible to our observation; they depend on us. A person can try to come out of his dream and remember the meaning of his existence; he can try to be present to himself, to be aware of what he is and of this real I which is in him. It is a long apprenticeship. But when he opens fully to what it is in him that needs his service, at that moment his functions are in tune with this wish: they change tempo, they harmonize. The thought is vigilant, the body lets go of its resistance and relaxes, and in the feeling, a joy arises which lends a warmth to support this mutual understanding. At that moment, there is unity; the true Master makes his appearance.

DMD: *He makes his appearance, but what then?*

PD: There is a lot to do, a lot to demand of oneself, before he can remain present. That is why I said to you at the beginning of this conversation that it was quite natural for these remarkable men, such as Gurdjieff depicted them, to show themselves indulgent toward the weaknesses of others. One must have verified in oneself the astonishing truth of the image of the hackney cab before one can make room for that which "every bearer of the name of Man should have": the true I, the real, whole individuality.

Note:

1   Kathryn Hulme, *Undiscovered Country: In Search of Gurdjieff* (Boston: Little, Brown & Co., 1972).

Parabola
Volume: 30.2
Restraint

ANOTHER AXIS WITHIN

An Interview with Paul Reynard

*Born in Lyon, Paul Reynard studied painting there and in
Paris, working under Fernand Léger. He came to New York
City in 1968, where he maintained a studio and for many
years taught at the School of Visual Arts. Reynard joined a
Gurdjieff group in Paris in 1946 and began to practice the
sacred dances known as the Movements with Jeanne de Salz-
mann, and later with G. I. Gurdjieff. In the United States he
was given the responsibility for Movements in The Gurdjieff
Foundation of New York and other U. S. as well as Canadian
Gurdjieff Foundations.*

—Lorraine Kisly

Paul Reynard: Perhaps we should begin by what it is you
mean by restraint. In the theme of this issue you imply
that restraint is not-doing. In French, restraint does not
mean not-doing but limitation. There is a tension in it.

Parabola: *Perhaps the genesis of the theme will help us here.
One impulse for the issue comes from something I heard long
ago about what's called fine-muscle development in infants.
You notice that very young babies move with the whole of their
bodies toward an object that excites their interest. Arms, legs,
mouth, everything is in motion. Over time, they do not develop
fine-muscle control at all but learn instead to restrain all but
those they need to pick up the tiny object. There's nothing to*

develop. The capacity is there. But with so much interference there is no freedom. And freedom after all is what's important in relation to restraint.

Secondly, this theme follows our thirtieth anniversary issue on Awakening, and it seems that a moment of awakening immediately plunges us into the realm of doing and not-doing in terms of search. It's an immediate paradox. A moment of awakening comes; it is given. Then I want something, I want to repeat it, I want to try.

PR: And I am back to where I was. It's finished.

P: *This is a situation that comes at the beginning—and goes on and on in a search.*

PR: It is a question of two levels appearing.

P: *And what are these two?*

PR: In your search you are waiting for God—or at least for another influence. You are looking for a different level that perhaps you experienced earlier sitting on that chair, for example. Now you are again sitting on that chair, and you try to reach that level, but with no success. It is why it is so difficult. The spiritual path is so difficult because one has to understand that one level has to be incorporated in the other. One life has to be incorporated in the other. And for a long time they are either side-by-side, or unaware of each other. When I go in one direction I forget the other one.

P: *I have to make an effort but who or what is it that makes the effort? Isn't effort a kind of doing?*

PR: Yes, in a way; it depends on how I look at it. You see, what interests me very much is the question of language. In the spiritual path, at the beginning you listen to what is said, or you read what is taught. And you learn the same way you learned in school. There is no difference. And when you meet someone who has a certain stature—a master— perhaps, of course he speaks in words, the same words you learned elsewhere. Except, for him, these words have a different source and a different meaning.

Sometimes it takes many years before you suddenly understand that a word you have used for a very long time doesn't mean exactly what you thought it meant. It is different.

For example, this notion of effort. This word at first means something you strive for. But you understand at a certain point that the kind of effort you need to comprehend is different; that what is meant by effort is letting go. It is an effort because I have to struggle against what is ingrained in me about the idea of effort: I want to *get* something, to *do* something. Finally, after years of trying, I begin to understand that the nature of effort is to *allow* something to appear. This new meaning of effort has to do with relaxation. And it is really an effort to understand relaxation when all my training was to strive, to battle against, to chastise some aspect of myself.

So over time the meaning of these outer words begins to change—not through an investigation of their etymology but through your experience; what they communicate to you is not the same as it was before.

P: *You spoke of the experience of encountering a master, or someone who has a certain development, for whom the two levels are active and present. They use words, as you say, and we take them in only according to our own understanding. At the same time one is being acted upon on both levels?*

PR: The master, if he is a master, lives in both levels at the same time. And I do not. I recognize both the gap and the presence of something that calls me.

P: *And yet I try to become like the master by taking his words in an ordinary way.*

PR: Pushing, forcing. … It is the same for the word "attention." With my ordinary attention, which is very useful, I can focus on a mathematical problem, a practical problem. It's needed. I begin that way also when I work on a spiritual path. There is no other way for me, I don't know any other attention except this focusing attention. Until there is a moment where, because I relate to other parts of myself, such as the body, for example, when I begin to be able to welcome another sort of attention which is no longer focusing, but embracing. Different.

P: *So when the mind encounters the idea of relaxation, it is just an idea.*

PR: Just an idea, and it doesn't know what to do.

P: *And it has to try something, so there is a doing.*

PR: I cannot help but to begin by doing. It is what and how I have learned. I have been told I must succeed. I have been taught how to do, not how to let go. It is something you learn in the end not through words but when you try. You meditate, for example, and at the beginning I try to force: "I'm here, I'm here." I'm here in my mind, my head, but I'm not here. And one day suddenly a different sensation comes, in my arm, in another part. I discover something new. Many years ago I had a friend, a sculptor. One day he called me and said I must come over right away. Something strange had happened to him. "I have sensation I never had before," he said. "I feel as though my hands have their own life."

I don't know what he learned from this experience afterwards but it was interesting. It is the way our experience begins. It is an awakening.

But where is the restraint?

P: *You have worked with the Gurdjieff Movements for many years. Someone might look at Peter Brook's film* Meetings with Remarkable Men *and see these Movements and say these people are not free. Outerly they have no freedom to move as they like; they must move in a prescribed and precise way. To some it may even appear mechanical.*

PR: It can be.

P: *So there is an outer restraint, would you say?*

PR: Yes and no. Yes and no because it can be completely mechanical. I've seen places where people do Movements for four hours in a row, completely mechanically; they expect that after four hours, God is going to descend upon them. But the work in Movements begins at the first moment, before the beginning—standing still.

On the other hand, you need a form, and you can be very free within it. Within a form which has been given to you, you may arrive at a point at which you are absolutely free. It is the same in a ritual; a Mass, for example, is a very strict form. But it is meant to bring you to a relation with another force, with a higher force.

P: *There are associations and tensions of all sorts, and when they are given a form and direction they are given another possibility?*

PR: Whether speaking of the Mass or of the Movements, you are given a certain form which is meant for a definite purpose—and sometimes through the windows, as it were, of this form you can see a little bit of this other life. Enough to give you a direction for your search.

P: *Every form can be empty or inhabited?*

PR: Certainly. I once went to a Christmas Mass at Notre Dame with thousands of tourists and it was like a gigantic party without the least sense of the sacred. On another occasion I attended an Easter Mass at the Abbey of Solesmes, also crowded with tourists, but so well ordered by the Benedictine monks that there was something very special there that you could neither forget nor ignore.

You need a form, you cannot do anything without a form, but where is the restraint?

P: *There is the Jewish teaching that in order to create, God had to restrain himself, to withdraw, so that form could appear. In your own work as a painter, how much is doing, and how much is not-doing?*

PR: That's a big question! There is a lot of doing, in the hope that you might express something. But even your expression is doing most of the time. I remember an instance where I worked on a painting for a long time, and thought I would cover it up. I thought it was finished. Nevertheless I continued and then the next morning, the painting was truly completed and meant something to me. But I didn't know when that completion had taken place. When the current was passing, I was not aware of it.

P: *It's necessary to try, to do something.*

PR: Absolutely. Sometimes I keep paintings that are not good but because I suffered there are traces of what we speak of. Others can be very well polished and be totally empty.

P: *When you begin a poem or painting there are thousands of impulses, and the problem is not to do but to discriminate, to hold back, to restrain. For what reason?*

PR: There is choice. I did a series of paintings on the idea of the crucifixion. I did not have a religious education but the symbolism of the cross, the suffering of the man on the cross, meant something to me. In Avignon there is a fifteenth-century painting of the Deposition of Christ by Enguerrand Quarton. It is an extraordinary painting. It might be said that the style of the painting is rigid but this feeling is so strong. So powerful. And my paintings in comparison were just a sort of illustration. Sometimes there was a little piece of something of that sort. But then the restraint is automatic.

I think it's why someone like Picasso has force: there is no restraint.

P: *In relation to what you say about restraint being automatic, something that under certain conditions comes naturally, Krishnamurti once said, "To understand something you have to pay attention, you have to love, and when you love something the very nature of love is discipline. ... When there is that state of attention which is care, affection, that in itself is discipline."*

So on one level restraint is an outer imposition and on another you are saying that it comes of itself, as a consequence of serving something. Then it comes of its own, not as something we do.

PR: It is not imposed. Yet, when I meditate I have to restrain myself from using my ordinary attention. And when words come back to my mind, I am closed and back in my prison.

P: *So for a long time there is an alternation of an imposed effort and one that comes of itself?*

PR: I begin to have a new appreciation, a new measure. As a result of my own experience. And meditation or Movements restrains the field of one sort of experience so it is possible to expand, to explore another field of experience. Otherwise you will be lost, swallowed up by too many impressions.

P: *But the Gurdjieff Movements can be very complicated. Why not just a simple movement of the arm, raising and lowering?*

PR: Because you cannot stay long with it. At a certain point your attention needs to be called a bit more. You cannot work one hour with only an arm up and down because your mind is going to begin to say, "Well … OK!" (*laughs*) And you will be gone. So then another demand will be given to reanimate your attention.

P: *It has been said that effort is really joining with something that is already offered, and this statement brings the wish to let go. …*

PR: That too needs to be questioned. To let go is not to collapse, to passively let go. I let go of a way of mind and body directing things but there is something that remains which is a relation with another energy. Otherwise there is nothing if you just let go. Another word is used often, stillness, "the mind is still." Yet when there is stillness you will see that there is also a great deal of movement of which you were not previously aware. You become aware of coarse movements like breathing, even the beating of the heart, of which you were not aware the moment before. But there are other movements, the movement of the energy of sensation for example. So I'm still, but my breathing continues, my blood circulates. But my mind is still—that means I am not busy with words, not explaining things to myself. And this itself can cause a reaction, a fear that I am being deprived of words; I am becoming stupid.

P: *So just as in Movements there is a demand on the attention so that dreaming doesn't begin, also in meditation there is a demand on the attention to include more? To include sensation, relaxation, to include all the levels of movement and stillness?*

PR: And for this to happen I cannot dream. Everything is there. Even the very finest energy is there. But I am not in touch with it. You know the story of the disciple who asks the Zen master, "What is the difference between you and me?" And the Zen master says, "It is very simple. When I eat I eat, and when I sleep I sleep." And of course the disciple doesn't understand it!

P: *And the student, when he eats?*

PR: He is dreaming … he is thinking about his girlfriend!

P: *Gurdjieff speaks of the need not to express negative emotions. How do you understand this?*

PR: Perhaps I can give you an example. I'm meditating in the morning and suddenly the telephone rings. Maybe I'm expecting an important call and so I stop and it is just someone wanting to sell me a radio. But it is not over—the whole morning I will continue to speak to the guy—"don't do that again," etc. And that is the expression of negative emotion. It eats me, it destroys me. Or I hear through the grapevine that you have a bad opinion of me—"how does she dare?!" And perhaps it isn't even true, but nevertheless it starts something in me that instead of lasting for one second is going to go on and on. "What have I ever done to her," etc.

P: *So the immediate reaction I am perhaps not responsible for?*

PR: I entertain it. And it continues. And that can destroy the whole of the day, it comes back and goes away and returns again.

P: *Of course, this doesn't matter unless I have an aim.*

PR: For the sake of the aim I have to see more, to see what the demand is. It begins by a question: the question of what my life is for. And it takes years to approach that.

P: *I read recently Pema Chödrön's advice that in the face of irritation or impatience or anger, one should "Sit still with the energy until it passes away." Does it pass away?*

PR: This is non-identification. What is important? You work with someone, maybe you have an apprentice and your apprentice drops and breaks your favorite cup and spills your coffee. You are going to be angry. Then life continues, and either you are going to make a sad face to him for the rest of the day or are you going to say, "I said that, and now it is finished, it is enough."

For me it has to do with trying to understand what is meant by the present. The cup breaks, and I'm in reaction. But then life goes on. My life is not a cup of coffee, my relation with you is not a cup of coffee. If I know what my aim is, I go on.

P: *So if you are there to experience it, the reaction doesn't just pass away? It passes into something positive, into presence?*

PR: It is not just to forget; it is not for the sake of being "cured"; it is not self-improvement. It is transformation. Self-improvement is to be better. To show you that I have made progress since the last time we met, that I'm a big guy. Inner transformation means a coming together with all of my parts, spiritual, physical, emotional.

P: *So it is not a choice between being and doing?*

PR: We must do, we must act, but the aim is to be able to do and at the same time to be here.

P: *This is where we began, when we spoke of encountering someone who lived on both of these levels, who embodied two strong currents, and even if we couldn't discriminate very well what it was we were attracted. And it takes a long time to understand what we saw, what we wish for ourselves.*

PR: The problem we have is that for a long time we are either on the level of doing, or of trying to be. And we know how difficult it is to put the two together. Just to be in the street: to be in relation with my body, with my feeling and walk in the street. A car passes by, or a light, and *whoosh*—I'm gone. But the aim is for the two to be together.

P: *To drink your coffee and not disappear into your cup?*

PR: Coffee is not so difficult—but when it is a beautiful cup! (*laughs*).

P: *Life also provides a form to fill or not.*

PR: Everything is a form but I can inhabit this form in two ways. Either completely mechanically, completely lost in it—or there can be another axis within which allows me to participate in the form but not be taken by it.

P: *This again is where restraint is a by-product. It comes along with the effort but it is in no way a suppression.*

PR: What I need to know—and that's not easy—is what to restrain. For example, take again the example of the Movements. A new Movement is given and it's apprehended by my mind. It is going to be very difficult at first to know what is going to be useful, and what is not going to be useful. I will need a different kind of attention, an attention that is in relation with sensation. At the beginning it is just the attention of my mind which is used. So I have to restrain that because that narrow attention will have a tendency to continue, to take over. And what is needed is something larger, an attention that can include the body, and sometimes the feeling as well. The Movement requires a support within and when the support within is lacking it is really like an empty skin.

P: *And without an elder, or a master, who embodies both currents there is no way to recognize the difference. Certainly this can never come from books. You end up with an empty Mass or empty Movements—and not even knowing they are empty.*

PR: Absolutely. I remember so well an experience I had with Gurdjieff himself. I was in a Movements class. I worked in the second row and someone in the front row was absent and so then I was in the first row. We had a Movement that went forward, file after file, so when it was my turn I went forward. Gurdjieff was in front of me and he said something I didn't understand, maybe it was that I was not coming far enough forward. So the second time he was waiting for me, and this time it was very strong, words I understood: "You *merde*. You *merde de merde*."

At that time I was still very shy. If you looked at me directly, I would blush, right away. And this man was insulting me, he was really insulting me. I stopped, and I said to myself, "What's going on?" I was not touched in the feeling. I was free. I stopped. And he walked away.

I was so shocked. I couldn't understand what was happening.

There was no reaction in my emotion. I froze. In that moment I learned a lot about not paying attention to the judgment of people. Not to be attached to that.

P: *How was it that you felt free at that moment?*

PR: Because I was not touched negatively. He was not hurting me. He was saying words, but the way he did it, they didn't enter as a blow the way they would have from other people. He was trying to help me. He was not trying to put me down as others would be doing in saying the very same words. He was playing the anger but he was not angry. And that was a positive shock, something absolutely new. He taught something very precise at that moment. It was love without restraint.

Parabola
Volume: 24.2
Prayer and
Meditation

INVITING HEAVEN INTO HELL

An Interview with William Segal

William Segal, painter and author, spent his life studying inner practices of esoteric schools. He came to regard an interior stillness as the final aim of prayer. With this in mind, I visited him in his New York apartment.
— *Marvin Barrett*

Marvin Barrett: *What is your definition of prayer?*

William Segal: I think we can accept that prayer is the expression of a human need. People want something, and prayer enables them to express their desire. Prayer may be at different levels, from supplication, wishing for something tangible, to a wishing for something that is neither tangible nor material.

MB: *That was my next question: What are the levels of prayer? Obviously there are very primitive forms of prayer, and prayer that can be humanity's ultimate activity.*

WS: Exactly. There is prayer which has to do with the simple needs of body and mind. And then there is prayer which has nothing to do with wanting something, where the impulse is for the highest.

Perhaps it is still asking for something, but what the highest prayer is asking for is unity with the supreme

•

being, communion. Questions of levels can be very important because most prayers are directed toward the material level, but the highest are toward the ultimate psychic energy.

MB: *Can we actually change ourselves through prayer and achieve a higher form of consciousness, a transformation?*

WS: Yes. Prayer certainly has to do with transformation. Transformation can only take place with a great effort, a commitment of time and knowledge. One transforms oneself from a captive of the associations of everyday life toward the highest energy, the indefinable.

MB: *Maybe we could consider prayer in the various traditions. It seems to me that there may be convergence as well as difference between the various traditions—the Buddhist, the Christian, the Jewish, the Islamic, the Hindu ...*

WS: They are all related and all—all, I am certain—take into account the law of levels. No matter what the religion, at the highest level prayer is related and emerges as a state of silence, inner silence, inner stillness. At a very high level one may believe that one is having a dialogue or directing a petition to God. Still, even this prayer is related to the tangible— something which one can objectify. All prayer in all traditions converges.
This is emphasized in the *Hannya Shingyo*, the Buddhist Heart Sutra: "No prayer, no you, no me ... no this, no that." It goes on until we come to "No thing. Nothing," where you can't put labels, you can't objectify. I think this view conceives of prayer as absolute emptiness, stillness.

MB: *How would you define the relationship between meditation and prayer?*

WS: I think that perfect meditation could be termed perfect prayer. A person in a state of purity, in a state of prayer, would be a person in meditation. There are no associations, the mind and the body are stilled, open to a force which might be called God. This openness to Godliness may be where one arrives after a period of deepest prayer, and deepest meditation.

MB: *What is the effect on a human being of that contact that experience?*

WS: It could be called a state of absolute equilibrium, a balance of all parts of oneself. Most of us are in our heads or in our feelings for much of the time.

There is a knowledge and effectiveness in a person who's come to this balanced state: a realization that "You are I and I am YOU." There is no discrimination, no for or against; there is an acceptance of the "Isness" of things. One still sees the difference between the sparrow and the human being, but the man in this higher state is able to harmonize every aspect of himself.

MB: *In the Christian tradition that would be called charity or love.*

WS: One has to love "being in a state of being" to love what is. To love oneself before being able to love a cat or God. To love is to be related to consciousness.

MB: *Can that come about through prayer? The love of oneself, the love of one's fellows, and the love of God seem to be a sequence.*

WS: Yes, and the highest state is a progression toward being present— which means a silence, inward and outward. One is not apart from the inner silence.

MB: *What would you say are the optimum conditions for prayer?*

WS: They would be a quiet place to sit, a relaxed erectness of posture, an awareness of breathing. One's body has to be relaxed, not tense. There should be a balance of the energies of the organism; the mind free of associations, the feelings quiet. A state of balance is essential.

MB: *How often and how long should one pray?*

WS: There is an Islamic tale about Moses going to God to ask how many times a day people should pray. "A hundred," God answered, and Moses went back to his people, who told him, "It is impossible—go back and ask again." Moses went back and forth until God finally reduced the number to five. And so it has been for the Muslims ever since. For others it may be quite different. But regularity I would say is essential. A regular commitment to prayer. Of course, ideally one should be praying at every moment. There is neither night nor day if one is in a proper relationship to this silence. This goes on whether one is sleeping or waking.

MB: *Would that be the same as "practicing the presence"?*

WS: I think that a person in a higher state, who is truly concentrating, would not be thinking about practicing anything. By his very being he will exert a beneficent effect on the world around him. He will not think of being of service—even that is a distraction—but no one will be of more use to humanity.

MB: *What about community, the presence of like-minded people?*

WS: Certainly we can help each other. Your stillness helps me. If you are agitated, nervous, aggressive, you pull me down. We're helped by being with others who are like-minded. Compassion for others helps. Recall Shantideva's Bodhisattva vow:

> *May I be the doctor and the medicine;*
> *And may I be the nurse*
> *For all sick beings in the world*
> *Until everyone is healed.[1]*

MB: *What about the rules, the commandments, in the various traditions?*

WS: Manifestations of greed, lust, cruelty … all these pull people down, drag them away from their reality. In all traditions the rules have to do with preventing that separation. In prayer one is free from the senses, from unworthy, unnecessary desires. The mind can be a help or a distraction.

MB: *Are there people in history or right now that are useful in terms of teaching us how to pray?*

WS: Certainly there are many who can impart knowledge of right posture, right thinking, mindfulness, right attitude, and so on. Much knowledge can be passed on. The true objective of prayer is for people to know their true nature and by establishing themselves in this true nature to gain liberation. Much knowledge can be passed on, but the highest knowledge comes from oneself and is in oneself.

MB: *So the teacher is transitional?*

WS: The guru or teacher can impart the principles relating to the importance of attention—to being present instead of distracted the way most people are. He or she can be an example, and impart lessons in being more awake, more attentive.

Prayer is here and now. The question of prayer is always concerned with the silence, the stillness.

MB: *What about the sacramental approach to life, ritual, thanksgiving, praise, adoration, etc., which we see in most traditions? How do they relate to prayer?*

WS: I think they are all valuable in invoking higher energies. They all have their place on the spectrum of awareness, and they all help, but in the final analysis it comes down to what we were speaking of before, the Buddhist Heart Sutra: "No virtue, no evil, no this, no thing. Nothing." This is the state of pure being. It has nothing to do with helping or hurting others.

There may be certain steps to come to this place where I am God and God is me. We come to the state, the place where there's no thought of God, no reliance on anything but the listening to one's innermost presence, when mentation of any kind ceases. There is a giving up, a surrender of all the functional aspects of the body, but the body is still here. Levels of prayer range from the gambler at the racetrack who prays to win a sum of money to the one who is in a state of purity and awareness and is not moved by any thought or feeling.

Perhaps this is where the question of love comes in. One comes to this state not through wanting but through loving. One can't bear to be separated from the presence of this vibration; one wants always to be in the presence or related, a state of unwavering love.

MB: *So beyond willing is loving.*

WS: Beyond desiring. Beyond all desire, except to be in a relationship to what we call God.

MB: *Is there a difference between the prayers of a young, a middle-aged, and an old man or woman?*

WS: There must be a maturity which comes with old age; at the same time, the ardent wish which can help one towards the ultimate comes more with youth. I think there is an openness in children. Bhagavan Maharishi tells of a child who was asked, "Did you say your prayers?" The child answered, "I don't have to say my prayers; I'm going to sleep now. Sleep is my prayer." The Maharishi agreed with her. Sleep is prayer. When you are in a sleep state, you don't have any wish, you don't have any ambition. Close to sleep we are close to prayer. You realize that when you are soundly sleeping you are well off.

MB: *If you don't have bad dreams.*

WS: Yes, but dreaming is not a sound sleep. When one is truly asleep, one is out—one has no associations. The mind is tranquil. One is in the prayerful sleep state that the child spoke about. When one wakes up, immediately thought comes in: "I want this." A desire comes in, an aggressive attitude, one is for or against something.

MB: *So you would say that the last thing you think before you go to sleep should be prayerful, and the first thing upon waking. ...*

WS: ... should be stillness. The last moments before you go to sleep should bring you to a state of relaxation in body and mind, an emptying of thoughts and feelings. In waking up one should again be aware of one's state of consciousness. An awareness persists however sleepy one is.

One's idea of prayer is most important. As we said, it can range from a wish for personal gain to a wish for contact with the highest.

MB: *William James says that prayer is the necessary core of religion: "Without prayer there is no religion."*

WS: But aren't they the same thing? A coming together of the human and the highest—coming together with this vibration of Godliness. A definition of religion can be close to a definition of prayer. Otherwise it is a question of calling yourself a Sufi, a Jew, a Christian, a Hindu, a Buddhist—each has one concept of religion, but the highest religion would be a oneness within oneself and others.

MB: *You mentioned the Buddhist Heart Sutra as an ideal prayer. What would be the Jewish equivalent?*

WS: I would say the *Shema*—"Hear O Israel, the Lord thy God is One"—is close to it. God is here, God is everywhere. There is no separation. Buddhism has many prayers that affirm the same truth in different words, even though there is no admission of the existence of God.

MB: *What about the Tibetan prayer at the time of death?*

WS: What is advised by the Buddhists for the dying is a following of the light. And the following of the light requires an awareness, a being there. If there's fear, or a wish, one is not concentrated in one's attention towards the light; and it is this concentration and attention to the moment of dying that is important. One must be entirely present. No thinking about one's will, one's heirs, one's regrets.

MB: *Wouldn't that be the ultimate prayer, the consciousness of light?*

WS: I don't know whether it is the *ultimate* prayer. It is very close to it, but when you say "consciousness of light," this is objectifying something, and for me in the ultimate prayer there would be no object, no light, no thing. So we are back to the Heart Sutra.

If we stop right now and are aware without being aware of any thing—that would be a very high state. As long as one objectifies, one hasn't reached the highest.

MB: *Would you say that prayer may be the principal means of knowing?*

WS: We live in a very complex world. We don't know who we are, we don't understand how our brain and our body function, we don't know who's guiding us, who is guiding the universe (in other words, who is running things)—we don't know any of that. But through prayer we might come to a state of knowing—not so much knowledge as knowing. An unknown knowing.

MB: *And well-being?*

WS: Certainly prayer, as much as any human activity, can bring us that feeling of well-being, that conviction of Julian of Norwich that "all is well."

MB: *Is prayer the answer to the problem of evil?*

WS: I think that prayer can diminish the amount of evil, though evil is also part of the scheme of things. It evidently has its place. We try to diminish it and to move towards a purity which is the opposite of evil. I think that prayer has this effect. There is the Zen Roshi's claim that "sleeping beside the waterfall, I stopped the war." Sleep as prayer again. Without doing or wishing anything, it diminishes evil.

Gurdjieff said that by going into a church and by opening yourself, being aware, you can receive an energy which has been deposited by people in prayer. In a church, synagogue, temple, or any place where people have seriously launched prayer, the atmosphere is good. One benefits from the vibrations generated and deposited by others.

MB: *What about other aids to prayer? Rosaries, prayer wheels, walking, dancing, singing, chanting. ...*

WS: They are all aids. Good posture, a gesture can be an aid to prayer. You lift your hand in a certain gesture and immediately the turbulence, the impulses, and the agitations of the body are stilled. Dances, simple forceful movements or smooth ones, like whirling—they all help to bring about concentration instead of diffusion of the energies within the organism. You can bring about a balance between different centers and parts of a human being. That can take years of training, and that is where a teacher comes in.

Almost every activity done with attention and presence can be a form of prayer. No matter what you are doing, if you do that with all your heart and soul and attention, it becomes a form of prayer which can lift you up.

MB: *That would include the arts.*

WS: Absolutely. And crafts.

MB: *Can ritual be used to move one away from the "I want this … I want an answer" type of prayer?*

WS: Ritual helps to prepare for prayer in its ultimate sense. Because the body and the mind do need preparation; the average person is distracted, manipulated—his body and his desires rule him. An evolved human being would have an inner intelligence which would understand that he's being worked on by many forces at many different levels. The seed of that true being which is prayer is in everyone. And ritual helps one to come close to it—to good morality. It helps to lift one. Prayer can lift us from level to level; we can't limit our idea of prayer.

Let us be still for a moment, and see if we can come to a prayerful state *now*. What would come out of being still and listening? Let's be quiet for just a moment. I wish to pray, to launch a prayer. What does it mean? What will it bring? How must I be? Am I able to pray? Am I fit? I need to calm my body, my mind, my emotions. As I speak with you I come closer to a relationship with another force; there is a greater sensitivity of the whole organism, an equilibrium. I'm not as taken with the noises of life. I've become a more intelligent, loving, even more poetical human being. I am not as distracted by that noise, the car alarm which is coming through the window. That sound is really useful: I am inviting hell into heaven.

Note:

1 Translated from the Tibetan by Robert Thurman.

Parabola
Volume: 22.3
Conscience and
Consciousness

Remembering the Self

P. D. Ouspensky

On one occasion while talking with G. I asked him whether he considered it possible to attain "cosmic consciousness," not for a brief moment only but for a longer period. I understood the expression "cosmic consciousness" in the sense of a higher consciousness possible for man in the sense in which I had previously written about it in my book *Tertium Organum.*

"I do not know what you call 'cosmic consciousness,'" said G., "it is a vague and indefinite term; anyone can call anything he likes by it. In most cases what is called 'cosmic consciousness' is simply fantasy, associative daydreaming connected with intensified work of the emotional center. Sometimes it comes near to ecstasy but most often it is merely a subjective emotional experience on the level of dreams. But even apart from all this before we can speak of 'cosmic consciousness' we must define in general *what consciousness is.*"

"How do you define consciousness?"

"*Consciousness* is considered to be indefinable," I said, "and indeed, how can it be defined if it is an inner quality? With the ordinary means at our disposal it is impossible to prove the presence of consciousness in another man. We know it only in ourselves."

"All this is rubbish," said G., "the usual scientific sophistry. It is time you got rid of it. Only one thing is true in what you have said: that you *can know* consciousness only in yourself. Observe that I say you *can know*, for you can know it only when you have it. And when you have not got it, you can know that you have not got it, not at that very moment, but afterwards. I mean that when it comes again you can see that it has been absent a long time, and you can find or remember the moment when it disappeared and when it reappeared. You can also define the moments when you are nearer to consciousness and further away from consciousness. But by observing in yourself the appearance and the disappearance of consciousness you will inevitably see one fact which you neither see nor acknowledge now, and that is that moments of consciousness are very short and are separated by long intervals of completely unconscious, mechanical working of the machine. You will then see that you can think, feel, act, speak, work, *without being conscious of it*. And if you learn to see in yourselves the moments of consciousness and the long periods of mechanicalness, you will as infallibly see in other people when they are conscious of what they are doing and when they are not.

"Your principal mistake consists in thinking that you *always have consciousness*, and in general, either that consciousness is *always present* or that it is *never present*. In reality consciousness is a property which is continually changing. Now it is present, now it is not present. And there are different degrees and levels of consciousness. Both consciousness and the different degrees of consciousness must be understood in oneself by sensation, by taste. No definitions can help you in this case and no definitions are possible so long as you do not understand *what* you have to define. And science and philosophy cannot define consciousness because they want to define it where it does not exist. It is necessary to distinguish *consciousness* from the *possibility of consciousness*. We have only the possibility of consciousness and rare flashes of it. Therefore we cannot define what consciousness is."

I cannot say that what was said about consciousness became clear to me at once. But one of the subsequent talks explained to me the principles on which these arguments were based.

On one occasion at the beginning of a meeting G. put a question to which all those present had to answer in turn. The question was: "What is the most important thing that we notice during self-observation?"

Some of those present said that during attempts at self-observation, what they had felt particularly strongly was an incessant flow of thoughts which they had found impossible to stop. Others spoke of the difficulty of distinguishing the work of one center from the work of another. I had evidently not altogether understood the question, or I answered my own thoughts, because I said that what struck me most was the connectedness of one thing with another in the system, the wholeness of the system, as if it were an "organism," and the entirely new significance of the word *to know* which included not only the idea of knowing this thing or that, but the connection between this thing and everything else.

G. was obviously dissatisfied with our replies. I had already begun to understand him in such circumstances and I saw that he expected from us indications of something definite that we had either missed or failed to understand.

"Not one of you has noticed the most important thing that I have pointed out to you," he said. "That is to say, not one of you has noticed that *you do not remember yourselves.*" (He gave particular emphasis to these words.) "You do not feel *yourselves*; you are not conscious of *yourselves*. With you, 'it observes' just as 'it speaks,' 'it thinks,' 'it laughs.' You do not feel: *I* observe, *I* notice, *I* see. Everything still 'is noticed,' 'is seen.' ... In order really to observe oneself one must first of all *remember oneself*. (He again emphasized these words.) Try to *remember yourselves* when you observe yourselves and later on tell me the results. Only those results will have any value that are accompanied by self-remembering. Otherwise you yourselves do not exist in your observations. In which case what are all your observations worth?"

These words of G.'s made me think a great deal. It seemed to me at once that they were the key to what he had said before about consciousness. But I decided to draw no conclusions whatever, but to try to *remember myself* while observing myself.

The very first attempts showed me how difficult it was. Attempts at *self-remembering* failed to give any results except to show me that in actual fact we never remember ourselves.

"What else do you want?" said G. "This is a very important realization. People who *know this*" (he emphasized these words) "already know a great deal. The whole trouble is that nobody knows it. If you ask a man whether he can remember himself, he will of course answer that he can. If you tell him that he cannot remember himself, he will either be angry with you, or he will think you an utter fool. The whole of life is based on this, the whole of human existence, the whole of human blindness. If a man really knows that he cannot remember himself, he is already near to the understanding of his being."

All that G. said, all that I myself thought, and especially all that my attempts at self-remembering had shown me, very soon convinced me that I was faced with an *entirely new problem which science and philosophy had not, so far, come across.*

I am speaking of the division of attention which is the characteristic feature of self-remembering.

I represented it to myself in the following way:

When I observe something, my attention is directed toward what I observe—a line with one arrowhead:

I   ⟶   the observed phenomenon.

When at the same time, I try to remember myself, my attention is directed both towards the object and towards myself. A second arrowhead appears on the line:

I   ⟷   the observed phenomenon.

Having defined this I saw that the problem consisted in directing attention on oneself without weakening or obliterating the attention directed on something else. Moreover this "something else" could as well be within me as outside me.

The very first attempts at such a division of attention showed me its possibility. At the same time I saw two things clearly.

In the first place I saw that self-remembering resulting from this method had nothing in common with "self-feeling" or "self-analysis." It was a new and very interesting state with a strangely familiar flavor.

And secondly I realized that moments of self-remembering do occur in life, although rarely. Only the deliberate production of these moments created the sensation of novelty. Actually I had been familiar with them from early childhood. They came either in new and unexpected surroundings, in a new place, among new people while traveling, for instance, when suddenly one looks about one and says: *How strange! I and in this place*; or in very emotional moments, in moments of danger, in moments when it is necessary to keep one's head, when one hears one's own voice and sees and observes oneself from the outside.

I saw quite clearly that my first recollections of life, in my own case very early ones, were moments of *self-remembering*. This last realization revealed much else to me. That is, I saw that I really only remember those moments of the past in which *I remembered myself*. Of the others *I know only that they took place*. I am not able wholly to revive them, to experience them again. But the moments when I had remembered myself were alive and were in no way different from the present. I was still afraid to come to conclusions. But I already saw that I stood upon the threshold of a very great discovery. I had always been astonished at the weakness and insufficiency of our memory. So many things disappear. For some reason or other the chief absurdity of life for me consisted in this. Why experience so much in order to forget it afterwards? Besides there was something degrading in this. A man feels something which seems to him very big, he thinks he will never forget it; one or two years pass by—and nothing remains of it. It now became clear to me why this was so and why it could not be otherwise. If our memory really keeps alive only moments of self-remembering, it is clear why our memory is so poor.

All these were realizations of the first days. Later, when I began to learn to divide attention, I saw that self-remembering gave wonderful sensations which, in a natural way, that is, by themselves, come to us only very seldom and in exceptional conditions. Thus, for instance, at that time I used very much to like to wander through St. Petersburg at night and to "sense" the houses and the streets. St. Petersburg is full of these strange sensations. Houses, especially old houses, were quite alive, I all but spoke to them. There was no "imagination" in it. I did not think of anything, I simply walked along while trying to remember myself and looked about; the sensations came by themselves. ...

Sometimes self-remembering was not successful; at other times it was accompanied by curious observations.

I was once walking along the Liteiny towards the Nevsky, and in spite of all my efforts I was unable to keep my attention on self-remembering.

The noise, movement, everything distracted me. Every minute I lost the thread of attention, found it again, and then lost it again. At last I felt a kind of ridiculous irritation with myself and I turned into the street on the left having firmly decided to keep my attention on the fact that *I would remember myself* at least for some time, at any rate until I reached the following street. I reached the Nadejdinskaya without losing the thread of attention except, perhaps, for short moments. Then I again turned towards the Nevsky realizing that, in quiet streets, it was easier for me not to lose the line of thought and wishing therefore to test myself in more noisy streets. I reached the Nevsky still remembering myself, and was already beginning to experience the strange emotional state of inner peace and confidence which comes after great efforts of this kind. Just round the corner on the Nevsky was a tobacconist's shop where they made my cigarettes. Still remembering myself I thought I would call there and order some cigarettes.

Two hours later I *woke up* in the Tavricheskaya, that is, far away. I was going by *izvostchik* to the printers. The sensation of awakening was extraordinarily vivid. I can almost say that I *came to*. I remembered everything at once. How I had been walking along the Nadejdinskaya, how I had been remembering myself, how I had thought about cigarettes, and how at this thought I seemed all at once to fall and disappear into a deep sleep.

At the same time, while immersed in this sleep, I had continued to perform consistent and expedient actions. I left the tobacconist, called at my flat in the Liteiny, telephoned to the printers. I wrote two letters. Then again I went out of the house. I walked on the left side of the Nevsky up to the Gostinoy Dvor intending to go to the Offitzerskaya. Then I had changed my mind as it was getting late. I had taken an izvostchik and was driving to the Kavalergardskaya to my printers. And on the way while driving along the Tavricheskaya I began to feel a strange uneasiness, as though I had forgotten something.—*And suddenly I remembered that I had forgotten to remember myself.*

At one of the following lectures G. returned to the question of consciousness.

"Neither the psychical nor the physical functions of man can be understood," he said, "unless the fact has been grasped that they can both work in different states of consciousness.

"In all there are four states of consciousness possible for *man*" (he emphasized the word "man"). "But ordinary man, that is, man number one, number two, and number three, lives in the two lowest states of consciousness only. The two higher states of consciousness are inaccessible to him, and although he may have flashes of these states, he is unable to understand them and he judges them from the point of view of those states in which it is usual for him to be.

"The two usual, that is, the lowest, states of consciousness are first, sleep, in other words a passive state in which man spends a third and very often a half of his life. And second, the state in which men spend the other part of their lives, in which they walk the streets, write books, talk on lofty subjects, take part in politics, kill one another, which they regard as active and call 'clear consciousness' or the 'waking state of consciousness.' The term 'clear consciousness' or 'waking state of consciousness' seems to have been given in jest, especially when you realize what clear consciousness ought in reality to be and what the state in which man lives and acts really is.

"The third state of consciousness is self-remembering or self-consciousness or consciousness of one's being. It is usual to consider that we have this state of consciousness or that we can have it if we want it. Our science and philosophy have overlooked the fact that we do not possess this state of consciousness and that we cannot create it in ourselves by desire or decision alone.

"The fourth state of consciousness is called the objective state of consciousness. In this state a man can see things as they are. Flashes of this state of consciousness also occur in man. In the religions of all nations there are indications of the possibility of a state of consciousness of this kind which is called 'enlightenment' and various other names but which cannot be described in words. But the only right way to objective consciousness is through the development of self-consciousness. If an ordinary man is artificially brought into a state of objective consciousness and afterwards brought back to his usual state he will remember nothing and he will think that for a time he had lost consciousness. But in the state of self-consciousness a man can have flashes of objective consciousness and remember them.

"The fourth state of consciousness in man means an altogether different state of being; it is the result of inner growth and of long and difficult work on oneself.

"But the third state of consciousness constitutes the natural right of man as he is, and if man does not possess it, it is only because of the wrong conditions of his life. It can be said without any exaggeration that at the present time the third state of consciousness occurs in man only in the form of very rare flashes and that it can be made more or less permanent in him only by means of special training.

"For most people, even for educated and thinking people, the chief obstacle in the way of acquiring self-consciousness consists in the fact that they think they possess it, that is, that they possess self-consciousness and everything connected with it: individuality in the sense of a permanent and unchangeable I, will, ability to do, and so on. It is evident that a man will not be interested if you tell him that he can acquire by long and difficult work something which, in his opinion, he already has. On the contrary he will think either that you are mad or that you want to deceive him with a view to personal gain.

"The two higher states of consciousness—'self-consciousness' and 'objective consciousness'—are connected with the functioning of the higher centers in man.

"In addition to [the thinking, emotional, and physical centers] there are two other centers in man, the 'higher emotional' and the 'higher thinking.' These centers are in us; they are fully developed and are working all the time, but their work fails to reach our ordinary consciousness. The cause of this lies in the special properties of our so-called 'clear consciousness.'

"In order to understand what the difference between states of consciousness is, let us return to the first state of consciousness which is sleep. This is an entirely subjective state of consciousness. A man is immersed in dreams, whether he remembers them or not does not matter. Even if some real impressions reach him, such as sounds, voices, warmth, cold, the sensation of his own body, they arouse in him only fantastic subjective images. Then a man wakes up. At first glance this is a quite different state of consciousness. He can move, he can talk with other people, he can make calculations ahead, he can see danger and avoid it, and so on. It stands to reason that he is in a better position than when he was asleep. But if we go a little more deeply into things, if we take a look into his inner world, into his thoughts, into the causes of his actions, we shall see that he is in almost the same state as when he is asleep. And it is even worse, because in sleep he is passive, that is, he cannot do anything. In the waking state, however, he can do something all the time and the results of his actions will be reflected upon him or upon those around him. *And yet he does not remember himself.* He is a machine, everything with him *happens.* He cannot stop the flow of his thoughts, he cannot control his imagination, his emotions, his attention. He lives in a subjective world of 'I love,' 'I do not love,' 'I like,' 'I do not like,' 'I want,' 'I do not want,' that is, of what he thinks he likes, of what he thinks he does not like, of what he thinks he wants, of what he thinks he does not want. He does not see the real world. The real world is hidden from him by the wall of imagination. *He lives in sleep.* He is asleep. What is called 'clear consciousness' is sleep and a far more dangerous sleep than sleep at night in bed."

Excerpts from *In Search of the Miraculous: Fragments of an Unknown Teaching,* by P. D. Ouspensky. Copyright © 1949 and renewed 1977 by Tatiana Nagro. Reprinted by permission of Harcourt, Inc.

Parabola
Volume: 29.3
Seeker

First Question

Ravi Ravindra

The struggle to know who I am, in truth and in spirit, is the spiritual quest. The movement in myself from the mask to the face, from the personality to the person, from the performing actor to the ruler of the inner chamber, is the spiritual journey. To live, work, and suffer on this shore in faithfulness to the whispers from the other shore is spiritual life. To keep the flame of spiritual yearning alive is to be radically open to the present and to refuse to settle for comforting religious dogma, philosophic certainties, and social sanctions.

Who am I? Out of fear and out of desire, I betray myself. I am who I am not. I cover my face with many masks, and even become the masks. I am too busy performing who I think I am to know who I really am. I am afraid: I may be nothing other than what I appear to be. There may be no face behind the mask, so I decorate and protect my mask, preferring a fanciful something over a real nothing.

I cling to the herd for comfort. Together we weave varied garments to cover our nakedness. We guard the secret of our nothingness with anxious agility lest we should be discovered.

Occasionally, I hear a voice uttered in some dark recess of myself. Sometimes it is the soft sobbing of a lonely child. At other times, it is the anguished cry of a witnessing conscience. At yet other times, it is the thundering command of a king. "Who are you?" I ask. I AM.

What am I asking when I ask "Who am I?" What sort of answer would be acceptable? Do I want a chart of my genealogical and social relations? A list of my racial and biological characteristics? A catalogue of my psychological features—my likes and dislikes, desires and fears? These are all the things that shape my personality. But whose personality is it? Who wears this mask? In response to a little knock at the door of my consciousness, I ask "Who is it?" No naming is sufficient. What I seek is to see and touch the face of the one who calls.

"Who am I?" does not ask for an enumeration of scientific facts: it expresses a certain restlessness, groping, and exploration. It is the beginning of a movement towards light, towards seeing things clearly, as a whole. It is the refusal to remain in the dark—fragmented and on the surface of myself. It is a state of searching for meaning, comprehensiveness, and depth. It is the desire to wake up.

Soon I betray this impulse and am lulled back to sleep by comforting caresses and fairy tales. I sleep, dreaming of great adventures and of quests for hidden treasures. I dream of many journeys, many peaks, and of lions guarding the mountain passes. Sometimes for a moment I wake up to find myself a prisoner of what I know and what I am. Even finding the door of my little prison open, I stay in it, afraid to leave, counting and recounting my possessions and my testimonials. ...

I share many walls with others. With vigor and imagination, I collaborate with others in building castles of science, art, philosophy, and religion in which we may rest secure, unmindful of our ignorance of who we are, why we are here, and why we do what we do. But the silent witness inside me asks, "What do you seek?"

From Ravi Ravindra, *Pilgrim Without Boundaries* (Sandpoint, Idaho: Morning Light Press, 2003), pp. 33-35. Copyright © 2003 Ravi Ravindra. Reprinted by permission of Morning Light Press, www.morninglightpress.com.

•

CHAPTER THREE

To a Man Who Is Searching with All His Being . . .

—Views from the Real World

Parabola
Volume: 31.3
Thinking

THE THINKING OF A MAN

Lord John Pentland

So let us ask now, what do we look for in a man of vision today? The number of adherents to a spiritual teacher, his personal charisma, proves nothing. The fact that it is traditional is not enough to make me know a teaching is for me. What should be our measure in speaking of a teacher? What are the virtues of a real thinker, what is important?

First of all, his thinking should be a service to the highest. Everything created, even down to the stones, must be alive because it has been created by the highest, by God, and it is to be respected because it is under God. And therefore to think about anything intelligently is itself also a sacred act.

Unfortunately we on the earth are on a very remote place, where we constantly forget the highest, where the influence from the highest is not strong. But it is through seeing this and being aware of our habit of forgetting that a change in accordance with the law can take place in us. So becoming aware of forgetting the highest, and that I wish to remember the highest, might be the first thinker virtue.

Secondly, a man with vision should think dangerously, without regard to the views of his fellows, or even the views of the greatest past thinkers whose influence has faded. Truth must be his only ethic. What he will propose of course can only be the same truth as was proposed in the past, but he states it in a new form, as if for the first time, in a manner which is directly appropriate to the contemporary confusion. He must not be afraid if in so doing he will give offense to others. The degree of fear in our vision of ourselves is what measures and limits our intelligence. The fear is what imprisons our thought. Breaking the tablets once is not enough. It has to be done again and again, both historically and for ourselves personally.

Thirdly, the thinking of a man of vision is from the heart as well as the head. Although it brings us the light and dark realities of life equally, it is felt on the whole as an encouragement to me, a manifestation of his love for me, a tough kind of love.

Fourthly and lastly, we ask of a man of vision that his teaching should be complete and consistent in itself, with no compromises, no exceptions and no self-contradictions. Although we are just beginners who fall far short, we want to see the teacher as an ideal, go the whole way with him. Although it begins with self-questioning like every other great teaching, although he emphasizes how far we are from the center and how weak and lazy our minds become through forgetting the highest, we want his teaching to provide answers also. It would not finally correspond exactly to the needs of our time unless it were a science, a sacred science which as well as putting questions to us fearlessly and lovingly, also depends on experiment, and provides a structure for understanding.

From "A Talk on the Ideas of G. I. Gurdjieff," Wagner College, Staten Island, June 1983.

Parabola
Volume: 29.3
Seeker

WITHOUT SLEEP, NO AWAKENING

Henri Tracol

Man is born a seeker. Equipped as he is by nature for vibrating to a vast range of impressions, is he not pre-destined to an endless wondering? Bound by necessity to select from these impressions those suitable for con-scious assimilation—and thereby to approach a genuine perception of his own identity—is he not singled out for continuous self-interrogation?

Such is his true vocation, his birthright. He may forget it, deny it, bury it in the depths of his unconscious being; he may go astray, misuse this hidden gift, and increase his own alienation from reality; he may even try to convince himself that he has reached, once and for all, the shores of eternal Truth. No matter; this secret call is still alive, prompting him from within to try, and to try increasingly, to realize the significance of his presence here on earth. For he is here to awake, to remember, and to search, again and still again.

Search for what? it could be asked. Surely there must be a definite aim, a purpose, a mark to be hit in due course. Have we not been warned only too often by modern sci-entists that "if you don't know *what* you are looking for, you will never know what you actually find"? According to their view, mathematical predictability must always prevail over the fertile challenge of uncertainty. And none of them will listen if you venture to remark that to "know" beforehand inevitably means that you will never "find" anything. Indeed there is no escape from the old bugbear of "whatness" unless we remember Scotus Erigena's dictum, "God does not know what He is, because He is not any 'what.'"

This cannot but remind me of my last meeting with an aging friend who was about to undertake what he sensed would be his last journey to sacred places and wise men of the East.

Bidding him goodbye, I said, "I hope you will find what you are seeking." He replied with a peaceful smile, "Since I am really searching for nothing, maybe I shall find it."

Let us get rid at once of a possible misunderstanding and clearly state that no real knowledge can ever be attained by mere chance. There is such fascination in the shifting lure of existence that it draws our interest away from the immediate perception of the essential. Letting oneself drift into persuasive "visions" and "discoveries," no matter how seductive, or yielding to the spell of what could be called "search for the sake of searching," is merely to indulge in daydreaming—a form of self-tyranny very much at variance with man's objective needs.

Then how is one to set about an authentic quest? Instead of surrendering at once to the call of any particular "way," one should first try with humility to discern some of the requisites for setting off on the right foot.

Is not the first essential an act of *recognition*—recognition of the utter necessity of the search itself, its priority, its urgency for him who aspires to awake and take upon himself as fully as possible his inner and outer existence?

Whenever a man awakes, he awakes from the false assumption that he has always been awake, and therefore the master of his thoughts, feelings and actions. In that moment, he realizes—and this is the shadow side of recognition—how deeply ignorant he is of himself, how narrowly dependent on the web of relationships by which he exists, how helplessly at the mercy of any suggestion that happens to act upon him at a given moment.

He may also awake—if only for a flash—to the light of a higher consciousness, which will grant him a glimpse of the world of hidden potentialities to which he essentially belongs, help him transcend his own limitations, and open the way to inner transformation.

At such a moment the call to search resounds in him and hope is born in his heart. But woe betide him if he believes himself safe from now on. The vision does not last—perhaps it is not meant to last—and once more he is left with the dizzying impression of having sunk back into his own insoluble contradictions.

Feeling lost, he may lose himself further in his search for self-recovery; experiencing his blindness, he may increase it in trying to see; becoming aware of his slavery, he may let his very search for freedom fetter him still more.

Until suddenly he awakes anew, and the whole process begins again. In the long run, by trying and failing over and over, he may come at last to attune himself to the specific part he has to perform in this enigmatic play.

Whenever a man awakes and remembers his purpose, he awakes to a fleeting miracle, and at the same time to an unanswerable riddle. He realizes, at moments, that in order for him to awake he was foredoomed to sleep; in order for him to remember, he was foredoomed to forget. Such is the law of this equivocal situation: without sleep, no awakening; without oblivion, no remembering. Hence, if he goes on looking for what is beyond ambivalence, it will prove to be merely another phantasm. In fact, there is, and always has been, a secret continuity in his being, which is partly reflected in the unchanging structure of his body and the regularly recurring activities of its functions. But in a perpetually moving world of energies, such a relative continuity can never be equated with immutability. The law of man's existence is to become—or to die. If a man were to stay still forever and merge into eternity, there would be little sense in his remaining here on earth.

Such is the human condition: a lucid and total acceptance of it is imperative. This alone will help the true searcher to reaffirm his inner determination. He must be ready to comply with a constantly shifting reality, ready to reconcile himself to the law of alternation, the law of successive turns of fate, ready to conform to whatever may be offered, either favorable or hostile, ready to reject all wishful thinking and to expect nothing in the way of result or reward.

Sooner or later, he will have to try not only to accept risks, but to take up the challenge *knowingly* and put himself in jeopardy. Only then will he truly respond to the call. Far from abjuring the revelations accorded him through teachings he may previously have come in contact with, he longs to "verify" them—that is, to prove them true for himself here and now. Conscious participation in what is self-evident is the goal of the genuine searcher—a goal so close and at the same time so remote, a goal so constantly offered and again withheld—in order that he may keep on searching.

For a man, far beyond his personal hopes and predictions, to search is a sacred task, and if he assents to it and persistently endeavors to fulfill it, he will experience it as truly corresponding both to his essential needs and to his specific capacities.

Patience—much patience, endurance and determination, watchfulness and readiness, availability and conscious flexibility—all these are indispensable to the seeker.

Maybe the time will come when he realizes that in order to develop these latent potentialities he needs guidance and support. Freed from any pretension to be a "knower," he will deliberately put himself under the authority of a master. To absorb his teachings and follow his directives? Yes, and even more important, to perceive and to study the way he deals with life and people, to watch how he conveys his understanding through behavior and tone of voice, and, ultimately, to be able to receive his wordless glance.

By serving such an apprenticeship the seeker gradually unbinds himself from prejudice and becomes sensitive to a wide range of manifestations or testimonies of search, wherever he may happen upon them—and this regardless of any apparent inconsistencies he encounters between their respective features. He will realize that they all refer to the same Unknown that he himself confronts.

From *Search*, edited by Jean Sulzberger (San Francisco: Harper & Row, 1979), pp. xv–xviii.

Parabola
Volume: 13.4
The Mountain

Mount Analogue: Traces

René Daumal

To reach the summit, one must proceed from encampment to encampment. But before setting out for the next refuge, one must prepare those coming after to occupy the place one is leaving. Only after having prepared them can one go on up. That is why, before setting out for a new refuge, we had to go back down in order to pass on our knowledge to other seekers.

•

You cannot stay on the summit forever; you have to come down again. So why bother in the first place? Just this: What is above knows what is below, but what is below does not know what is above. In climbing, take careful note of the difficulties along your way; for as you go up, you can observe them. Coming down, you will no longer see them, but you will know they are there if you have observed them well.

There is an art of finding one's direction in the lower regions by the memory of what one saw higher up. When one can no longer see, one can at least still know.

•

When you strike off on your own, leave some trace of your passing which will guide you coming back: one stone set on another, some grass flattened by a blow of your stick. But if you come to an impasse or a dangerous spot, remember that the trail you have left could lead

•

people coming after you into trouble. So go back along your trail and obliterate any traces you have left. This applies to anyone who wishes to leave some mark of his passage in the world. Even without wanting to, you always leave a few traces. Be ready to answer to your fellow men for the trail you leave behind you.

·

Keep your eye fixed on the way to the top, but don't forget to look right in front of you. The last step depends on the first. Don't think you're there just because you see the summit. Watch your footing, be sure of the next step, but don't let that distract you from the *highest goal*. The first step depends on the last.

·

Never halt on a shifting slope. Even if you think you have a firm foothold, as you take time to catch your breath and have a look at the sky, the ground will settle little by little under your weight, the gravel will begin to slip imperceptibly, and suddenly it will drop away under you and launch you like a ship. The mountain is always watching for a chance to give you a spill.

·

Shoes, unlike feet, are not something you're born with. So you can choose what you want. At first be guided in your choice by people with experience, later by your own experience. Before long you will become so accustomed to your shoes that every nail will be like a finger to feel out the rock and cling to it. They will become a sensitive and dependable instrument, like a part of yourself. And yet, you're not born with them: when they're worn out, you'll throw them away and still remain what you are.

Your life depends to some extent on your shoes: care for them properly. But a quarter of an hour each day is enough; for your life depends on several other things as well.

·

By our calculations, thinking of nothing else; by our desires, abandoning every other hope; by our efforts, renouncing all bodily comfort, we gained entry into this new world. So it seemed to us. But we learned later that if we were able to reach the foot of Mount Analogue, it was because the invisible doors of that invisible country had been opened for us by those who guard them. The cock crowing in the milky dawn thinks its call raises the sun; the child howling in a closed room thinks its cries open the door. But the sun and the mother go their way, following the laws of their being. Those who see us, even though we cannot see ourselves, opened the door for us, answering our puerile calculations, our unsteady desires, and our awkward efforts with a generous welcome.

Parabola
Volume: 4.1
The Trickster

THE WAY OF BLAME

Michel Waldberg

The name Gurdjieff almost always arouses suspicion or hostility. The man is usually described as a kind of werewolf, a cynical tyrant, demanding much of others and little of himself, making use of his disciples for some mysterious aims, seeking power rather than virtue, with an absolute contempt for the whole of humanity.

His teaching is considered forbidding, sterile and dry. His "objectively impartial" critique of man's life is merciless and ferociously funny; it is radical and nothing which constitutes the "human treasure" escapes it. In a supposedly Christian civilization, Gurdjieff denounces the fallacy by which inconsistency is forgiven in the name of mercy; like all the great masters, he reminds us of the primary truths, and tells us that a Christian "is not a man who calls himself a Christian, nor whom others call a Christian, but a man who lives in accordance with the precepts of Christ." The way he proposes, the way of consciousness, seems arrogant to the ordinary eye, and he is reproached for not yielding its place to love.

In contrast to the "humanity" of the understanding and compassionate master, Gurdjieff is accused of "inhumanity" because he exposes what he calls "the terror of the situation," and proposes a "dry" path to his disciples.

But it must be emphasized that in ordinary language the notions of benevolence or compassion are unduly

associated with the notion of gentleness. Gurdjieff is not alone in reject-
ing the usual paths, accepted ideas, and ordinary morality, in reproaching
men and using humor and vulgarity to act effectively on their psyches:
the "way of blame." Whatever may have been said about him, benevolence and compassion—and above all, goodness—are qualities which he
developed to the highest degree in himself, while never associating them
with any useless and harmful softness. It is precisely in the apparently
brutal relationship with the disciple that these qualities are manifested.
For to love the disciple is not to console, but to heal him. And the more
serious the illness, the more violent the cure. Sometimes it is even necessary to amputate: "If thy right eye offend thee," said Christ, "pluck it out
and cast it from thee."

But Gurdjieff is not only a physician or a surgeon. He also shows paths
toward wisdom and happiness, paths which are often painful, arduous,
barren to the eyes of those men whose "personality" (that rigid monster)
lacks the flexibility necessary to overcome obstacles, but easier for those
whose hearts have not yet hardened, for those "ordinary men" who have
not systematically "sought difficulties where there were none" and who
have set themselves to listening, humbly and attentively, to the "inner
voice." For besides the harsh path of the school, there exists the path
of life, of so-called popular wisdom, the importance of which Gurdjieff
has always emphasized. Thus, in the first chapter of *Beelzebub's Tales,* he
writes: "I am a confirmed believer in popular wisdom whose sayings have
been established for many centuries; and I am a believer not only in
theory, like contemporary men, but in practice."

This path of life is the path of the *obyvatel.* "Obyvatel," Gurdjieff
said, "is a strange word from the Russian language. It has the current
meaning of 'inhabitant'; nothing more. It is also used for disdain or
derision: obyvatel!—as if there could be nothing worse. But those who
speak in this way do not understand that the obyvatel is the healthy,
vigorous core of life."

It is also on the road of the obyvatel that we meet the legendary Persian master Mullah Nassr Eddin, to whom Gurdjieff constantly refers
in his books, borrowing his most popular aphorisms and most baffling
and wisest commentaries. A body of anecdotes which make up a whole
legend in the Islamic world have for their hero this paradoxical master,
for the Mullah is the wisest of initiates as well as apparently the most

foolish of villagers. It matters very little whether this character actually existed. He is the protagonist of hundreds of "good stories" which are also excellent fables, some of which can rival the best of the "Zen stories" collected by Suzuki in his *Essays*.

One can find a number of the Mullah's stories, intelligently annotated, in the fourth chapter of Idries Shah's book *The Sufis*.

One of the most typical of these stories is the following: "The Mullah was thinking aloud. 'How do I know whether I'm dead or alive?' 'Don't be stupid,' said his wife, 'if you were dead, your limbs would be cold.' Some time later, the Mullah was in a forest, cutting wood. It was the middle of winter. He suddenly realized that his hands and feet were ice cold. 'I'm unquestionably dead,' he thought, 'so I should stop working, since corpses don't work.' And since corpses don't move either, he lay down on the ground. A pack of wolves approached, and attacked the Mullah's donkey, which he had tied to a tree. 'Go ahead!' said the Mullah; 'take advantage of the fact that I'm dead. But if I had been alive, I wouldn't have allowed you to take such liberties with my donkey!'"

In *Beelzebub's Tales* as well as in *Meetings with Remarkable Men*, Mullah Nassr Eddin is constantly making his opinions known, either in pronouncing one of his "just and caustic judgments," or in commenting briefly on a situation which Gurdjieff considers typical of man's inconsistency.

Mullah Nassr Eddin appears as a reminder of the limits of the intellect; unless the whole being is involved experience is empty, and knowledge evaporates. The Mullah attains his ends by seemingly improbable means. He is a master of the "way of blame," where the initiator assumes the role of the fool, the simpleton, the madman. But the predicaments, however ticklish they may be, always turn to his advantage.

Another master of the "way of blame," at certain moments, was Christ. We live in a society where, consciously or not, the image of a "sweet Jesus" is dominant. Gurdjieff affirms that we suffer "from the crystallization of the consequences of the properties of the maleficent organ kundabuffer," the organ which causes us to see reality backwards. What better verifies this admirable myth than our application of the term "sweet Jesus" to the man who said: "Think not that I am come to send peace on earth: I came not to send peace, but a sword." Nobody, however, would dream of speaking of Christ's inhumanity.

Gurdjieff is often reproached for the manner in which he ousted the curious, whose questions he refused to answer. But this same "sweet Jesus" said: "Give not that which is holy unto the dogs, neither cast ye your pearls before swine, lest they trample them under their feet and turn again and rend you."

One other remark must be made here: we are even more intolerant of Gurdjieff because he speaks to us in *our* language; he tells us, in *our* language: you must recognize your nothingness. If he had been, for example, a Zen master, we would accept him much more easily. However, in reading *Essays on Zen Buddhism* by Suzuki, one cannot ignore the violence that marks the relationship between master and disciple. But Zen is fashionable. It is acceptable, therefore, that a master treats his disciple like a "punching bag," that he beats him with a stick or slaps him—it's exotic. Or, worse yet, we sweeten Zen as we have sweetened Christianity. In Zen, we no longer consider anything but the bliss of *satori*, forgetting the incredible efforts made by the disciples to attain it. At worst, we come to confuse this or that rare emotion with the true satori.

Gurdjieff, understanding the psyche of men, protected himself against such abuses. He multiplied the obstacles, emphasized the difficulties, and demanded much of those who wished to follow him. He rejected the lukewarm, and for that they have not forgiven him.

Gurdjieff tells us: "Men are not men." This is a scandalous proposition; because if there is one thing we have never questioned, it is our humanity. We have accepted our sinfulness, of course, but we have always thought that however serious our weaknesses were, we could become aware of them and correct them. Gurdjieff denies that we have this capacity for understanding and for doing. We haven't really seen the "terror of the situation," we take what is normal as accidental. We believe that with all its ups and downs, humanity progresses; that war, for example, is an exceptional phenomenon. When a master appears who tells us that most men are irresponsible machines, wholly enslaved by their own automatism, incapable of developing even the embryo of a soul, we react with indignation. However cynical we might be, such propositions threaten the humanistic ideas we have nurtured about ourselves: we have not heard the lessons of the masters.

We have not listened to Chateaubriand, Balzac, Baudelaire, Lautréamont or Rimbaud, nor taken seriously Breton's warning cry. We have grown fond of these writers in a sentimental way, admiring them for the beauty of their style or their noble bearing, but we have not listened to them.

Folly and error, avarice and vice,
Employ our souls and waste our bodies' force.
As mangy beggars incubate their lice,
We nourish our innocuous remorse.

Our sins are stubborn, craven our repentance.
For our weak vows we ask excessive prices.
Trusting our tears will wash away the sentence,
We sneak off where the muddy road entices.

These are the first verses of *Les Fleurs du Mal.* We should also listen to Lautréamont:

All my life, without a single exception, I have seen narrow-shoul-dered men doing many stupid things, brutalizing their fellow men, and perverting souls in every conceivable way, motivated by their desire for "glory."

Or then again, the cry of Rimbaud in *Lettre du Voyant:*

If the old fools had not found merely the false meaning of the "I," we would not have had to sweep out those millions of skeletons that, over an infinite amount of time, have accumulated, vaunted products of their distorted thinking.

Baudelaire wrote in his diary:

It is impossible to skim through a newspaper, of any day, month or year, without finding on every line signs of the most atrocious human perversity, coupled with the most astonishing claims to integrity, charity and good will, and the most barefaced statements about progress and civilization.

> *The whole newspaper, from the first line to the last, is but a web of*
> *horrors, a drunken orgy of wars, crimes, thefts, obscenities, tortures,*
> *crimes of states, of nations, of individuals.*
>
> *And it is with this disgusting apéritif that civilized man accom-*
> *panies his morning meal. Everything in this world oozes crimes: the*
> *newspaper, the walls, and man's face.*
>
> *I do not understand how a clean hand can touch a newspaper*
> *without a shudder of disgust.*

These poets, seers and clairvoyants were not mistaken nor lulled to sleep by the fatal illusion of progress. But they died from it. They died of this hunger which Gurdjieff says is essential in order to find the true path, murdered by the monstrous arrogance of those who ignore or deny the existence of a path, convinced that they possess a soul upon which a semblance of morality and the sacraments confer a blessed immortality.

Gurdjieff says the same thing when he describes those whom he calls "the three-brained beings of the planet Earth":

> *As regards their general psyche itself and its fundamental traits, no*
> *matter upon what part of the surface of their planet they arise, these*
> *traits in all of them have precisely the same particularities, among*
> *them being also that property of the three-brained beings there, thanks*
> *to which on that strange planet alone in the whole of the Universe*
> *does that horrible process occur among three-brained beings which is*
> *called the 'process of the destruction of each other's existence,' or as it is*
> *called on that ill-fated planet, 'war.'*
>
> *Besides this chief particularity of their common psyche, there are*
> *completely crystallized in them and there unfailingly become a part*
> *of their common presences—regardless of where they may arise and*
> *exist—functions which exist under the names 'egoism,' 'self-love,'*
> *'vanity,' 'pride,' 'self-conceit,' 'credulity,' 'suggestibility,' and many*
> *other properties quite abnormal and quite unbecoming to the essence*
> *of any three-brained beings whatsoever.*

Humanity is thus unworthy, and can only achieve freedom by becoming conscious of its unworthiness:

Individuality, a single and permanent 'I,' consciousness, will, the ability to do, a state of inner freedom—none of these qualities belong to the ordinary man. ... Man must realize that he doesn't exist; he must realize that he can lose nothing, because he has nothing to lose; he must realize his nothingness, in the strongest sense of the word.

This is the fundamental lesson of Gurdjieff's teaching, the prerequisite to any serious work in the spiritual domain. But how can men become aware of their monstrosity? What weapons can be sharpened to awaken them from this sleep which they presumptuously call their life?

The chief weapon, in this battle of consciousness against sleep, is humor, even vulgar humor. Freud said that this kind of humor "not only had something liberating about it, but something sublime and lofty." Breton labeled it "black humor," and took pains to dissociate it "from foolishness, skeptical irony, and frivolous fun." He called it "the mortal enemy of sentimentality."

This is where the shoe pinches. We have the automatic tendency to associate notions that do not belong together. For instance, we assume that science, philosophy, theology, mysticism—in short, the search for truth—must be taken "seriously." But how do we understand the word "serious"? Of course, it means "worthy of consideration"; but it can also mean "dangerous or threatening."

We tend to confuse seriousness and gravity. Breton denounced this confusion and Gurdjieff exposed it. We don't think of a wise man, philosopher, theologian, or mystic as one who laughs. We say a moral life is serious, as if we were describing an illness.

When we come to Gurdjieff with a question and he does not answer it with the seriousness we expect, we are baffled and upset by his apparently improper or even scandalous attitude. We then reason according to the following sophism: a real spiritual master is always serious; Gurdjieff is not serious; therefore, Gurdjieff is not a real spiritual master. But what about the Zen masters, with their use of laughter, cries and blows?

One evening, Yao Chan climbed a mountain. Seeing the moon suddenly appear from behind the clouds, he laughed heartily. The echo of his laugh was heard ninety li to the east of Li-Yang, where his monastery was situated. The villagers thought that the voice came from their neighborhood. In the morning, it was discussed from door to door until it reached the monastery, and the villagers concluded: "Last night, on the mountaintop, the master let us hear the biggest laugh of his life."

André Breton was the first writer who tried to restore the true and vivifying function of humor:

It is more and more likely, considering the specific demands of modern sensitivity, that any poetic, artistic, or scientific work, any philosophical or social system that lacks this kind *of humor will be doomed to perish more or less swiftly. ... We touch here upon a burning question ... and expose ourselves to heated controversy when we dare to bring into the open this sort of humor—whose manifest results we nevertheless single out with such satisfaction in literature, in art, and in life.*

This text can clarify Gurdjieff's approach; it may eliminate much ill-founded reserve and false shame. *Beelzebub's Tales to His Grandson*, which is often considered forbidding, should be read not as one is used to reading a didactic text, but as one of the highest expressions of an art form addressed to the heart and body as well as to the mind. It produces the "explosion" without which, as both Baudelaire and Breton emphasized, there would be no comedy.

True comedy is what Baudelaire called "absolute comedy"—which, as he said, is vertigo. In the *Tales*, this vertigo is produced by comic descriptions of the depth of man's foolishness and perversion. Any other approach would be unbearable.

One of the unique virtues of Gurdjieff's books is that they establish a distance between the reader and all that is banal and ordinary, and show him that what is banal and ordinary is horrible because it is in fact utterly foreign to him. The reader cannot escape the bewildering effect of Gurdjieff's writing. To bewilder, uproot and disorient is the master's first task, for we are in fact lost, taking the wrong road, going in the wrong direction.

Gurdjieff said to Ouspensky: "Awakening begins when a man realizes that he is going nowhere and does not know where to go." The master is the awakener, and his most effective weapons can be humor and vulgarity. His intervention has to be rough; otherwise, a man lets his conscience be rocked to sleep on the waves of daily life. To be persuaded of this, one has only to think of the meanings taken by the word "disillusionment." The dictionaries define it as "loss of an illusion." That should be positive and reassuring to men who claim to be searching for truth. But evidently it is not, for vexation, letdown, disappointment, disenchantment, error, are analogous terms. Man is too attached to his mistakes to allow anyone to point them out to him.

This is why the master is so often obliged to use the "way of blame," the way of scandal, seeming madness, paradox, contradiction. For what is wisdom in God's eyes is madness in the sight of men; what is true in the spiritual order is absurd in the social order. I would like to illustrate this fact with two anecdotes of the legendary master of the way of blame, Mullah Nassr Eddin.

In the village plaza, under a blazing midday sun, the Mullah, sweating and covered with dust, is on all fours looking for something in the sand. One of his neighbors sees him, approaches, and asks: "What have you lost?" "My key," answers the Mullah, who continues to search while his neighbor kneels down to help him. After several minutes, sweating and panting, the latter asks: "Are you sure that this is where you lost it?" "Oh no," replies the Mullah, "I lost it at home." "But then why look for it here?" "Because here, my dear neighbor, there is more light!"

The stories of Mullah Nassr Eddin, besides being "funny," have a "metaphysical" value. They are troubling and perturbing, and Gurdjieff delighted in telling them, even when he didn't invent them. Mullah Nassr Eddin, often the embodiment of popular wisdom, assumes above all the role of the fool whose apparently absurd logic subverts established notions:

One day, the Mullah goes into a shop. The shopkeeper comes forward to help him. "First things first," says the Mullah. "Are you sure you saw me enter your shop?" "Of course!" "Have you ever met me before?" "Never." "But then how would you know it's me?"

These anecdotes are shocking; everything that we take for granted is turned upside down.

Gurdjieff often behaved like the Mullah. One of his students writes: "He never hesitated to arouse doubts about himself by the kind of language he used, by his calculated contradictions, by his behavior—to such a point that people around him, particularly those who had a tendency to worship him blindly, were finally obliged to open their eyes to the chaos of their reactions."

On the "way of blame," the initiator can appear brutal, inconsistent, or outrageous.

The master, first of all, is the one who knows *me* and *my* needs (I don't know myself; I am unaware of what I really need). I am Nathaniel and the master saw me under the fig tree. He is the only one who knows what happened there. The master knows the paths that lead toward the Good I covet. But he cannot simply tell me these things. He can only help me to understand them with all my mass, as Gurdjieff says. He can only indicate these things to me, not explain them: the finger doesn't explain the moon, the Zen saying reminds us—it merely points to it, and woe to him who mistakes the finger for the moon.

How does the master make reality known? He has recourse to what Zen calls "clever stratagems," responding to the disciple's question with a pointing finger, outstretched arms, brandished stick, or shouts and blows. He uses paradoxes, contradictions, repetitions, exclamations, seemingly irrelevant answers (or even refusals to answer) and many other unexpected means.

"A monk asked Chao-chu: 'Does a dog have Buddha-nature?' Chao-chu answered '*Mu!*'"

"Ling-ien was asked: 'How were things before Buddha came into the world?' Ling-ien brandished his stick."

It seems to me that the essence of the "way of blame," which I have tried roughly to describe, is this refusal of the empty question, and provocative behavior that causes the often painful awakening of the disciple.

Gurdjieff offers his disciples, for the most part "intellectuals," a system of exemplary coherence, whose study makes real progress possible. The cohesion of this system is seductive, but it may discourage the follower by its complexity and by the demands of its method. The master, who embodies the system, seems distant, even inaccessible. Yet in his intimate relationship with the pupil, Gurdjieff lessened this distance by his patriarchal attitude and his benevolence. When necessary, however, he also played the role of the madman—the master of the way of blame.

"When he assumes this role," writes Charles Duits, "the master becomes a mirror in which the disciple sees himself. He caricatures and exaggerates the disciple's weaknesses, feigning anger, arrogance or decadence when necessary, shocking the disciple who has a long way to go before understanding that the odious character the master is showing him is himself." When he finally sees himself in the mirroring master, many apparent contradictions are resolved; reproaches and bitterness fade away.

In this way, Gurdjieff, in his life as in his writings, accomplished the first of the tasks he set himself:

"To destroy, mercilessly, without any compromises whatsoever, in the mentation and feelings of the reader, the beliefs and views, by centuries rooted in him, about everything existing in the world."

It is in this sense that he can appear "inhuman," for his undertaking is anything but "normal," in the ordinary sense of the word.

"*What is necessary,*" he said to Ouspensky, "*is conscience. ...* We do not teach morality. We teach how to find conscience. People are not pleased when we say this. They say that we have no *love.* Simply because we do not encourage weakness and hypocrisy, but, on the contrary, take off all masks."

Quotations from Gurdjieff and Ouspensky are from *Beelzebub's Tales to His Grandson,* by G. I. Gurdjieff (E. P. Dutton & Co. Inc., New York, 1950) and *In Search of the Miraculous,* by P. D. Ouspensky (Harcourt, Brace and Company, Inc., New York, 1949).

Parabola
Volume: 11.3
Sadness

The Sound of Gurdjieff

Laurence Rosenthal

Although in the past few years various recordings of the music of G. I. Gurdjieff have been issued and are generally available, it may still surprise many who are aware of this Armenian-Greek teacher to learn that he was, in fact, the composer of an impressive number of musical works, mainly for the piano.

Gurdjieff's master-pupil relationship with the Russian composer Thomas de Hartmann has been affectionately chronicled by de Hartmann and his wife, Olga, but the unusual and surely unique musical collaboration between the two men remains an uncanny phenomenon, producing a result which would have been patently impossible for either one of them alone.

The sheer volume of work that emerged from this joining of forces attests to the importance which Gurdjieff seems to have attached to music as an element in his teaching, perhaps even as a repository of precise knowledge. His cosmological ideas make extensive use of the language of musical structure and function.

While the earliest and crucially important phase of their collaboration was involved with music for the sacred dances—or Movements, a vital component of Gurdjieff's method—the compositions included in a recently released four-record album, performed by de Hartmann himself, are not related to the Movements, but are pieces of absolute music, albeit with richly evocative titles. These recordings, made in the 1950s under somewhat casual conditions and with amateur tape equipment, sometimes even without de Hartmann's knowledge, have now been reengineered with the most advanced techniques. Considering the modesty of the original effort, the results are remarkably good. What we have is a clean, quiet recording of performances which, without a doubt, set the standard for the interpretation of these deceptively simple pieces. As a pianist, de Hartmann was not only a superb technician, but played with great depth of understanding and poetic sensibility; and then, of course, it was his own music. Unlike, therefore, any other recording of these works, this one gives the sense of the pianist-composer going to the very heart of each phrase. The music emerges in all clarity and integrity; the pianist and his personality disappear entirely from the scene. One cannot ask more from any musical rendering.

The greater part of these works was composed in the years from 1924 through 1926 at Gurdjieff's institute in Fontainebleau, near Paris. Many of the compositions bear specific dates which indicate periods of a literally daily musical output and suggest the great intensity of the collaborative-creative process, often for weeks at a stretch.

The compositions which comprise the present album [*The Music of Gurdjieff/de Hartmann*] have been well chosen, offering a broad view of various aspects of the Gurdjieff/de Hartmann work. There are hymns of a solemn or contemplative nature, quite unlike our usual idea of that form, often drawing from the idiom of the Russian Orthodox liturgy, or else echoing music Gurdjieff remembered hearing in remote Asian temples and monasteries. At the other end of the spectrum are the ingenuous dancelike evocations of simple, ethnic folk melodies. And in between are suggestions of the Near-Eastern improvisation known as the *taksim*; subjective songs of intimate, personal expression in the music of the sayyids, proverbial descendants of Mohammad; melodies of great warmth and humanity rather more in the Western harmonic style, such as the *Bokharian Dervish*, and *Rejoice, Beelzebub*, and also excerpts from the score of Gurdjieff's unproduced ballet, *The Struggle of the Magicians*.

Describing the external forms and styles of this music does not, however help to illuminate its inner essence, which remains strangely enigmatic.

What is the source of its compelling force, its ineffable atmosphere, its capacity to cast a spell on the listener while bringing him more intensely into contact with himself?

To begin with, the genesis of these pieces, the method of their composition, is singular, to say the least. De Hartmann has engagingly adumbrated the process, in which Gurdjieff, who could improvise movingly on the harmonium but was in no way a trained composer, would whistle or pick out with one finger on the piano some characteristically Near-Eastern phrase. This and other melodic fragments were somehow assembled and shaped by de Hartmann under Gurdjieff's watchful eye. Harmonies would attach themselves, rhythmic patterns would add momentum, gradually a form would appear. Yet despite de Hartmann's schooled and polished compositional mastery, the influence of Gurdjieff on this "fleshing-out" process seems unquestionable. De Hartmann's own personal style in his numerous orchestral, chamber, and operatic works reflects the transition from an elegant and charming Russian-French neoromanticism into an early 20th-century modernism, peculiarly related to the contemporary cubist and expressionist schools of painting, with an almost naïve use of dissonant tone-clusters, a tendency toward mechanistic rhythms, a taste for ironic or sarcastic harmonic configurations.

With very rare exceptions, none of this appears in the music de Hartmann created with Gurdjieff. Occasional dissonances are transformed into something subtle and mysterious; the entire musical stance is a different one. These works seem, in fact, almost devoid of any device designed for effect. They are characterized rather by a directness of feeling and simplicity of structure, even when the ultimate "meaning" is more recondite. The melodies are often oriental in idiom, occasionally even verging on the trite. The harmonic underpinning (a Western adaptation, nonexistent in Eastern music) is mostly triadic or made of fourths and fifths, or else uses the familiar organ-point or drone. When the harmony is on occasion more complex (de Hartmann's touch, to be sure) it is rarely with intent to weave elaborate chordal progressions, but rather to make more emphatic, pungent, or poignant some melodic movement. The rhythms are almost primitively straightforward. One might say this music, whether it is being lyrically introspective, dancelike, or prayerful, always feels stripped down, its bones showing. Textures are of minimal interest, embellishments only for the intensification of expression.

On the other hand, in rare instances, the music may seem, for a moment, awkward, ungainly, taking an incomprehensible turn for no apparent reason, as though some subtle intention is eluding us. What feels at first like a mistake leaves us later not so sure. Has de Hartmann deliberately allowed a touch of Gurdjieff's amateurism to remain "uncorrected"? Or, finally, is it absurd to apply here the ordinary academic principles of musical procedure? Is Gurdjieff eschewing also, as he did with the "literary," the "bon ton *musical* language"?

But leaving aside these relatively subtle points, one might guess that the trained listener will very possibly, on first hearing, instantly dismiss this music as typically folkloristic, indigenous to the ethnic and religious crossroads where Gurdjieff was born and spent his early years, and as a characteristic example of the incorporation of such source material into concert works, so common among Russian composers of this period, for whom this style seemed attractively exotic.

But a deeper contact with the Gurdjieff music will quickly show the error in likening it either to traditional folk or religious music itself or to any trivial popularization of it. The similarity is principally one of vocabulary, all on the surface. Gurdjieff obviously used it because it was quite simply the language he knew and, as it happens, a language rich in a kind of natural, universal, human expression. But his purpose in music went much deeper.

In Gurdjieff's view, most art we know is subjective, both in its creation and its reception. He saw objective art—much rarer—as having a specific relationship to the properties of feeling, as emanating precise vibrations which influence the feelings, directly, organically, predictably. Objective art, he said, affects all people in the same way.

Unavoidably we are drawn to ask: Is Gurdjieff's music an example of objective art? Of course, it is impossible to say. His various works are clearly on different levels. And yet one may well wonder, for example, when hearing the last composition in this series of records, entitled "Remembrance." Here is the archetype of the essential Gurdjieffian "sound." Anything that could evoke sentiment, nostalgia, charm, or sadness, is nowhere to be found. The music is naked, unadorned, and yet not stark or severe. Instead, a profound, searching tone follows the questioning single line, an angular, unpredictable melody that seems to find no resting place, hesitating, feeling its way from moment to moment, supported by a three-voiced harmonic base, likewise elusive, curiously unwilling to resolve itself. And all haunted by a deep, indescribable feeling, as though gazing intently inward, without comment. Objective.

To compare this music with other, more familiar, kinds of music, classic or otherwise, is pointless. Although its materials are utterly simple, recognizable, even conventional, it defies classification. It seems to have been created with a special aim, a special intent. It is, finally, *sui generis*. It makes statements and asks questions not to be found elsewhere.

Parabola
Volume: 29.2
Web of Life

Segal-san

Roger Lipsey

Marielle Bancou-Segal has just published *A Voice at the Borders of Silence: The Autobiography of William Segal*, based on recorded talks with her late husband, and with her own additions to fill the gaps and provide both perspective and warmth. Her book is an extended love letter, a spiritual biography, a family scrapbook and photo album, a travelogue, a *Bildungsroman*, an essay in art criticism, and shelter for a voice that will surely continue to be heard.

This list summons another. A skilled and resourceful teacher of the Gurdjieff ideas and practice, yet equally and profoundly at home in Zen; an entrepreneur in fashion publishing who had made his first fortune by the age of thirty-one; a bridge builder between Japan and the United States in the years after World War II; a painter and printmaker who applied the eyes of an artist to all things; and in later years a trustworthy sage to whom people from many walks of life turned for counsel— William Segal was a man among men. His writings and a number of interviews have appeared in the pages of *Parabola* where he was a much appreciated collaborator.

To respect journalistic custom, I must record here that I knew Bill Segal over a period of nearly forty years and never called him Bill. He was always "Mr. Segal," a dignity well deserved. We first met on a Sunday at Franklin Farms, a center for study of the Gurdjieff teaching in rural

New Jersey, and, strictly speaking, I did not know that I had met him: I saw a well set-up man in his middle years, bald like a Zen priest and of comparable bearing, dressed in work clothes that included a worn quilted vest, an enigmatic touch of style. I didn't learn his name until later. I was assigned to his team for the day, and he in turn assigned me to fork over a steaming manure pile. I was to transfer some of it to wheelbarrows that other men pushed to fields elsewhere on the property. Mr. Segal left me to my work, executed with astonishment at the acrid, hot steam released with every shovelful from the inner layers of manure. I had never before encountered a phenomenon that demonstrated so many laws of Nature at one go. Some hours later he returned with a number of men considerably older than myself and invited us to jog across the property. We ran behind him in single file—he proved to be remarkably fit—until he stopped on a low height of land overlooking the fields and bid us look around. "This," he said, "is when a man can truly be 'the center of world.'"

Toward the end of the day, he gathered four or five of us unto a tight circle and said, "Let's try an experiment." We stood in silence, Mr. Segal and these older men who seemed to me like weathered trees. I felt acutely my youth and inexperience. I waited for the experiment to begin. After three minutes or so, Mr. Segal perceptibly relaxed and said, "Well, that's enough."

I shall never know what the experiment was.

In later years I came to know his mind. He often spoke at gatherings that explored great ideas and the more elusive, challenging aspects of human experience, and after such meetings I adopted the custom of periodically walking with him the few blocks northward in midtown Manhattan to his home. He did not walk as if committed to a scheduled arrival. We would walk, and stop and speak, and walk more. The stops were unpredictable, like his insights. They were also intimate: other pedestrians would fade from view as we stood in the middle of the sidewalk to engage on some matter as if alone.

Mr. Segal stepped up to the challenge of formal discussion in a most deliberate way. He would state the topic as if it were a magical koan, a challenge to think and increase our understanding that we could not and should not evade. And as he developed the theme from his perspective, he would often linger over a vast, Latinate word, seemingly chosen from a dictionary of obsolete terms known to him alone, which captured to his satisfaction some aspect of what he wished to convey. I can recall only one now: potentiation. As that particular talk took place in the years when the Human Potential movement was at its height, this swaying word—part electrical engineering, part medieval mysticism—seemed to seize the whole notion of human development and cast it into a setting where we, his listeners, had to begin again, look afresh. He revered Meister Eckhart: those complex writings and sermons, offered by an incomparably knowing soul, were of the texture of his own mind. Yet he was also pragmatic in his approach to great ideas and challenges. He respected the push and pull of daily life, knew that human limitations are high and wide, recognized that most of us are awkward and less than ideally gifted.

Mr. Segal was one of that group of American thinkers and artists, soon after World War II, who studied with D. T. Suzuki at the time the great Japanese scholar returned to the United States to give seminars at Columbia University and develop a private circle of people with an interest in Zen. Soon he and Dr. Suzuki became friends who saw each other both in the United States and in Japan. Traveling to Japan for business purposes—among other projects, he advised a major Japanese textile manufacturer—Mr. Segal also spent periods of time in Zen monasteries and took part in the rigorous life of extended sittings, practical work, and spare food. He shared this interest with his intimate friend, Paul Reps, author of *Zen Flesh, Zen Bones*, whose life and works can be read as a brotherly parallel to his own. These experiences and friendships marked him: Mr. Segal was truly a Zen man. The wisdom of his late years was Zen wisdom; it circulated around the experience of just watching, just listening, just sitting, *shikantaza*. Zen practitioners accepted him. If there is a scent or pheromone specific to each teaching, they detected theirs in him and welcomed Segal-san as one of their own.

Yet he was a loyal student of G. I. Gurdjieff, the independent sage and master whom he had met in the late 1940s after years of study with Gurdjieff's noted follower, P. D. Ouspensky, at Franklin Farms. There was some bedrock of truth and experience that took shape in him thanks to Gurdjieff. In retrospect, it seems to me that all else—Zen and his way of doing business, art, and the much appreciated pleasures of daily life—grew from that base and revealed it. I do not know why this was so, although he would occasionally say that he had met no one like Gurdjieff, and he evoked Gurdjieff's ideas and perspectives like a man reading Braille, with intimacy and almost physical contact. I suppose that one could sort it all out, or very nearly: what was Gurdjieff and what was Zen. But Mr. Segal never did within my hearing. He must have felt that there is one teaching, to be experienced as fully as one can and expressed as one can.

I cannot write of him without remembering the accident: a brutal car crash in the summer of 1971, from which it took him something on the order of a year to recover. In *A Voice at the Borders of Silence*, he speaks movingly of this time. He emerged from that period a different man: physically different, as his face had been reassembled and now, oddly handsome, was no longer the same, spiritually different in ways that can hardly be expressed, though his friend Soen Nakagawa Roshi told him that one accident is worth a thousand meditations.

If there is in the end a single feature, activity, or accomplishment that most closely typifies each of us, then Mr. Segal's single activity was sitting meditation. This was his world, a world with no props or accessories, where each person can encounter an inner life of unknown dimension and light. It was here that all charm dropped away, all preconception, all pattern. He loved this world with a primal love, and he did his best to share his sense of endless discovery of the inner world in a way that might in time set us free to love it in turn, each in his or her own way.

He lived long and contributed much in the years following his accident. When the time came to die, he chose to share it with some of us who had been his friends and students. We would meet with him as usual, but now at his home, where he would receive us wrapped in blankets in a chair. Mrs. Segal was never far away. I have had the impression that individuals of his kind impersonate old age; inwardly they are not old, but they are obliged by circumstances to act and look as if they are old. Mr. Segal was persuasive in the role of a very old man. At these late gatherings, he was often nearly as animated and inquiring as ever, but at times he sat motionless at length with closed eyes, scarcely breathing, while we waited with growing anxiety for him to awaken and engage. These incidents made it clear that he would go soon. He was ninety-six years of age. A few years earlier, after a conversation about art, he had walked me to the elevator in his apartment building and commented that he didn't care any longer whether he lived or died, and I felt that it was true. He had lived completely, accomplished surely more than he had set out to accomplish, and could depart at any time without regret.

He might not forgive me if I said nothing of his art. He was—or so I thought—haunted by three, perhaps four painters: the Rembrandt of the self-portraits, Cézanne as a creator of still life, Bonnard and perhaps Vuillard (or Vuillard and perhaps Bonnard) for their muted, mobile rendering of color. He was also well aware of Sengai and Hakuin, Zen artists of whom he must have spoken at length with Dr. Suzuki. This was the company, Western and Eastern, he kept. Trained young as a painter, he had turned to business and made several fortunes in publishing but never forgot his other calling as a painter and resumed it when he retired from business. Art had not been the ground on which we met over the years, though we spoke of it and could readily share our interest in it. For this reason, others are more able than I to evoke his art.

But I trust I have evoked the man.

Parabola
Volume: 5.3
Obstacles

FOOTNOTE TO THE GURDJIEFF LITERATURE

Michel de Salzmann

The increasing spate of books about Gurdjieff should not blind us to their almost unfailing and therefore tragic irrelevance to what is essential. "Well and good," we might say, if we are willing to accept the offerings of ill-informed commentators who provide us with every possible shade of misinformation. But how not to be baffled when those who claim some relation to Gurdjieff's teaching contribute, by the subjectivity of their approach, to the distortion of its real perspective?

Of course, one cannot blame premature attempts for their failure to meet an almost impossible challenge, for their failure to convey, outside its proper ground, the metaphysical essence of the teaching, which is self-realization and the correlative capability for true action. But did those responsible for these attempts ever consider that naïve and pretentious intentions in this realm could very well engender in others thought and reactions that are deeply misleading? We must admit that the problem is not an easy one, and is fraught with ambiguity.

Ambiguity already arises in the uncontrollable phenomenon of Gurdjieff's increasing fame. He was almost unknown in his lifetime. But now the spreading literature about him and the filming of *Meetings with Remarkable Men* have made his name widely known to the general public; and it will probably not be long before he will sit in the ranks of popular figures. On the one hand, we are justifiably irritated insofar as this mounting wave of interest is based largely on a caricature of the reality. On the other hand, we cannot object to it if we recognize, underneath it all, its profound legitimacy.

Ambiguity appears again when we observe that, in spite of all the dilutions, distortions, and mystifications that Gurdjieff's message has undergone, it nonetheless preserves an awakening power.

Ambiguity, or rather the lack of understanding from which it arises, will of necessity always be found near Gurdjieff. It pertains, in fact, to the kind of knowledge he tried to transmit and to the inherent requirements of this transmission, which are beyond ordinary understanding. Failure to recognize this essential point ends any chance of avoiding the misunderstandings.

It is not possible to present here a conventional review of all that has been written about Gurdjieff. Neither censure nor arguments, nor judgments in general, can be helpful when trying to approach a reality that is beyond them. The words of Heraclitus wonderfully point to an alternative ideal: "Among those who sleep, each one lives in his own world; only those who are awake have a world in common."

So, until the definitive book appears, it seems preferable to suggest, and perhaps make acceptable by means of a candid commentary, the idea that different levels are expressed—levels which are necessarily to be found in the Gurdjieff literature as well as in any other human endeavor. It may also become apparent that what has been written on this subject has for the most part only touched the deceptively visible portion of the iceberg or, to use a better image, merely commented on the facade behind which the "path" begins.

Books "of" the Teaching

A definitive characteristic of a living teaching or way is that it cannot be found in any book. Many books may make us sensitive to the existence of the path and help us find the threshold, but rare are those which can go further to serve as a precise map for orientation along the way. As for the journey itself, it cannot go far without a guide, or without a "school," in the original meaning of the term.

It would serve little purpose to set forth here the principles that necessarily apply to Gurdjieff's teaching as they do to any other traditional teaching, since they are, in essence, universal. But it may be useful to point out two widespread misunderstandings.

The first is the complete inappropriateness, from a traditional perspective, of designating as a teaching a mere dealing with ideas. The word "teaching" should refer strictly to a direct relational experience that takes place in the presence of a teacher, in particular through oral transmission.

The other misunderstanding, which in fact arises from the first, is reflected in the indiscriminate usage of the word "esoteric." Wholly apart from etymological and more abstract considerations, we should realize that esotericism is not at all to be found in ideas themselves, whatever they may be, but in the capacity to understand them correspondingly. It involves an experiential and practical aspect in which the meaning of an idea may even acquire a new taste. It implies, so to say, a conscious control over higher states of being, where what is reflected by the ideas corresponds effectively to what is actualized in the dynamics of the state, and vice versa. This refers to the fundamental identity between "Knowledge" and "Being." Esotericism therefore is not something voluntarily hidden; it is by nature self-protected, since it cannot be grasped without the corresponding inner preparation.

These considerations may help us not to misuse the word "esoteric" when speaking of mere books, and also clarify why, besides Gurdjieff's own writings, there has thus far issued from his pupils only one book that can be considered, without any prejudice, definitely useful in the teaching. This is P. D. Ouspensky's *In Search of the Miraculous: Fragments of an Unknown Teaching* (Harcourt Inc., 1949). Gurdjieff's pupils have always felt deeply indebted to Ouspensky for this exceptional and as yet unrivaled contribution to his work. It is a brilliant, honest, and faithful exposition of the author's memory of what had been transmitted to him. If one realizes that note-taking was never permitted, the book is all the more extraordinary. Although it corresponds to an initial stage of Gurdjieff's work both in time (1915 to 1923) and as regards the pupils' preparation, it retains a remarkable strength and freshness in orienting an active questioning for those on the path.

Ouspensky's qualifications and motivations were doubtless unusual, but the secret quality emanating from his book comes from the fact that it carries us as near as possible to the conditions of oral teaching, in which the influence of the teacher gives life to the ideas.

Books "on" the Teaching

What is stated above should not imply that other serious books on the teaching are without interest. They can—and do, in some cases, include a special insight, reveal original aspects, or bring new information. They may also be more accessible for people outside the teaching. And evidently they can serve as excellent mirrors for its followers, impelling them towards a personal confrontation in regard to their own understanding. At least in the latter case they have the much-to-be-desired advantage of not engendering excessive misinterpretations. But even though serious, these books are usually pale reflections of Ouspensky's as concerns the doctrine; and because of their more subjective motivation, they cannot escape from altering its spirit.

It was Ouspensky's destiny at a certain moment to separate from Gurdjieff, and thus disassociate the teacher from his teaching. This certainly brings up the vital question of fragmentation or of the effective continuation and transmission of a teaching. If it is deprived of the influence from which it originates—which all traditions recognize as being beyond the human level—and which is the only force that can animate it, a teaching essentially and substantially becomes a different "apparatus," unfitted for fulfilling the same purposes. A spiritual teaching, without a noticeable change in its formal aspect, may well become a merely moral or psychological doctrine. In any case this depends upon the level reached by the pupil.

Ouspensky himself gave the word "psychology" a traditional and higher significance, but it is hardly deniable that his more or less distant followers who wrote about the teachings gave it increasingly the taste of tidy and endless "psychological knitting." This process is evidently culminating in much more exterior forms of what is, unfortunately, still called the "work," which seem to flourish now in many places and sometimes appear to have firmer links with a search for publicity and social acceptance than with Ouspensky, much less with Gurdjieff.

It seems unnecessary to speak extensively about what we might call the classical books, dealing with the "system" of Gurdjieff. As was said before, they are mostly an expression of Ouspensky's line of thought and refer to conceptions adapted for early stages of the work. We could mainly include here the books of Maurice Nicoll, Kenneth Walker, and J. G. Bennett; C. S. Nott might also be mentioned in this context. All these authors were British, associated with Ouspensky or else deeply marked by his influence. All, at one time or another in their lives, were in direct contact with Gurdjieff and his teaching, although briefly, and clearly felt something near him that they did not receive from Ouspensky. Bennett nevertheless had a particular itinerary, being a follower of many teachers in succession and making a mixture of teachings that is difficult to sort out. At the end of his own life, he established a center of his own, returning more frankly to what he considered to be the "Gurdjieff way." His last book, *Gurdjieff: Making a New World* (Harper & Row, 1973), is interesting because of its profusion of informative material, but unfortunately indulges in highly speculative interpretations of Gurdjieff's works and life—which, needless to say, have been thoroughly exploited by commentators of all breeds.

A more recent contribution, that may well represent a significant reflection of the development of Gurdjieff's teaching after his death, is Jean Vaysse's *Toward Awakening* (Harper & Row, 1979), which gives a special importance to the experience of attention and bodily sensation —oddly missing in Ouspensky—and hence the taste of a more advanced stage of involvement.

At least, all these authors had a personal evaluation of Gurdjieff's work. And they have paid, largely through their own strivings and inevitable sacrifices, a tribute to it. They were and are respected as worthy men by all those whom they have helped to become more genuine human beings. The background of the teaching's concrete demands enabled them to convey the ideas with a realistic goal and a sense of relativity.

Books "about" the Teaching

When this background in experience is lacking, one is unable to give the "work" ideas their real weight; they become abstract, lose their depth, and are manipulated more or less happily under the sole control of subjective appreciation. Kathleen Speeth's *The Gurdjieff Work* (And/Or Press, 1976) may appear to be a clear and unquestionable digest of facts, but no substance is left. Moreover, naïveté here, as elsewhere, has the inevitable result of a completely undiscriminating mixture, all on one level, of information of diverse sources, qualities, and credibility. Although more practical and more limited in its objective, Colin Wilson's recent essay on Gurdjieff's philosophy, *The War Against Sleep* (The Aquarian Press, 1980), shows the same lack of background, which his intelligence cannot make up for and which he may be unconsciously justifying when he writes: "Ouspensky's peculiarly narrow and puritanical view of the 'work' convinced him that writing was somehow forbidden. In fact, the final publication of his book, as well as that of many brilliant books by others involved in the 'work', proved beyond all doubt that the essence of Gurdjieff's ideas can be conveyed perfectly well on the printed page."

We must agree that in all fields ideas can be well conveyed by properly prepared people. It is, however, evident that in the case of "experiential" disciplines, which are normally included in spiritual teachings at a very high degree of sophistication, ideas taken too literally can only lead to sterile theorizing and distortion when their symbolic or practical significance is not understood. And we should not forget that the most important part of Gurdjieff's teaching is necessarily conveyed under the cloak of analogy and symbolism.

Nevertheless, among people not actively following the teaching, it may happen that an authentic personal interest (perhaps associated with scholarly skills and patience) can very well convey fresh impressions and insights, notwithstanding big errors: as is the case, for instance, with Michel Waldberg's work based on Gurdjieff's books. Such really spontaneous undertakings should certainly not be discouraged.

The recent book by James Webb, *The Harmonious Circle* (G. P. Putnam's Sons, 1980), should also be mentioned here as an apparently serious attempt to decipher, through books and interviews, the phenomena of and around Gurdjieff and Ouspensky. Unfortunately, however, it is also overloaded with misinterpretations, quotations taken out of context, and mere rumors.

Further Misunderstandings About the Teaching

It is important to recall that Gurdjieff practically disappeared for more than twenty years, at the turn of the century, before reappearing in the "world"—bearing a knowledge of an overwhelming dimension. The teaching he brought represented, in Colin Wilson's view, "probably the greatest single-handed attempt in the history of human thought to make us aware of the potential of human consciousness."

It is also clear that Gurdjieff did not invent a "philosophy" of his own in order to be original and create a sensation. Nevertheless, his teaching can indeed astonish us. While connected with the most profound sources of traditional thought, it brings an illumination, a form, and a language which can be found nowhere else, notwithstanding the simplistic and misleading efforts to track down their sources by writers such as Boris Mouravieff, Idries Shah, and J. G. Bennett. Being unable to place the teaching within an established "way" with a regular lineage, others, like Whitall Perry, have not hesitated to brand it as purely and simply antitraditional, an argument that can only be ventured by assuming a "hearsay attitude" toward the facts and with a total disregard for intuition.

Gurdjieff's teaching (of which one can find a fragmentary exposition in Ouspensky's book) contains a properly metaphysical aspect, a cosmology, and a detailed explanation of that complex transformer of energy represented by the whole of each human individual. But its specific character appears not only in the doctrine. It is also evident in the multiple means or supports—representing the praxis, or "works" as one would say in Christian terminology—which are basic to it. It is these supports that make it possible to harmonize the different elements of the ordinary functional level in order to become able to correspond, and participate in, higher levels of being, themselves in relation with more subtle influences.

This inner process obeys laws and develops in stages that are precise. One of the particularities of Gurdjieff's teaching is the noteworthy emphasis on the importance of the first phase of harmonizing the functions and acquiring a center of gravity of the individual presence (which reminds us of the Hara). The definite and complete realization of this phase Gurdjieff named "self-consciousness." He pointed out that it was the normal and primordial state, which modern man finds himself very far from, but which he ought *naturally* to wish for and be able to attain. He was merciless in not allowing those who followed him to dream of other, distant possibilities before having worked thoroughly toward actualizing this one. The assiduous and all too often visible work linked with this phase, in spite of the progressive transformation of "effort" into "non-effort," has undoubtedly contributed to the superficial conclusion that Gurdjieff's teaching is "voluntaristic," without love, humanistic, etc.

Gurdjieff's ideas appear to correspond especially to the psyche of modern man. The edgy resistances of today's "areligious" man are not provoked, since the teaching apparently does not call upon any belief, any cult or worship, or any ritual; at first it simply proposes that one should know oneself as one is, in order to allow the chaos of the inner functioning to be remedied. But let us make no mistake; awakening to oneself necessarily involves the discovery of a unifying inner dimension of being which was not perceived at the beginning: an "I" deeply hidden, a "Knower" that illumines and experiences what is lived as an immediate, non-discursive knowledge. Thus the etymology of the word "re-ligion" (that which re-connects) or of "yoga" (union) becomes again meaningful.

The teaching brought by Gurdjieff cannot, in its essence, be in contradiction to any of the traditional teachings. On the contrary, when one is sufficiently prepared, this teaching makes possible a true correspondence in depth with other traditions. And it is not at all astonishing that at a certain level a very direct and mutual appreciation becomes possible, since the actualization of inner development and its corresponding states of being is everywhere subject to the same laws.

Books "on" Gurdjieff

Another aspect, and not the least as regards the specific character of Gurdjieff's teaching, was the special awakening influence conveyed by his own presence. All who approached him on a right basis were unforgettably marked by it. Though he certainly made a strong impact on people in general, it is particularly interesting to consider the different and special relationship that he established with his pupils.

One might be tempted to explain this influence by Gurdjieff's unusual charisma, or his mastery in dealing with what psychoanalysts call "transference." But such interpretations lead only to giving importance to his person, to inducing a personality cult which he himself would have mercilessly destroyed; there are no golden legends to be built around him. The only purpose of an authentic teacher is to awaken others. And this awakening always takes place through laws—simple but difficult to apply—according to which real consciousness awakens consciousness just as true love awakens love. There would be no transmittable teaching if it were attached, so to say, to the individual person and not inherent in the high potentialities of being. This does not conflict with the view that a man is great insofar as he truly succeeds in lifting others above their ordinary limitations. And it was indeed this that one felt so strongly near Gurdjieff.

What was furthermore remarkable was his way of teaching and addressing each one according to his particular capacities, inadequacies, and needs. He evidently gave Ouspensky more material about ideas than most of the others; with Thomas de Hartmann, the Russian composer, he specially developed a certain work on music; with some others he went more deeply into the study of the flow of energies through intensive work on various exercises and "sacred movements." Along with the conditions provided in common, everyone received an appropriate food. More generally speaking, near him there seemed to be no limits for transforming daily life into meaningful conditions for inner work. Seeing around him a representation of humanity *in toto* was a powerful help in raising one above a too personal vision. But notwithstanding this example, some of his pupils later formed their own groups of a definitely elitist character.

It is therefore not surprising that the personal accounts about Gurdjieff can have such a diversity of expression. But all of them—although they often fall into awkward misinterpretations, or gossip, or even vanity and name-dropping—give flashes or flavors of the same fundamental experience. One cannot remain indifferent to the intimate happenings of these accounts. And depending on the reader's own capacity to separate the wheat from the chaff, he can find some wonderful glimpses of Gurdjieff: in the early years of his teaching, with Thomas and Olga de Hartmann; somewhat later, with Kathryn Hulme and Fritz Peters; and later still, in books by William Welch and René Zuber. Margaret Anderson also conveyed personal impressions, perhaps in a more dilettantish fashion; and more recently, A. L. Stavely and Anna

Butkovsky-Hewitt have offered their contributions, among still many more, in the delicate area of personal testimony.

Voluntary and Involuntary Mystifications

Writing has certainly lost its ethical standards and books their aura of credibility. One nevertheless cannot avoid wondering what kind of special perversion is involved in a certain category of books about Gurdjieff, in which we have searched but could not find even a vehicle for humor. Here, for their glory, must be cited the intentionally abusive inventions of *The Teachers of Gurdjieff* presented under the pseudonym of Rafael Lefort, the tasteless hoax of *Secret Talks with Mr. G.* by E. J. Gold, and the imaginative *Dialogues of Gurdjieff* by Jan Cox.

The current year's crop includes *Gurdjieff, Seeker of the Truth* (Harper & Row, 1980) by Kathleen Speeth and Ira Friedlander, which is not intentionally fallacious but nevertheless exploits—as if it were unquestionably factual—the now fashionable subject of Gurdjieff's book *Meetings with Remarkable Men* (E. P. Dutton, 1963). An extensive bibliography at the end cannot suffice to give weight to such an incredibly feeble production.

Of course, we must cite here the long-time source of the most unworthy legends, *Monsieur Gurdjieff* (Samuel Weiser, 1972), by Louis Pauwels who never met Gurdjieff, as he publicly acknowledged. Though the book was an unfortunately stimulating example that almost anything can be written with impunity, Pauwels himself later regretted his dubious achievement, which he called "a sin of youth."

The Silent Ones

It may be interesting to note that, at least until now, none of Gurdjieff's closest pupils, except Ouspensky, has written a book concerning him. What matters most to disciples is the life and continuation of the teaching; and that is far from a literary or historical preoccupation. What is really promising is that today the tree has borne fruit. The written accounts returning to the past, linked with anecdotal or even historical comments about Gurdjieff, seem rather idolatrous to those of us for whom Gurdjieff is more alive than he ever was.

For us, the only true creativity gives testimony to the real life of a teaching. We find much more alive, for instance, the works of those who, because they were especially linked to writing, tried to pass on what they understood in a form that was original and appropriate to them. Let us name here A. R. Orage, Jean Toomer, P. L. Travers, and René Daumal, among others. Maurice Nicoll likewise furnishes an interesting example through his attempt, in particular his books, *The New Man* and *The Mark* (Stuart and Watkins, 1950, 1954), to go more deeply into the Gospels by means of keys offered by the teaching.

Certainly, one always hopes for a more holistic view that will show Gurdjieff's place in relation to the great traditions. But will it save us from ambiguity? When he saw us lost in our painfully dualistic gropings, at just the right moment Gurdjieff would address us, smiling, with his Taoist-like expression: "A stick always has two ends ... however you take it."

First published in *Gurdjieff: An Annotated Bibliography*, by J. Walter Driscoll and the Gurdjieff Foundation of California (New York: Garland Publishing, 1985).

Parabola
Volume: 8.3
Words of Power

BROTHER AHL AND
BROTHER SEZ

G. I. Gurdjieff

I must tell you that in our brotherhood there are two very old brethren; one is called Brother Ahl and the other Brother Sez. These brethren have voluntarily undertaken the obligation of periodically visiting all the monasteries of our order and explaining various aspects of the essence of divinity.

Our brotherhood has four monasteries, one of them ours, the second in the valley of the Pamir, the third in Tibet, and the fourth in India. And so these brethren, Ahl and Sez, constantly travel from one monastery to another and preach there.

They come to us once or twice a year. Their arrival at our monastery is considered among us a very great event. On the days when either of them is here, the soul of every one of us experiences pure heavenly pleasure and tenderness.

The sermons of these two brethren, who are to an almost equal degree holy men and who speak the same truths, have nevertheless a different effect on all our brethren and on me in particular.

When Brother Sez speaks, it is indeed like the song of the birds in Paradise; from what he says one is quite, so to say, turned inside out; one becomes as though entranced.

●

His speech "purls" like a stream and one no longer wishes anything else in life but to listen to the voice of Brother Sez.

But Brother Ahl's speech has almost the opposite effect. He speaks badly and indistinctly, evidently because of his age. No one knows how old he is. Brother Sez is also very old—it is said three hundred years old—but he is still a hale old man, whereas in Brother Ahl the weakness of old age is clearly evident.

The stronger the impression made at the moment by the words of Brother Sez, the more this impression evaporates, until there ultimately remains in the hearer nothing at all.

But in the case of Brother Ahl, although at first what he says makes almost no impression, later, the gist of it takes on a definite form, more and more each day, and is instilled as a whole into the heart and remains there forever.

When we became aware of this and began trying to discover why it was so, we came to the unanimous conclusion that the sermons of Brother Sez proceeded only from his mind, and therefore acted on our minds, whereas those of Brother Ahl proceeded from his being and acted on our being.

Parabola
Volume: 25.3
The Teacher

Spiritual Masters: Linking Heaven and Earth

An Interview with William Segal

A few weeks after he granted this final interview, William Segal died at the age of ninety-six.
　　　　　—Marvin Barrett

Marvin Barrett: *What is the function of a spiritual master, and what is the difference between personal contact with a master and contact through writing?*

William Segal: The aim of the master is to link heaven and earth. Contact with a master is a definite physical event where energy is transferred between two people. From that point of view, a direct relationship is vital. That happens very rarely. But a group of people can utilize one master's time very well. Maybe a master can't devote all his attention to a single individual, but a little cluster around him can serve as a stimulation for others. Even a modicum of relationship with a master gives rise to an openness and a reception of energies that is not possible without the teacher's presence. The question is, is the ultimate master inside you? It may be that the ultimate master arises at the moment that I'm still and I recognize this ever-abiding presence that has nothing to do with me as I generally conceive of myself.

MB: *What is the relationship between the exterior master and the interior master that you're describing? Does the outer activate the inner?*

WS: There is a relationship between the exterior and the interior. My stillness has its effect on you. So does the wind. In a sense, we are called to live between two worlds—between the objective and subjective worlds. It is possible to encompass all the richness of impressions that are offered by nature and at the same time remain in contact with one's subjective "I." I can sit here with all my fantasies and dreams, but if I can't be still for a moment and stop the movements that generally go on, I cannot partake of certain vibrations that are always present. It comes to include people in the deepest sense, and we begin to know what we cannot know with our ordinary limitations—the voice of God.

MB: *Is the master someone intervening between you and God?*

WS: Not in the strict sense. It's only when an opening to the intrusion of another force appears that the recognition of what might be called God is possible. But it has nothing to do with whether a master acts or not.

MB: *In the Zen tradition, the master is the one who is the instrument of your illumination.*

WS: It seems that the master is there to help clear the way. As long as one lusts for food or sex and is beset by such thoughts, nothing is possible. So the master challenges the disciple, sometimes quite harshly, until he is willing to give up those attachments. A master carries the responsibility of refining the capacities of the disciple so that he can begin to realize his true nature.

MB: *There is also the concept of those in other fields becoming so masterful that they really become masters in spirituality. For instance, the singer Marian Anderson, whom I met briefly, was a consummate artist who had no ego. She had a presence that conceivably grew out of her mastery of the art of singing. Of course, it may have been something that was there from the beginning. But that is an example of someone in the arts who has developed this quality.*

WS: It's a question of levels. In the teaching of art or music, the master passes on a very high level of technique together with the ability to sustain an effort. Even an athlete receives this kind of training. It's a question of holding the student's attention. Certainly a strong teacher can really give you the works.

MB: *Or hit you in your ego.*

WS: I would say D. T. Suzuki was a master. He consciously and very nobly undertook to educate a dull American. He gave me what he could. Gurdjieff, of course, was too big to teach you directly. You had to watch him. So I watched.

MB: *You had to extract it from him.*

WS: Yes. And I saw it in the way he walked, the way he handled people, the way he helped them. He kept his cool, as it were. And so we learned. We learn from the bad things and the good things. We're continually learning, whether we know it or not. There's a constant input of impressions, knowledge, and energies received in your head, your stomach, your hands, that is present even in the feel of a cup of tea. It goes on every moment of the day. But we're too small. We can't grasp it. Shakespeare put it very well: "What fools these mortals be."

MB: *Blake said if a fool persists in his folly, he will become wise. Everything has meaning, if you observe in the proper way. It's there to teach you.*

WS: That doesn't disprove the first part at all.

MB: *But it gives you hope.*

WS: One has to be intelligent enough to analyze it. Otherwise we waste our substance on negativity and throw away our birthright.

MB: *There's the phenomenon of someone like Caravaggio, who has this remarkable power of attention and was totally disorganized in other areas.*

He had this incredible ability to interpret reality, yet his own life was a willful nightmare. It's very mysterious.

WS: The mystery we must all take into consideration lies in the moment that transforms everything. What is it in that moment that brings God into our sphere of being? For me, there is this silence. If we're able to evoke this silence, it would be a very clear sign of the presence of a master—not a master in the formal sense, but in our ability to change things around us, *to do without doing.* It's very difficult to evoke or to sustain, but the great masters are able both to evoke this mysterious opening to the new energy and to sustain it. Gurdjieff used the expression the "Omnipresent-Okidanokh."

In the midst of my mechanical living, if I stop and I make contact with my breath, I may be evoking this ever-present Okidanokh, which opens us up to a new quality of energy. I've witnessed this in very few people. Gurdjieff could do it. There would be silence in those moments with him where we would possess a much greater attention. This is the mysterious quality that I think the masters possess, either through knowledge, development, or inheritance. The Japanese express this as *satori.* I recall coming out of a Japanese monastery after two or three months of sitting. I bought a loaf of bread and a box of strawberries on my way to the railway station. As I stood on the platform and took a bite of a strawberry, with the sun hitting my face, I suddenly realized, "Oh, this is what the old boys meant." It was so simple. It was as the Bible says—to "be still and know that I am." If we know this secret, we've been able to receive mastership from the masters.

MB: *There are a number of individuals who are recognized as masters because they put their teachings down on paper or lecture about it. The Dalai Lama has the ability to do what Gurdjieff did, which is to emanate a certain quality, and he also writes and articulates it.*

WS: There are people who are better fitted to opening people up without talk and intellection. And there are others who can express themselves verbally in such a way that a disciple is able to follow and be helped by it.

MB: *The real master gives it directly, without articulation.*

WS: The masters are there, if we're ready to recognize them. There are a few. You meet a man and he may seem like a simple man, but he's got something that you would like to know more. You would like to feel him more. And that's an opening. That raises a question of whether one can be called a master without having a following.

MB: *It requires an interaction. Yet they can speak across the ages and have disciples right now. How do we explain that in terms of being a master?*

WS: The call coming from a true master is so strong that it reverberates over the ages and is able to attract people after the master himself has gone. The teaching is fortified, not by the will of the master, but by the energy with which he imbues everything he says and touches.

MB: *Does it have any definite connection with sanctity? Do you have to be a saint before you can become a master, or is it irrelevant?*

WS: I can be a great individual, but unless I have that spark or energy which makes contact, nothing essential can develop. I won't really be able to call up this quality of openness that can help others.

MB: *At the end of his life, St. Thomas Aquinas said that all the extraordinary writing he had done was worthless compared to the illumination he had received.*

WS: Yes, all this wonderful information is nothing compared to the evocation of a moment, which penetrates to a deeper level.

MB: *Instantaneously?*

WS: It has nothing to do with time.

MB: *Have you known any other masters?*

WS: I'm trying to visualize my own relationships with different people, and it's difficult to come to someone whom I would unquestionably call a master. I would say, speaking quite honestly, that my relationship with Ouspensky was one of going through a teaching. I imbibed what he had to offer. But for me, he was not a master. He passed along what he knew, but what he knew had been given to him by someone else.

MB: *Does your search continue even if you find a master? You said earlier that the ultimate master is within yourself. That's where the search ends. But I don't think you ignore help in the process.*

WS: We need help to reach a certain point. But at a later stage, one doesn't believe in anything. Neither in God nor in himself.

MB: *Do you think a master is necessary as a preliminary?*

WS: It's necessary to acquire a certain amount of training, knowledge, and experience, which can be given from one person to another. But there comes a time, as I was saying, when all of the teaching and all that one can give to another doesn't help, so he's left empty, blank. And then he's ready to truly search. He can only find it within himself. I'm sure there are people nowadays who question whether it is worthwhile looking for a master. How do I know if I have found someone who qualifies? What would help me? What kind of contact is necessary with a master? Is there such a thing as a pure spirit that makes one qualified?

MB: *We have to be critical. It seems to me there are obviously false masters that are accepted as the true thing.*

WS: Do you know the story of the man who tells his disciples to jump off the cliff? His first disciple jumps over the cliff and lands on his feet unharmed. The second jumps over and also lands safely on his feet. The third one goes over the cliff and it's the same thing. Now the master leans over the edge of the cliff, thinking these guys should be dead. So he says to himself, gee whiz, I have great power. So he jumps over and is killed. I suppose that faith overcomes everything, even a false master.

MB: *You met Sai Baba in India. What was your opinion of him?*

WS: My Western intellect says he is so obviously a fake it isn't even funny. On the other hand, who am I to judge, when all of a sudden he says, "Give me your hand," and in my hand appears a watch. But my opinion is personal. I can never accept him, but that doesn't mean others can't.

MB: *You've also spoken about meeting Muktananda.*

WS: Yes, he straightened out the eyes of my little Siamese cat.

MB: *I love that.*

WS: He had a knowledge that I didn't have. For instance, he explained the significance of the fire god in some pieces of sculpture we have. He obviously had a thorough knowledge of these things. But again, for me he was not a master. It's really so subjective. One man believes in the master. Another doesn't. What is it a master gives that doesn't touch you but touches me?

MB: *In the past, you've spoken of Jeanne de Salzmann, who was connected with the Gurdjieff Work. Was there some point in her life where you felt she moved into the category of a master?*

WS: Yes, there was a point where she came into touch with this spark within herself, which changed her to the extent where she could look at you and have a very different relationship than she had before.

MB: *When did this happen?*

WS: She was in her early sixties. She suddenly emerged from being one of us and we began to look up to her. We accepted her. There was no reason for me to accept her in 1947. In fact, I just thought of her as another woman. A talented woman, certainly. Then when Gurdjieff died, she began gradually to take over his relationships. She showed acumen, courage, intelligence, and a level of understanding that was impressive to me. And then I was willing to give a little. In the beginning, I had a similar attitude toward Gurdjieff. I wasn't sure at first. To me, he was just another man. But then you have a moment where something passes between you, and you're more inclined to be open, more open to the possibility of his being quite special.

MB: *Is there an explanation for that?*

WS: I think you will agree that it's possible to find an opening that was not there, to find within ourselves an inspirational quality that wasn't there before. For instance, I see how these people at *Parabola* are trying to carry the torch, trying to inject something into the world, and I become more open to what they bring. It's the wish to meet something.

MB: *Can that be artificially produced? Would asceticism be a way of achieving it?*

WS: We could be helped by the study of Milarepa's transformation. How did that come about? At what cost? What eventually made Milarepa a master was the determination to follow, to obey the instructions of his master, Marpa. As you said, if a fool persists in his folly, he shall become wise. If I have enough commitment to a course of action, where commitment means a higher level of attention, then I have the possibility of becoming a master.

MB: *This rhythm of withdrawing and then feeling at a certain moment that you must go back into the world and make a contribution is what could be called a bodhisattva approach. Are masters bodhisattvas?*

WS: I think a true master doesn't care about anything but persistently relating to this mysterious energy that is always present. He doesn't care whether a formal training exists and whether he has it or not. He's only concerned with his own relationship to the highest. There's a freedom and an openness about him that in turn generates an energy which touches others.

MB: *He's generous. He is not reclusive and he doesn't keep it to himself. Otherwise he wouldn't be a master. Do you think generosity is an overflowing of this?*

WS: A master is someone who makes poetry. He doesn't think about it. Like a child artist. He just paints something. He doesn't say "I'm a master." Just as a child doesn't say "I'm going to create." He doesn't think about those things at all. No generosity. He doesn't even think he's giving anything. As soon as I think I can give you anything, I fall. But if we just act naturally, we come together, and between us arises a feeling that cannot be so easily identified. To have any goals is not it either. It's like that Buddhist sutra: no wisdom, no attainment, no thought, no feeling, no non-feeling, no love, no non-love—until one arrives at that pure emptiness which we are sometimes able to recognize and value. But as soon as we take it seriously and think or talk about it, we lose it. I think one must be a master naturally—one does not try to be one. As soon as you try to help, you're lost.

MB: *There's no anxiety.*

WS: No anxiety. No ambition. No wish to help. I was taking part in a lecture one time, and I made the statement that wishing doesn't help in this work. I was speaking on a rather ordinary level. A woman on the panel responded with a harangue about how it's necessary to have a wish. And I was thinking all the while, this poor woman is being held back by her wish to help others. She was not free of her wish. I was struck by the fact that any wishing, any desire to become something, any desire to help or change others, is not it.

MB: *No wish, no desire.*

WS: No desire, no wish. Evidently, in the life of a human being, there are moments when the purity of the inner world is so great that it needs room for the appearance of something that is truly celestial. What can God be for you and me? As soon as one names it, one has lost it.

MB: *It has to do with faith, with confidence in a greater power.*

WS: Isn't faith tinged with mental conception?

MB: *You say "Thy will be done." That to me is faith. I trust that whatever's happening has some meaning.*

WS: If you carry out that idea, "thy will be done" also can signify absolute non-identification.

MB: *Freedom.*

WS: Yes. I would say that simple word, "freedom," is closer to it. Freedom unattached to anything, even God. If God appeared now, I'd punch him in the face. I'd ask Him, what are you doing around here? You're not going to help me, and I'm not going help you. You go your way and I'll go mine. Then I'm open to real freedom. That would be faith.

MB: *And then you are open to God. When you reject him, you open yourself.*

WS: All these teachings are full of contradictions. Yet we are given many hints—in the silence. Kabori used to say that between zero and one a soul is born. Now if you ponder that, it's really zero. In other words, what I think he was saying is that between the human being with all its attributes and feelings and the silence, between me and nothing, a soul is born.

MB: *Does it have anything to do with love?*

WS: One has to have the knowledge that enables one to be free of any negative energies. Impatience or anger in me spoils everything. We live in a very delicate, subtle world where every word spoken has its place. I speak and it produces an effect in you. If my words are negative, impatient, or angry, it spoils the relationship. One must have an understanding of one's effect as a human being. Within each of us there is a well of energy that is untapped. One quality of the master is to refine or purify the energy in the people he encounters.

MB: *What can we hope for from masters?*

WS: All we can do is prepare ourselves for the encounter. Preparation is very important. Preparing for the advent of a relationship means one has to be more or less pure, a true human.

MB: *Do you think the preparation itself produces a master? Is there a cumulative effect that demands the presence of a master?*

WS: Yes, but don't have any dreams of meeting a master. Simply set about preparing yourself.

MB: *How can the danger of embracing a false master be avoided? Is there any technique for preventing that?*

WS: We have to be very practical. It requires intelligence. One should have a discriminating mind in order to know the false from the true. But it's difficult. We live in a world where all our values are distorted. We are confronted with all sorts of scandals. This is where your discrimination comes in. The help is there, but we still bear a certain responsibility for our own judgment and common sense.

MB: *Are you optimistic about the appearance of masters?*

WS: Yes, I am. If the master doesn't want to deceive people. If he's not acting out of egotism. If he is not trying to gain anything but is trying to live his own life as purely as he can. That way, as an example, he can help others. In that sense, I'm optimistic. On the other hand, if the so-called master is not aware that his every word is having an effect, the results can be quite damaging. But if he acts purely, out of the purity in himself, and the disciple is ready to receive it, I think the good can happen.

MB: *If you read* The New York Times, *there seem to be very few areas where such a person could emerge. Maybe that in itself is significant.*

WS: I believe there are groups of individuals who are on the right track. I see them come every week and listen to people like me talk. If they do it with an openness week after week, something accrues, and I do notice a transformation. Their being changes. They're more human. They are able to give a finer quality of attention.

MB: *It's important to have a commitment to something of value, something that in itself is a serious endeavor.*

WS: When there are enough people, yes. Certainly in the Gurdjieff Work I notice that there are maybe thirty or forty people who little by little have become more open. I'm optimistic because I see that it takes a long time. And one never knows. I remember one time I expressed impatience with someone in whom I saw so little progress. And a friend said, no, we must be patient. It takes time to develop understanding.

Parabola
Volume: 25.1
Threshold

THE NATURE OF A THRESHOLD

An Interview with William Segal

Painter and author William Segal, who was a lifelong student of traditional ways of being, responds to questions about life's thresholds put by Parabola's senior editor Marvin Barrett.

Marvin Barrett: *What is the nature of a threshold?*

William Segal: It is an interruption in the ordinary response of our lives. It is difficult to realize how many reactions are merely mechanical. But sometimes our response to a certain situation can surprise or even astonish us. It is in such moments that a change in consciousness appears and enriches us in a quite unexpected way.

I remember seeing my first Noh play in Kyoto almost fifty years ago. I was struck by the initial appearance of the main player. It was the moment when he was crossing the bridge that separates the back of the stage from the stage itself. His was not the walk of an ordinary man. It sprang, instead, from an inner relatedness. It gave rise to a tension that became almost unbearable, bringing the waiting audience to a high degree of attention. All our concentration was focused on the deliberate movement of the slightly bent, robe-clad figure.

His voice, too, in the few words he spoke, carried a weight. This slowly moving figure produced a vibration that spoke to each one in the audience. There was no escaping the fact of being present to something different from ordinary existence, a change in the conditions that were a result of the being of the player. Time was surely being examined in front of our eyes. Something new was about to unfold. One passed a threshold in oneself to a different level of being.

MB: *It was a transformation of some sort?*

WS: It was the beginning of a transformation. It was as if the player was in between a world he had left and an entirely new world. In that moment, he embodied stillness.

MB: *Is stillness itself a threshold?*

WS: Stillness is a nurturing element to help one rise instead of being entirely subject to the negative principle of mechanical deterioration and its downward path.

MB: *How do you perceive the relation between stillness and the threshold?*

WS: Being cognizant of the threshold itself, a kind of stillness appears. And with it, perhaps, a realization that one has been asleep. There can be a dawning of consciousness in these moments of transition, if one is able to become still enough to perceive them.

MB: *What are some of the thresholds one has to cross on the way to stillness?*

WS: A realization of the prevalence of sleep, a dawning of a new consciousness, an opening towards a hidden existence.

MB: *What aids us in crossing thresholds?*

WS: The seeing of one's position and of reality in general—one sees the reality, even the terror, of existence. Man has a small margin of will. Within this margin he can make an effort to move actively in the direction of transformation.

MB: *Is the present moment a threshold?*

WS: A very interesting question, because each moment is a prelude to a new beginning. If one is able to stop, one can become sensitive to the presence of another energy. It is as if an abyss fraught with possibilities has appeared. We are in front of a call.

MB: *What gives real hope for an individual's crossing the next threshold?*

WS: The real hope is that a union with the higher is within reach—the beginning of an understanding of the destiny of the human race.

MB: *One hears that humankind is on the threshold of a new age. What do you think this means?*

WS: There is a realization that something is being asked of us: to come into contact with a subtle vibration of consciousness. Unless this threshold is better understood, it may be that we will fail in our comprehension of our role. Great nature may dispense with the earth itself, unless there is an understanding on our part.

MB: *Are we being addressed by that which lies on the far side of the threshold?*

WS: There is a call for a revaluation of our values. This is something which is being felt more and more. We know when something is amiss, and unless something is brought of another nature, woe betide us.

MB: *Do you consider birth and death thresholds?*

WS: We don't have much to do with our birth. But there is a great deal that has to be done in relation to one's death. There is a preparation for perhaps a new turning.

MB: *Are there different kinds of thresholds in any given life? In a profession or a craft you have an apprentice/journeyman/master. Is there some sort of parallel in life itself?*

WS: Yes. Almost any profession, any calling, any work done honestly and with attention can open us to the possibility of stopping a moment, which in itself brings about more favorable conditions for passing from one condition to another.

MB: *Do initiation rites have a connection with threshold?*

WS: In many traditions, initiatory rites are the indication of a sound understanding of the necessity for effort at a certain point. Take the case of a young person entering into adulthood. The question of threshold becomes a living question. To view one's life as consisting of a series of thresholds would instill a creative attitude into the process of living. This attitude can bring a realization of the infinite possibilities of one's existence.

MB: *There are also thresholds like the tests you find in myths and fairy stories.*

WS: Most fairy tales contain the idea of challenge, calling for the best qualities of its principal characters. It requires completing a passage that demands a wholehearted involvement of oneself. That means that readiness is essential—with a developed mind, feeling, and body—so that all parts of oneself are engaged in confronting the challenge of this threshold. For such a passage, cleverness alone is not enough.

MB: *Well, the whole concept of "happily ever after" seems a contradiction to the concept of thresholds.*

WS: One is always called upon to meet the next challenge.

MB: *Is looking back a dangerous thing to do?*

WS: Yes, because the whole idea of threshold is neither looking forward nor back. It is being here and now. Always there is the time factor. When does one act and when should one forbear? Isn't Hamlet the classic example of a man paralyzed on a threshold? Students of time may find the investigation of this phenomenon especially rewarding. Is it not true that there are an infinite number of "time bits" in every second—bits in which we pass from one experience to another, hardly realizing the movement that is taking place?

MB: *Are there negative or false thresholds?*

WS: In our everyday lives there are numerous false beckonings. We can be easily deluded into thinking that we are approaching a threshold when we are only reacting to past associations. Some thresholds may merely be blind alleys, leading to paralysis. One can become stuck in delusion.

With so many opportunities, there is the risk of being overwhelmed. How do we tune in to the stillness of a true threshold when its appearance normally coincides with a noisy period in one's life? One should treat each threshold seriously. Here a moment of stillness would be appropriate. Would it not help to explore the intrinsic significance of this stop in relation to a deepening comprehension of the threshold? Each of us can remember a moment when a door seemed to open, together with the feeling that it might not remain open for long. A decision was required. Our task at such times is to bring being into doing.

Parabola
Volume: 14.2
Tradition and
Transmission

THE TRANSPARENT VEIL
OF SYMBOLISM

P. D. Ouspensky

"One of the most central ideas of objective knowledge,"
said G., "is the idea of the unity of everything, of unity in
diversity. From ancient times people who have understood
the content and the meaning of this idea, and have seen
in it the basis of objective knowledge, have endeavored to
find a way of transmitting this idea in a form comprehen-
sible to others. The successive transmission of the ideas of
objective knowledge has always been a part of the task of
those possessing this knowledge. In such cases the idea of
the unity of everything, as the fundamental and central
idea of this knowledge, had to be transmitted first and
transmitted with adequate completeness and exactitude.
And to do this the idea had to be put into such forms as
would insure its proper perception by others and avoid
in its transmission the possibility of distortion and corruption. For this purpose the people to whom the idea
was being transmitted were required to undergo a proper
preparation, and the idea itself was put either into a logical form, as for instance in philosophical systems which
endeavored to give a definition of the 'fundamental principle' or ἀρχή from which everything else was derived, or
into religious teachings which endeavored to create an
element of faith and to evoke a wave of emotion carrying people up to the level of 'objective consciousness.' The

attempts of both the one and the other, sometimes more sometimes less successful, run through the whole history of mankind from the most ancient times up to our own time and they have taken the form of religious and philosophical creeds which have remained like monuments on the paths of these attempts to unite the thought of mankind and esoteric thought.

"But objective knowledge, the idea of unity included, belongs to objective consciousness. The forms which express this knowledge, when perceived by subjective consciousness, are inevitably distorted and, instead of truth, they create more and more delusions. With objective consciousness it is possible to see and feel the unity of everything. But for subjective consciousness the world is split up into millions of separate and unconnected phenomena. Attempts to connect these phenomena into some sort of system in a scientific or a philosophical way lead to nothing because men cannot reconstruct the idea of the whole starting from separate facts and they cannot divine the principles of the division of the whole without knowing the laws upon which this division is based.

"Nonetheless the idea of the unity of everything exists also in intellectual thought, but in its exact relation to diversity it can never be clearly expressed in words or in logical forms. There remains always the insurmountable difficulty of language. A language which has been constructed through expressing impressions of plurality and diversity in subjective states of consciousness can never transmit with sufficient completeness and clarity the idea of unity which is intelligible and obvious for the objective state of consciousness.

"Realizing the imperfection and weakness of ordinary language the people who have possessed objective knowledge have tried to express the idea of unity in 'myths,' in 'symbols,' and in particular 'verbal formulas' which, having been transmitted without alteration, have carried on the idea from one school to another, often from one epoch to another.

"It has already been said that the higher psychic centers work in man's higher states of consciousness: the 'higher emotional' and the 'higher mental.' The aim of 'myths' and 'symbols' was to reach man's higher centers, to transmit to him ideas inaccessible to the intellect and to transmit them in such forms as would exclude the possibility of false interpretations. 'Myths' were destined for the higher emotional center;

'symbols' for the higher thinking center. By virtue of this all attempts to understand or explain 'myths' and 'symbols' with the mind, or the formulas and the expressions which give a summary of their content, are doomed beforehand to failure. It is always possible to understand anything, but only with the appropriate center. But the preparation for receiving ideas belonging to objective knowledge has to proceed by way of the mind, for only a mind properly prepared can transmit these ideas to the higher centers without introducing foreign elements to them.

"The symbols that were used to transmit ideas belonging to objective knowledge included diagrams of the fundamental laws of the universe and they not only transmitted the knowledge itself but showed also the way to it. The study of symbols, their construction and meaning, formed a very important part of the preparation for receiving objective knowledge and it was in itself a test because a literal or formal understanding of symbols at once made it impossible to receive any further knowledge.

"Symbols were divided into the fundamental and the subordinate; the first included the principles of separate domains of knowledge; the second expressed the essential nature of phenomena in their relation to unity.

"Among the formulas giving a summary of the content of many symbols there was one which had a particular significance, namely the formula *As above, so below,* from the 'Emerald Tablets of Hermes Trismegistus.' This formula stated that all the laws of the cosmos could be found in the atom or in any other phenomenon which exists as something completed according to certain laws. This same meaning was contained in the analogy drawn between the *microcosm*—man, and the *macrocosm*—the universe. The fundamental laws of triads and octaves penetrate everything and should be studied simultaneously both in the world and in man. But in relation to himself man is a nearer and more accessible object of study and knowledge than the world of phenomena outside him. Therefore, in striving towards a knowledge of the universe, man should begin with the study of himself and with the realization of the fundamental laws within him.

"From this point of view another formula, *Know thyself,* is full of par-ticularly deep meaning and is one of the symbols leading to the knowl-edge of truth. The study of the world and the study of man will assist one another. In studying the world and its laws a man studies himself, and in studying himself he studies the world. In this sense every symbol teaches us something about ourselves.

"The understanding of symbols can be approached in the following way: In studying the world of phenomena a man first of all sees in everything the manifestation of two principles, one opposed to the other, which, in conjunction or in opposition, give one result or another, that is, reflect the essential nature of the principles which have created them. This manifestation of the great laws of *duality* and *trinity* man sees simultaneously in the cosmos and in himself. But in relation to the cosmos he is merely a spectator and moreover one who sees only the surface of phenomena which are moving in various directions though seeming to him to move in one direction. But in relation to himself his understanding of the laws of duality and trinity can express itself in a practical form, namely, having understood these laws in himself, he can, so to speak, confine the manifestation of the laws of duality and trinity to the permanent line of struggle with himself on the way to self-knowledge. In this way he will introduce the *line of will* first into the circle of time and afterwards into the cycle of eternity, the accomplishing of which will create in him the great symbol known by the name of the *Seal of Solomon*.

"The transmission of the meaning of symbols to a man who has not reached an understanding of them in himself is impossible. This sounds like a paradox, but the meaning of a symbol and the disclosure of its essence can only be given to, and can only be understood by, one who, so to speak, already knows what is comprised in this symbol. And then a symbol becomes for him a synthesis of his knowledge and serves him for the expression and transmission of his knowledge just as it served the man who constructed it.

"The more simple symbols:

or the numbers 2, 3, 4, 5, 6, which express them, possess a definite meaning in relation to the inner development of man; they show different stages on the path of man's self-perfection and of the growth of his being.

"Man, in the normal state natural to him, is taken as a *duality*. He consists entirely of dualities or 'pairs of opposites.' All man's sensations, impressions, feelings, thoughts, are divided into positive and negative, useful and harmful, necessary and unnecessary, good and bad, pleasant and unpleasant. The work of centers proceeds under the sign of this division. Thoughts oppose feelings. Moving impulses oppose instinctive craving for quiet. This is the duality in which proceed all the perceptions, all the reactions, the whole life of man. Any man who observes himself, however little, can see this duality in himself.

"But this duality would seem to alternate; what is victor today is the vanquished tomorrow; what guides us today becomes secondary and subordinate tomorrow. And everything is equally mechanical, equally independent of will, and leads equally to no aim of any kind. The understanding of duality in oneself begins with the realization of mechanicalness and the realization of the difference between what is mechanical and what is conscious. This understanding must be preceded by the destruction of the self-deceit in which a man lives who considers even his most mechanical actions to be volitional and conscious and himself to be single and whole.

"When self-deceit is destroyed and a man begins to see the difference between the mechanical and the conscious in himself, there begins a struggle for the realization of consciousness in life and for the subordination of the mechanical to the conscious. For this purpose a man begins with endeavors to set a definite *decision*, coming from conscious motives, against mechanical processes proceeding according to the laws of duality. The creation of a permanent third principle is for man the *transformation of the duality into the trinity*.

"Strengthening this decision and bringing it constantly and infallibly into all those events where formerly accidental neutralizing 'shocks' used to act and give accidental results, gives a permanent line of results in time and is the *transformation of trinity into quaternity*. The next stage, the transformation of quaternity into quinternity and the *construction of the pentagram* has not one but many different meanings even in relation to man. And of these is learned, first of all, one, which is the most beyond doubt, relating to the work of centers.

"The development of the human machine and the enrichment of being begins with a new and unaccustomed functioning of this machine.

We know that a man has five centers: the thinking, the emotional, the moving, the instinctive, and the sex. The predominant development of any one center at the expense of the others produces an extremely one-sided type of man, incapable of further development. But if a man brings the work of the five centers within him into harmonious accord, he then 'locks the pentagram within him' and becomes a finished type of the physically perfect man. The full and proper functioning of five centers brings them into union with the higher centers which introduce the missing principle and put man into direct and permanent connection with objective consciousness and objective knowledge.

"And then man becomes the *six-pointed star*, that is, by becoming locked within a circle of life independent and complete in itself, he becomes isolated from foreign influences or accidental shocks; he embodies in himself the *Seal of Solomon*.

"In the present instance the series of symbols given—2, 3, 4, 5, and 6—is interpreted as applicable to one process. But even this interpretation is incomplete, because a symbol can never be fully interpreted. It can only be experienced, in the same way, for instance, as the idea of *self-knowledge* must be experienced.

"This same process of the harmonious development of man can be examined from the point of view of the law of octaves. The law of octaves gives another system of symbols. In the sense of the law of octaves every completed process is a transition of the note *do* through a series of successive tones to the *do* of the next octave. The seven fundamental tones of the octave express the law of seven. The addition to it of the *do* of the next octave, that is to say, the crowning of the process, gives the eighth step. The seven fundamental tones together with the two 'intervals' and 'additional shocks' give nine steps. By incorporating in it the *do* of the next octave we have ten steps. The last, the tenth, step is the end of the preceding and the beginning of the next cycle. In this way the law of octaves and the process of development it expresses, include the numbers 1 to 10. At this point we come to what may be termed the *symbolism of numbers*. The symbolism of numbers cannot be understood without the law of octaves or without a clear conception of how octaves are expressed in the *decimal system* and vice versa.

"In Western systems of occultism there is a method known by the name of 'theosophical addition,' that is, a definition of numbers consisting of two or more digits by the sum of those digits. To people who do not understand the symbolism of numbers this method of synthesizing numbers seems to be absolutely arbitrary and to lead nowhere. But for a man who understands the unity of everything existing and who has the key to this unity the method of theosophical addition has a profound meaning, for it resolves all diversity into the fundamental laws which govern it and which are expressed in the numbers 1 to 10.

"As was mentioned earlier, in symbology, as represented, *numbers* are connected with definite *geometrical figures*, and are mutually complementary one to another. In the Cabala a *symbology of letters* is also used and in combination with the symbology of letters a *symbology of words*. A combination of the four methods of symbolism by numbers, geometrical figures, letters, and words, gives a complicated but more perfect method.

"Then there exists also a *symbology of magic*, a *symbology of alchemy*, and a *symbology of astrology* as well as the system of the *symbols of the Tarot* which unites them into one whole.

"Each one of these systems can serve as a means for *transmitting* the idea of unity. But in the hands of the incompetent and the ignorant, however full of good intentions, the same symbol becomes an 'instrument of delusion.' The reason for this consists in the fact that a *symbol* can never be taken in a final and definite meaning. In expressing the laws of the unity of endless diversity a symbol itself possesses an endless number of aspects from which it can be examined, and it demands from a man approaching it the ability to see it simultaneously from different points of view. Symbols which are transposed into the words of ordinary language become rigid in them, they grow dim and very easily become 'their own opposites,' confining the meaning within narrow dogmatic frames, without giving it even the very relative freedom of a *logical* examination of a subject. The cause of this is in the literal understanding of symbols, in attributing to a symbol a single meaning. The truth is again veiled by an outer covering of lies and to discover it requires immense efforts of negation in which the idea of the symbol itself is lost. It is well known what delusions have arisen from the symbols of religion, of alchemy, and particularly of magic, in those who have taken them literally and only in one meaning.

"At the same time the right understanding of symbols cannot lead to dispute. It deepens knowledge, and it cannot remain theoretical because it intensifies the striving towards real results, towards the union of knowledge and being, that is, to *Great Doing*. Pure knowledge cannot be transmitted, but by being expressed in symbols it is covered by them as by a veil, although at the same time for those who desire and who know how to look this veil becomes transparent."

Excerpts from *In Search of the Miraculous: Fragments of an Unknown Teaching,* by P. D. Ouspensky. Copyright © 1949 and renewed 1977 by Tatiana Nagro. Reprinted by permission of Harcourt, Inc.

•

CHAPTER FOUR

WHEN YOU HAVE SEEN YOUR TWO NATURES, THAT DAY, IN YOURSELF, THE TRUTH WILL BE BORN.

—Gurdjieff, "The First Initiation"

Parabola
Volume: 6.3
Mask and Metaphor

A Quiet Life or to Work on Oneself?

P. D. Ouspensky

You must realize that each man has a definite repertoire of roles which he plays in ordinary circumstances. .... He has a role for every kind of circumstance in which he ordinarily finds himself in life; but put him into even only slightly different circumstances and he is unable to find a suitable role and *for a short time he becomes himself.* The study of the roles a man plays represents a very necessary part of self-knowledge. Each man's repertoire is very limited. And if a man simply says "I" and "Ivan Ivanich," he will not see the whole of himself because "Ivan Ivanich" also is not one; a man has at least five or six of them. One or two for his family, one or two at his office (one for his subordinates and another for his superiors), one for friends in a restaurant, and perhaps one who is interested in exalted ideas and likes intellectual conversation. And at different times the man is fully identified with one of them and is unable to separate himself from it. To see the roles, to know one's repertoire, particularly to know its limitedness, is to know a great deal. But the point is that, outside his repertoire, a man feels very uncomfortable should something push him if only temporarily out of his rut, and he tries his hardest to return to any one of his usual roles. Directly he falls back into the rut everything at once goes smoothly again and the feeling of awkwardness and tension disappears. This is how it is in life; but in the work, in order to observe oneself, one must become reconciled to this awkwardness and tension and to the feeling of discomfort and helplessness. Only by experiencing this discomfort can a man really observe himself. And it is clear why this is so. When a man is not playing any of his usual roles, when he cannot find a suitable role in his repertoire, he feels that he is undressed. He is cold and ashamed and wants to run away from everybody. But the question arises: What does he want? A quiet life or to work on himself? If he wants a quiet life, he must certainly first of all never move out of his repertoire. In his usual roles he feels comfortable and at peace. But if he wants to work on himself, he must destroy his peace. To have them both together is in no way possible.

— G. I. Gurdjieff

Parabola
Volume: 7.4
Holy War

Holy War

René Daumal

Translated by D. M. Dooling

I am going to write a poem about war. Perhaps it will not be a real poem, but it will be about a real war.

It will not be a real poem, because if the real poet were here and if the news spread through the crowd that he was going to speak—then a great silence would fall; at the first glimpse, a heavy silence would swell up, a silence big with a thousand thunderbolts.

The poet would be visible; we would see him; seeing him, he would see us; and we would fade away into our own poor shadows, we would resent his being so real, we sickly ones, we troubled ones, we uneasy ones.

He would be here, full to bursting with the thousand thunderbolts of the multitude of enemies he contains—for he contains them, and satisfies them when he wishes—incandescent with pain and holy anger, yet as still as a man lighting a fuse, in the great silence he would open a little tap, the very small tap of the mill of words, and let flow a poem, such a poem that it would turn you green.

What I am going to make won't be a real, poetic, poet's poem, for if the word "war" were used in a real poem—then war, the real war that the real poet speaks about, war without mercy, war without truce would break out for good in our inmost hearts.

For in a real poem words bear their own facts.

But neither will this be a philosophical discourse. For to be a philosopher, to love the truth more than oneself, one must have died to self-deception, one must have killed the treacherous smugness of dream and cozy fantasy. And that is the aim and the end of the war; and the war has hardly begun, there are still traitors to unmask.

Nor will it be a work of learning. For to be learned, to see and love things as they are, one must be oneself, and love to see oneself as one is. One must have broken the deceiving mirrors, one must have slain with a pitiless look the insinuating phantoms. And that is the aim and the end of the war, and the war has hardly begun; there are still masks to tear off.

Nor will it be an eager song. For enthusiasm is stable when the god stands up, when the enemies are no more than formless forces, when the clangor of war rings out deafeningly; and the war has hardly begun, we haven't yet thrown our bedding into the fire.

Nor will it be a magical invocation, for the magician prays to his god, "Do what I want," and he refuses to make war on his worst enemy, if the enemy pleases him; nor will it be a believer's prayer either, for at his best the believer prays, "Do what you want," and for that he must put iron and fire into the entrails of his dearest enemy—which is the act of war, and the war has hardly begun.

This will be something of all that, some hope and effort towards all that, and it will also be something of a call to arms. A call that the play of echoes can send back to me, and perhaps that others will hear.

You can guess now of what kind of war I wish to speak.

Of other wars—of those one undergoes—I shall not speak. If I were to speak of them, it would be ordinary literature, a makeshift, a substitute, an excuse. Just as it has happened that I have used the word "terrible" when I didn't have gooseflesh. Just as I've used the expression "dying of hunger" when I hadn't reached the point of stealing from the food-stands. Just as I've spoken of madness before having tried to consider infinity through a keyhole. As I've spoken of death before my tongue has known the salt taste of the irreparable. As certain people speak of purity, who have always considered themselves superior to the domestic pig. As some speak of liberty, who adore and polish their chains; as some speak of love, who love nothing but their own shadows;

or of sacrifice, who wouldn't for all the world cut off their littlest finger. Or of knowledge, who disguise themselves from their own eyes. Just as it is our great infirmity to talk in order to see nothing.

This would be a feeble substitute, like the old and sick speaking with relish of blows given and received by the young and strong.

Have I then the right to speak of this other war—the one which is not just undergone—when it has perhaps not yet irremediably taken fire in me? When I am still engaged only in skirmishes? Certainly, I rarely have the right. But "rarely the right" also means "sometimes the duty"—and above all, "the need," for I will never have too many allies.

I shall try to speak then of the holy war.

May it break out and continue without truce! Now and again it takes fire, but never for long. At the first small hint of victory, I flatter myself that I've won, and I play the part of the generous victor and come to terms with the enemy. There are traitors in the house, but they have the look of friends and it would be so unpleasant to unmask them! They have their place in the chimney corner, their armchairs and their slippers; they come in when I'm drowsy, offering me a compliment, or a funny or exciting story, or flowers and goodies—sometimes a fine hat with feathers. They speak in the first person, and it's my voice I think I'm hearing, my voice in which I'm speaking: "I am ..., I know ..., I wish ..." But it's all lies! Lies grafted onto my flesh, abscesses screaming at me: "Don't slaughter us, we're of the same blood!"—pustules whining: "We are your greatest treasure, your only good feature; go on feeding us, it doesn't cost all that much!"

And there are so many of them; and they are charming, they are pathetic, they are arrogant, they practice blackmail, they band together ... but they are barbarians who respect nothing—nothing that is true, I mean, because they cringe in front of everything else and are tied in knots with respect. It's thanks to their ideas that I wear my mask; they take possession of everything, including the keys to the costume wardrobe. They tell me: "We'll dress you; how could you ever present yourself properly in the great world without us?" But oh! it would be better to go naked as a grub!

The only weapon I have against these armies is a very tiny sword, so little you can hardly see it with the naked eye; though, true enough, it is sharp as a razor and quite deadly. But it is really so small that I lose it from one minute to the next. I never know where I stuck it last; and when I find it again, it seems too heavy to carry and too clumsy to wield—my deadly little sword.

Myself, I only know how to say a very few words, and they are more like squeaks; while *they* even know how to write. There's always one of them in my mouth, lying in wait for my words when I want to say something. He listens and keeps everything for himself, and speaks in my place using my words but in his own filthy accent. And it's thanks to him if anyone pays attention to me or thinks I'm intelligent. (But the ones who know aren't fooled; if only I could listen to the ones who know!)

These phantoms rob me of everything. And having done so, it's easy for them to make me feel sorry for them: "We protect you, we express you, we make the most of you, and you want to murder us! But you are just destroying yourself when you scold us, when you hit us cruelly on our sensitive noses—us, your good friends."

And an unclean pity with its tepid breath comes to weaken me. Light be against you, phantoms! If I turn on the lamp, you stop talking. When I open an eye, you disappear—because you are carved out of the void, painted grimaces of emptiness. Against you, war to the finish—without pity, without tolerance. There is only one right: the right to *be* more.

But now it's a different song. They have a feeling that they have been spotted; so they pretend to be conciliatory. "Of course, you're the master. But what's a master without servants? Keep us on in our lowly places; we promise to help you. Look here, for instance: suppose you would want to write a poem. How could you do it without us?"

Yes, you rebels—some day I'll put you in your place. I'll make you bow under my yoke, I'll feed you hay and groom you every morning. But as long as you suck my blood and steal my words, it would be better by far never to write a poem!

A pretty kind of peace I'm offered: to close my eyes so as not to witness the crime, to run in circles from morning till night so as not to see death's always-open jaws; to consider myself victorious before even starting to struggle. A liar's peace! To settle down cozily with my cowardices, since everybody else does. Peace of the defeated! A little filth, a little drunkenness, a little blasphemy for a joke, a little masquerade made a virtue of, a little laziness and fantasy—even a lot, if one is gifted for it—a little of all that, surrounded by a whole confectioner's-shopful of beautiful words; that's the peace that is suggested. A traitor's peace! And to safeguard this shameful peace, one would do anything, one would make war on one's fellows; for there is an old, tried, and true formula for preserving one's peace with oneself, which is always to accuse someone else. The peace of betrayal!

You know by now that I wish to speak of holy warfare.

He who has declared this war in himself is at peace with his fellows, and although his whole being is the field of the most violent battle, in his very innermost depths there reigns a peace that is more active than any war. And the more strongly this peace reigns in his innermost depths, in that central silence and solitude, the more violently rages the war against the turmoil of lies and numberless illusions.

In that vast silence obscured by battlecries, hidden from the out-side by the fleeing mirage of time, the eternal conqueror listens to the voices of other silences. Alone, having overcome the illusion of not being alone, he is no longer the only one to be alone. But I am sepa-rated from him by these ghost-armies which I have to annihilate. Oh, to be able one day to take my place in that citadel! On its ramparts, let me be torn limb from limb rather than allow the tumult to enter the royal chamber!

"But am I to kill?" asks Arjuna the warrior. "Am I to pay tribute to Caesar?" asks another. Kill, he is answered, if you are a killer. You have no choice. But if your hands are red with the blood of your enemies, see to it that not a drop spatter the royal chamber, where the motionless conqueror waits. Pay, he is answered, but see to it that Caesar gets not a single glimpse of the royal treasure.

And I, who have no other weapon, no other coin, in Caesar's world, than words—am I to speak?

I shall speak to call myself to the holy war. I shall speak to denounce the traitors whom I nourished. I shall speak so that my words may shame my actions, until the day comes when a peace armored in thun-der reigns in the chamber of the eternal conqueror.

And because I have used the word 'war', and because this word 'war' is no longer, today, simply a sound that educated people make with their mouths, but now has become a serious word heavy with meaning, it will be seen that I am speaking seriously and that these are not empty sounds that I am making with my mouth.

—*Spring, 1940*

Translated by D. M. Dooling from the original French text, "La Guerre Sainte," in the collection, *Poesie Noire, Poesie Blanche,* by René Daumal, Copyright © Editions Gallimard (Paris), 1954. Reprinted with permission of Editions Gaillimard and J. Daumal.

Parabola
Volume: 27.1
The Ego and the "I"

AWAKEN TO THE QUESTION

Michel de Salzmann

We have, all of us, something in common—together with the fact that we just exist now: it is that to everyone present here, whether he recognizes it or not, the most important thing, the thing that really matters to him, is *himself.* I am not referring now to some specific ego features such as selfishness, self-love, or self-importance, but to something very simple, factual, quite unavoidable. Am I not extremely important since everything that exists exists because I am? And if I think the opposite, is it not again I who think it? Everything passes through me. I am the only one who can experience or live my life. It is not a secondhand life, although unfortunately most of the time we seem to forget that.

This fact brings us immediately to the most difficult question. What is myself?

Let us try to consider that, avoiding as far as possible our "ready-made" patterns of thought. We are of course immediately tempted to refer to a philosophical point of view, or to recall the Buddhist or Hindu conception of the self, or to approach the problem in terms of depth psychology, behaviorism, or any other of our personal "idiosyncrasies." Let us try to face the question in a more provocative way, I would say in a naïve way. So I come back to myself. What is it? Do I have anything of my own?

My life? I may say, in a way it was given to me. I have done nothing for that. It is now given to me as an existential fact. I can become aware of it. It operates through my body.

This body given to me works by itself according to definite laws. It is the site of myriads of processes and of constant exchanges with the outer world. Various determining influences have given it its peculiarities: race, heredity, climate, food; and also more distant influences: astrological, cosmic, etc., of which we know very little. Anyhow, it works, and most of the time I am unconscious of it. It is like an animal. An animal in itself is a great thing, as the etymology reminds us: "anima," like "spiritus," refers to the breath, to the mysterious "animation" of the body. Thus animated, the body goes and comes, eats, sleeps, evacuates, has sex affairs and sometimes calls on me to be recognized, to be taken care of; but it usually works as well without me. In the best moments of awareness it appears to me as an integrated part of a greater whole, from which it is inseparable. Made of matter, my body obeys the causality of what we call the physical world.

Now there is another, greater whole of which I am a part, to which I belong, in which I bathe. That is culture or society. I may sometimes realize that everything I have, all my thoughts, my words, all my feelings, my body's learned ways of behavior—all the contents as well as most of the dynamics of what is called my psychological life—have been "inputted" into me.

My only originality seems to lie in the way it is put together. Everyone has a style, some characteristic habits and associations; but so it is in a computer also. The way all this has been put together has merely happened. It came about through contingency—through accidental events— and developed quite unconsciously. My computer deals with new inputs according to its own conditioned program. Nothing completely new can ever come out of it. None of us, for instance, would be able to draw an entirely new animal. Known elements or features would inevitably be made use of. I may say, roughly, and provocatively, that everything, including my character and equipment, has been given to me. My psychic life, even though it obeys the causality of intentionality, is also given to me and is basically conditioned or motivated by its cultural world.

At least something seems to remain undoubtedly my own, something that gives me the sense of my identity: I, myself, the one who pretends to be aware of all that. But here again, is it not one of those deeply rooted assumptions that we never put into question? Our "ego" actually turns out to be just as much of a gift, maybe a poisonous gift, but nevertheless a grand gift from our culture.

We are not just simply born into human existence. As existentialists would say: human existence is initially ego-consciousness. And this only appears in a child born and reared in a human society, usually after the age of two, when the neurological system has completely matured. Ego-consciousness appears then, altogether, as affirmation of oneself as I-ego; as discrimination of oneself from what is not I—the other; and as a fact presented to oneself and recognized by the ego. Immediately dissociation arises in the ego: the ego in ego-consciousness being simultaneously ego as subject and ego as object. In spite of all its dramatic attempts to escape this conditioned subjectivity, the ego seems never able to be a subject without an object ... unless, with some help, it can go down to the very root of its fundamental contradiction.

Should I conclude that I am just a specific conjunction of outer influences, a sort of metabolic link within the cosmos? Something remains evidently irreducible to such a perspective. However deeply I realize that what I am is altogether "imported," conditioned, and divided, I still believe in a mysterious and compelling vocation: that of being myself. Like Isis desperately trying to gather the dispersed members of Osiris, the ego is ever in quest of a unified, meaningful identity.

In fact with ego-consciousness and its provocative ambiguity there has been awakened in us a strange and immediate sense of responsibility. This brings me much nearer to what I can recognize as my own. Especially if I recall that to be responsible means properly to respond, to answer. All I can possibly do, as a matter of fact all I am doing, is responding, responding to my existence. What really defines and shows us a man is his response. If there is for me the slightest possible choice in the midst of operating laws, whether from hazard or necessity, is it not in the way I respond—that is, in the quality of my participation in all that is given to me through the immediate experience of my life?

Let us be clear that my genuine responsiveness is not to be found in any of the formal responses that my programmed computer never fails to produce. It has to be sought beyond that. It is an intentional act of knowing, which has a singular capacity for freedom since it can exist beyond my "formal" conditioning. This primary, free response is my attention. My attention is my own and fundamental answer to my existence. It is both my response and what I can be responsible for. An opening as well as an engagement, it is my becoming present to what is, it is *hic et nunc* my participating in the actuality of being. Arising as a basic act of knowing through actual being, my attention is simultaneously awakening to myself and to the world. All the rest, I mean all the other responses which are formal, all my acting out, all my outward manifestations proceed, so to say, by themselves, depending in their quality on the quality of my attention.

The idea of quality of attention is not familiar to us, nor is the idea of different possible levels of attention. But this would need an elaboration we cannot make here. Let us just say that our attention is much more than we generally think. It is much more than a simple mental or cerebral mechanism. It concerns our whole being. If its potentialities are far from being fully actualized in our usual life, maybe it is precisely because it is not recognized as a multidimensional keyboard and as the unifying principle of our being.

Paradoxically this basic act of knowing, which is attention, is only actualized when we don't know—that is, when there is a question. Its level and, so to say, its degree of "totalization" are proportional to our questioning. You have surely noticed that when a question is vital—when it takes us in the guts, as you say—it suspends all unnecessary movements, emotional and physical as well as mental. It clears the way for real awareness and sensitivity, which are components of my total power of attention. It is only between my not knowing and my urge to know that I find myself present, mobilized, open, new—that is to say, attentive.

Attention in its active form is therefore inseparable from interrogation; it is essentially, in its purity, an act of questioning. This act is the privilege of our human existence. An animal contents itself with being. The responsibility of man is to question himself on the meaning of his being.

In our society, mainly concerned with production and efficiency, the drama is that our capacity for questioning, still so vivid in early childhood, is very quickly eradicated or pushed aside for the benefit of our capacity for answering. When a child has a real question, most of the time he is immediately given a stupid answer. In the best cases the educator goes to the dictionary to be sure his answer is accurate. But anyhow, unconsciously, if not proudly, he closes the question. From school to the end of our life it is always necessary to answer. We are compelled to learn how to answer. If we don't know how to answer, we are just no good. So little by little we become some kind of model machine able-to-answer-all-situations with all the necessary blindness as regards its own contradictions. That kind of answering, whose degree of sophistication may sometimes hide from us its conditioned character, is required by our life. But under its dominating necessity, is it possible to keep alive in ourselves our most authentic and precious capacity, which is questioning?

This is the whole problem confronting us, actually. But are we strong enough, free enough, concerned enough, to really question ourselves while answering? The challenge is just as difficult as facing a Zen koan. While playing our part, while being engaged without cheating in the situation that calls us, can we at the same time neither affirm nor deny, neither resist nor follow, assume that we neither know nor don't know, that we are able or unable? Can we be acutely present to what is, without judgment or indifference, without any solution or escape? It would mean being aware on all fronts, renouncing the known for the unknown, withstanding the inevitable principle of repetition, staying still within our movement.

Total questioning in our living is the key to being, but whoever ventures unprepared into the experience will meet a wall of resistance in himself, if not simply fear that he is stupid, incapable, and so on. Only exceptionally motivated searchers will take the risk and leave room for questioning—and get beyond the phantasms of insecurity. Most of us are so busy with successful answering and so identified with our own image that we need severe shocks such as death, suffering, illness, deep frustration, or "supergratification" to awaken to the question.

The question is here, waiting for us, following us everywhere, since we ourselves are that very question. I have started with it, asking, "What am I?" but this approach has kept me an outsider, a mere on-looker of myself. When born in the mind, the question calls forth an answer through the mind and keeps me divided under my compulsion for explanation and for power over my object world. Understanding needs more. It needs experiencing—that is, to be put to the test and to pass through. I have to engage myself, to respond totally in the act of knowing myself. Arising from being, the question finds an answer through being. Our question has thus shifted from a ratiocentric point of view to an ontocentric point of view and has become "Who am I?"

Behind the misleading screen of all our other questions it is the question of each one of us in our human existence. It is humanity's first and last question. It is today as it was centuries ago. Throughout human history, dim, bright, or enlightening lights have repeatedly reactivated that question. It is the axis around which moves in a spiral the eternal revolution of human culture.

Parabola
Volume: 2.4
Relationships

Because You Are My Friend

René Daumal

Our friendship, all friendship, consists of this: I have
understood, acquired, realized something only if you also
have understood, acquired, realized it. For the moment
our friendship consists in knowing and remembering
that we are incapable of friendship. Friendship, complete
union in search, exists between us only in flashes which
we do not know how to produce. In these flashes, there
is no difference between what is good for you and what
is good for me. The rest of the time we live together only
on the memory of these flashes. And to prepare for future
flashes, the first condition is to know that it is only a
memory. A friendship has to be remade, continually, and
if we imagine that it already exists in a permanent and
stable way we shall make no effort to build it. In order to
build it, we have to establish mutual relations as though
this friendship *did* exist, as though we really had forged
something lasting between us. This presupposes that each
effort must be twofold for each of us: I make it for me
and for you.

Our first task in order to make the friendship real is
to break with everything that is ordinarily called friendship: confederacy in lying, familiarity (complicity in falling), convenience, connivance in going to sleep, one of us
shifting our responsibility onto the other and so forth.

In front of every human being, I should support him, understand him, be free of him and respect his freedom, and remember what we have in common; yes, in front of *all* others. But I know I am not capable. Let me at least try to be like that in front of you, because you are my friend, because you prepared the way for me and made the task easier for me. So in your presence at any rate I should not allow myself any weakness; all our meetings should be sacred moments.

You exist for me—I *touch* your unique existence—only in moments when I am aware of my own nothingness. The rest of the time you are a "thing" in my subjective world. You are a "person" when I feel myself nothing. At that moment, I can understand you, but I can have no right to judge you. I can at most judge your opinions, your outer actions, productions, etc., *in relation to you*, and to our common aim. But I cannot judge *you*, the person. Our common aim should more truly be called our common *wish* (hardly more than the wish for that wish), since the true wish for something "better," permanent and immovable, we do not have.

And so our friendship cannot be fulfilled "in this world," in this world alone. It would be empty without the certainty which we share of a higher world to which our friendship would wish to belong, in order to serve.

Chaque fois que l'aube parait, by René Daumal (Paris: Gallimard, 1953), translated from the French.

Parabola
Volume: 9.1
Hierarchy

THE TASTE FOR THINGS THAT ARE TRUE

Henri Tracol

This essay from Henri Tracol's book, The Taste for Things That Are True, *was written when the author was in his twenties and at the beginning of his search, or as he puts it in his book, "some thirty years before May 1968"—the date of the student uprisings in Paris.*

We young ones were hungry. Our appetite was law; we absolutely had to taste everything, know everything, satiate ourselves with everything. We had read, reread, and catalogued all the most variegated and extravagant bills of fare. Our eyes shone at the mere sight of the appetizers; when the main dishes appeared, we shouted with enthusiasm.

Poor innocents. There are no words for what this banquet was—and still is. Under the sauces which were too skillful to be honest, there was only spoiled meat, vegetables no longer fresh, fruit three-quarters rotten. The few morsels that were good were all mixed up with the worst. The more appetizing the plate looked, the less it contained. Everything smelled of adulteration, artifice, machine oil, and the chemical factory.

For this is the way it is: with our cooks, whether they are philosophers, politicians, industrialists, sportsmen, economists, writers, or artists, the aim is to imitate or to conceal *the taste of things that are true*. And so keen is our appetite at first that we devour everything eagerly. We lick the plates and ask for more. But soon enough weariness, the memory of imaginary feasts, and sluggish digestion have their effect. Tired of stuffing ourselves to no purpose, we beg (or demand) to be given at last nourishment worthy of the name; and immediately our pseudo-master-cooks bestir themselves and bustle about arguing, only to wind up offering us (or forcing on us) some new concoctions. But under other names, we are always served the same dishes.

No words, indeed, for such a banquet. But I ask you, what then can we say about the guests? Because the worst of it is that in spite of everything we should still be sitting today at the same table with the same disgusting messes in front of us, and to crown it all, that we have wound up by acquiring a taste for them.

No doubt, such persistence is laughable; but all the same, it's a serious matter. For if we go on cheating our hunger, tomorrow we will kill it. All that will remain will be that artificial hunger, at once tyrannical and servile, that obeys instantly the smallest solicitation from without—and makes us its slaves.

Do you remember how we experienced with all our being the need to live fully? Life, naked life, was in front of us. We wanted to chuck into the fire all that cheap finery that decked our purpose; sweep away the dubious company of half-truths, half-feelings, half-decisions; the crowd of walk-ons made up as scholars, poets, civilizing heroes, with their big empty words and their spectacular gestures; tear down finally all the cardboard stage sets in front of which they played out their comedy for us, but behind which, surely, *something* must be happening. ...

Remember how so many questions had us by the throat, which have gone unanswered. And since then, we've dared to make fun of them, we've dared to deny them, because it's the fashion to be skeptical, reasonable—that is, not to search *sincerely* any more to understand.

And yet—at the start, for us, *to understand* didn't mean to penetrate the skillfully arranged labyrinth of some philosophical theory; it didn't mean to accumulate thousands of fragments of information in order to fit them ingeniously together in the laboratory; on the contrary, it meant to seize reality with open arms, in the midst of life; and to look at it bravely, as the only way to become men.

I see you shrug your shoulders; I hear you snicker. But remember how it was: to understand, for us, then, meant the opposite of words. We had to act, to risk our safety, our lives, make dangerous experiments; we had to measure ourselves in action, to know our possibilities and our limits not in the abstract but in the full exercise of our functions. We felt the need to play to the hilt our role among other people, so as to discover the meaning of our presence in the world. We felt the need to believe, to love, to commit ourselves, to march shoulder-to-shoulder towards a common ideal.

Do you remember? We had no words harsh enough, then, for the lukewarm, the sleepyheads, for sulking adolescents, for cowards and mollycoddles, for "philosophizers" in bedroom slippers and abstainers of every kind. For all those defeated before they began, all those who accepted to be bought off cheaply to lead a dog's life, we had only one cry: "Back to your kennels!"

But I ask you: what have we ourselves made of our enthusiasms? We have been traitors and perjurers; we in our turn have become deceivers, sleight-of-hand artists; we know all the ins and outs of performing con-jurers' tricks with the only real, living questions. We have learned to be crafty with ourselves, to manipulate irony, to "philosophize," to dismiss, kindly, as "infantile," the manliness of our former search.

Already lethargy is creeping up on us. Already, at the least alarm, with our snail-like reflexes, we rush to reenter the deepest hollow in our mental shells. We take our stand in previously established positions; we refuse to expose ourselves.

What then has happened? Why have we deserted? From whence comes this progressive numbness, this sliding toward death of all that was most alive in us?

It came on by itself, stealthily, like a creeping infection—as the con-sequence of who knows what dangerous illusions or premature discour-agement. From one disappointment to another, the sickness has taken a progressively deeper hold, gradually chasing us out of ourselves.

For that is where the trouble lies: what we didn't have courage enough to look for *inside*, we have thought we could find *outside*. Not that we have given up hope of a change, of a better use of our powers; but with-out knowing it, we have stopped really counting on ourselves to bring that about. Not that we have given up entirely, but now we wait for a miracle from outside. And we have begun to have wild dreams of favorable circumstances, of better conditions of life, or of some exceptional encounter. To feed our hopes, we have pounced greedily on the most absurd fictions and the stupidest arguments; we have flung ourselves at the stockpile of ready-made notions, at the leftovers of the great thinkers, at the whole doctrinal flea market. Anything would do to save us from the terrible effort of facing ourselves.

We were afraid, of course, in front of life, and tried to escape. But the endless circle of the imagination is vicious indeed. Between the tyranny of our dreams and the bitterness of our awaking, we were wholly caught in the cogwheels. In the too-bright light of the sun, we preferred the shadows of our dreams, and then blamed the whole universe because they vanished.

So we began demanding everything from others; from society or from chance—and nothing from ourselves. Soon it was on these others, on society or misfortune, that we were heaping the blame for all our defeats.

We cry that we have been cheated, hoaxed, duped. But who began it? We have deserved these falsehoods a hundred times over. What am I saying? It was we who called them, adopted them, warmed them in our bosoms, fattened, pampered, and cherished them in order to flaunt them and carry them around in triumph. Who among us doesn't daily take his wishes for reality? If we fool ourselves like this, where will we find the strength to resist the lies that flatter our secret preferences?

"Whose fault is it?" That's our great cry. For every one of our failures, individual or collective, we must have at all costs someone to blame. At all costs we must find out who is responsible and chastise him thoroughly—sometimes one, sometimes another; there is always a scapegoat.

But our worst misfortune is that *no one is responsible*—ourselves less than anyone. We spend our time refusing all responsibility, even for our thoughts. We claim to have an answer for everything, but no longer wish to be answerable for anything.

In our frantic flight away from ourselves, we nevertheless feel a need for brotherhood, for walking side by side, which draws its strength from the same source as our deepest and truest emotions. But after the first professions of faith have been exchanged, why do we come together? To congratulate ourselves, to complain, to lull each other to sleep—or to make common property of all our hate and rancor. So in the group we are part of, we hurry to repeat the mistakes we already made with ourselves. It is always "the others" who are wrong; we, collectively, are excused. We consolidate our lies, we multiply them; and above all, we convince ourselves that we are strong. But the union of the worst weaknesses has never created strength.

When will we understand true brotherhood? If you are my brother, it's not flattery or sympathy I expect from you, but questions, provocations, a challenge; then you can help me, not before. If you are my brother, don't leave me in peace, don't let me go to sleep; my life is at stake. If we are brothers, we will discover together the hunger we knew when we were twenty, and the questions that had us by the throat—questions that have no answer except in the struggle for self-mastery and the conquest of our lives. Only that struggle can give us the taste for things that are true.

If we are sick to death of the sham banquet, who keeps us here? Let's leave this table of deceptions and go together in search of real food. Let us, too, return to earth—return to the abandoned field of our own lives, and clear, plow, fertilize, and cultivate this unworked ground that has been invaded by weeds. And when harvest time comes, we will go and tell our other comrades how bread tastes that one has kneaded with one's own hands.

Parabola
Volume: 3.2
Sacrifice and
Transformation

SACRIFICE AND WILL

Christopher Fremantle

The idea of sacrifice as a *making sacred* has always been very much a part of Western thought. Today the word remains, but it is more often used in the political and economic sense of belt-tightening or of accepting inconveniences necessary for the common welfare; or even as a sort of trade-off or exchange. There is no other word to carry its primal meaning, so it is necessary to restore the word to its original significance and bring it back into currency; for it is not only a word but a dynamic idea, as alive now as ever, although seemingly out-of-date. And it is also a paradox.

If, as tradition says, the universe is created, then everything must be sacred, because this quality derives from the Creator; so the idea of "making sacred" is redundant. But if in accord with some present-day thought, our universe is accidental, arising from an unknown beginning, then nothing in it is or will become sacred. And our understanding of this contradiction is not helped by the traditional Christian outlook which, leaning on the words, "Greater love hath no man than this, that a man lay down his life for his friends," speaks of death as "the supreme sacrifice"; nor is it helped by traditional sacrificial rites in which the blood of victims is offered. How can the destruction of life—whether on the altar or the battlefield—render life itself sacred?

I think the reconciling elements between these conflicting aspects of meaning must be looked for in the view of sacrifice as an essential part of the life process, rather than as an isolated act of expiation. There is a striking, though very brief, passage in the Gospel of St. John in which Christ says (apparently referring to the Eleusinian mysteries, since Philip had just announced that two Greeks wished to speak with him): "Except a corn of wheat fall into the ground and die, it abideth alone, but if it die it bringeth forth much fruit." In this statement, and in the context of the Greek mysteries, the idea of sacrifice and death is linked together with that of rebirth and fulfillment. That is, the idea of sacrifice and that of immortality, life beyond time; "before Abraham was, I am." In joining sacrifice, suffering and death with the concept of transformation and of the continuity of life as a total process, all the apparent contradictions are resolved. The perspective that life itself does not die, but is expressed in constant transformation and movement, lies at the root of major religious traditions in both East and West.

Here in the light of modern investigative thought, the question arises: what actually is the transforming action of sacrifice and suffering upon the person who offers it? The first contemporary teaching to have posed this question seems to have been that of Gurdjieff, with his emphasis on "conscious labors and intentional suffering." Every sacrifice involves suffering, sometimes beneficial and sometimes not; what seems to distinguish "useful," strengthening and transformative suffering from that which is useless and distorting is precisely its intentional quality. If the suffering is not voluntarily accepted, it turns into bitterness, as Lot's wife turned into salt.

But with the idea of voluntary sacrifice other questions arise. Today, the medieval Christian asceticism that expressed itself in self-torture seems remote; any such tendency is suspect, as masochism or at best just another ego-trip. So the question becomes important: what is the nature of, and whose is the *will* behind this voluntary action? What is the transforming role of personal will in sacrifice? What, indeed, is it that we call "will"? We know so much more about "self-will," with its ego-motivations, than about human will itself; and how are we to separate real will from the conditioned responses and defenses formed around a person from birth?

Ramana Maharshi, who died in 1952, once commented that to gain control of the attention is the sole aim of all spiritual exercises and disciplines—thus aligning himself with Ramakrishna who, a century earlier, had followed for twelve years different disciplines of great traditional religions and concluded that they did not differ in essence. Gurdjieff, too, pointed to attention as the unique tool for acquiring objective, nonegoistic will. The attention to which they refer is certainly not that which is continually darting from one thing to the next, distracted by every happening and every association; nor that which is helplessly absorbed in some problem. Neither kind has the activity and stability capable of resisting the automatic, conditioned responses which rule our behavior. When suffering appears, these automatic impulses push us towards escape; where sacrifice is involved, towards compromise or complacency. Only an independent and stable attention can be aware of the moment of decision and choice, and detect a deviation from the decision before it gathers momentum.

Perhaps it can be said that real will is the product of intention and of the strong forces released in us by suffering. Suffering and danger free vast amounts of fine energy which have observable physical manifestations: under threat from a charging bull a man leaps obstacles he could never clear in cold blood; when a child is in danger a mother can forego sleep for days and nights because an extraordinary energy is present. But except at such moments we are not in control of these capacities and not even aware of them, so they are not available to us.

All teachings regarding conscious transformation seek ways of coming into relationship with these inner powers. Traditional counsels of "action without attachment," ascetic practices of various kinds, deep meditation and contemplation, are means proposed for reaching and studying an attention which can transform: that is, an attention which can link a man with his deepest aspiration and the power to resist the automatism of flight in the face of suffering.

Modern scientific psychology has begun to study those areas crucial to development in man's psyche, and to acquire some information about them. This direction interested the late Abraham Maslow and other researchers who have pursued it through psychological studies or through laboratory measurement of the physiological effects of meditation; but not nearly enough is yet known. In medicine, current research is reported to be revealing the part played by fine energies—sub-atomic particles—in the processes of physiological and neurological response. Looking further ahead, particle physics will surely throw new light on the action on man's psyche of fine energies entering our world from the cosmos. When these aspects of the natural sciences reach their flowering, it may well be found that they restate, more lucidly and in contemporary terms, ancient traditional teachings concerning the true role of sacrifice. The last thirty years have brought about a rapprochement between metaphysical and scientific thought, and it seems quite possible that a new understanding, confirmed by research, will show the role of sacrifice and suffering as vital forces in the chain of life's evolution and transformation.

Parabola
Volume: 6.3
Mask and Metaphor

THE HISTORY OF THE HOLLOW-MEN AND THE BITTER ROSE

René Daumal

The Hollow-Men live in solid rock and move about in it in the form of mobile caves or recesses. In ice they appear as bubbles in the shape of men. But they never venture out into the air, for the wind would blow them away.

They have houses in the rock whose walls are made of emptiness, and tents in the ice whose fabric is of bubbles. During the day they stay in the stone, and at night they wander through the ice and dance during the full moon. But they never see the sun, or else they would burst.

They eat only the void, such as the form of corpses; they get drunk on empty words and all the meaningless expressions we utter.

Some people say they have always existed and will exist forever. Others say they are the dead. And others say that as a sword has its scabbard or a foot its imprint, every living man has in the mountain his Hollow-Man, and in death they are reunited.

In the village of Hundred-Houses there lived the old priest-magician Hunoes and his wife, Hulay-Hulay. They had two sons, two identical twins who could not be told apart, called Mo and Ho. Even their mother got them mixed up. To tell them apart the day of name giving, they had put on Mo a necklace bearing a little cross and on Ho a necklace bearing a little ring.

Old Hunoes had one great unconfessed worry. According to custom his eldest son should succeed him. But which was his elder son? Did he even have an elder son?

At the age of adolescence Mo and Ho were already accomplished mountaineers. They came to be called the two mountain goats. One day, their father told them, "To whichever one of you brings back to me the Bitter-Rose I shall hand on the great knowledge."

The Bitter-Rose is found only at the summit of the highest peaks. Whoever eats of it finds that whenever he is about to tell a lie, aloud or to himself, his tongue begins to burn. He can still tell falsehoods, but he has been warned. A few people have seen the Bitter-Rose: According to what they say, it looks like a large multicolored lichen or a swarm of butterflies. But no one has ever been able to pick it, for the tiniest tremor of fear anywhere close by alerts it, and it disappears into the rock. Even if one desires it, one is a little afraid of possessing it, and it vanishes.

To describe an impossible action or an absurd undertaking, they say: "It's like looking for night in broad daylight," or "It's like wanting to throw light on the sun in order to see it better," or "It's like trying to catch the Bitter-Rose."

Mo has taken his ropes and pick and hatchet and iron hooks. At sunrise he is already high up on a peak called Cloudy Head. Like a lizard, sometimes like a spider, he inches upward across the high red precipice, between white snow below and the blue-black sky. Little swift-moving clouds envelop him from time to time and then expose him suddenly to the light again. And now at least, a little distance above him, he sees the Bitter-Rose, shimmering with unearthly tints. He repeats to himself unceasingly the charm that his father has taught him to ward off fear.

He's going to need a screw ring here, with a rope sling, in order to straddle this outcropping of rock like a rearing horse. He strikes with his hammer, and his hand breaks through into a hole. There is a hollow under the stone. Shattering the crust around it, he sees that the hollow is in the form of a man: torso, legs, arms, and little tubes in the shape of fingers spread in terror. He has split the head with the blow of his pick.

An icy wind passes across the stone. Mo has killed a Hollow-Man. He has shuddered, and the Bitter-Rose has retreated into the rock.

Mo climbs back down to the village and tells his father, "I killed a Hollow-Man. But I saw the Bitter-Rose, and tomorrow I shall go to look for it."

Old Hunoes became grave. Far off he saw one misfortune after another coming in procession. He said: "Watch out for the Hollow-Men. They will seek vengeance. They cannot enter our world, but they can come up to the surface of things. Beware of the surface of things."

At dawn the next day Hulay-Hulay gave a great cry, rose up, and ran toward the mountain. At the foot of the red cliff lay Mo's garments, his ropes and hatchet, and his medal with the cross. His body was no longer there.

"Ho," she cried, running back. "They've killed your brother. They've killed my son."

Ho rises up with his teeth clenched and the skin tightening on his scalp. He takes his hatchet and prepares to set out. His father says to him, "First, listen to me. This is what you have to do. The Hollow-Men have taken your brother and changed him into a Hollow-Man. He will try to escape. He will go in search of light to the seracs of the Clear Glacier. Put his medal around your neck as well as your own. Go to him and strike at his head. Enter the form of his body, and Mo will live again among us. Do not fear to kill a dead man."

Ho gazes wide-eyed into the blue ice of the Clear Glacier. Is the light playing tricks on him, are his eyes deceiving him, or is he really seeing what he sees? He watches silvery forms with arms and legs, like greased divers under water. There is his brother, Mo, his hollow shape fleeing from a thousand Hollow-Men in pursuit. But they are afraid of the light. Mo's form seeks the light and rises in a large blue serac, turning around and around in search of a door. Despite his bursting heart and the blood clotting in his veins, Ho steps forward. To his blood and to his heart he says, "Do not fear to kill a dead man." Then he strikes the head, shattering the ice. Mo's form becomes motionless; Ho opens the ice of the serac and enters his brother's form like a sword fitted into its sheath, a foot into its imprint. He moves his elbows and works himself into place, then draws his legs back out of the mold of ice. And he hears himself saying words in a language he has never spoken. He feels he is Ho, and that he is Mo at the same time. All Mo's memories have entered his mind—the way up Cloudy Head and where the Bitter-Rose has its habitation.

With the circle and the cross around his neck, he comes to Hulay-Hulay. "Mother, you will have no more trouble telling us apart. Mo and Ho are now in the same body; I am your only son, Moho."

Old Hunoes shed a few tears, and his face showed happiness. But there was still one doubt he wished to dispel. He said to Moho, "You are my only son; Ho and Mo can no longer be distinguished."

Moho told him with conviction, "Now I can reach the Bitter-Rose. Mo knows the way; Ho knows the right gesture. Master of my fears, I shall have the flower of discernment."

He picked the flower, he received the teaching, and old Hunoes was able to leave his world peacefully.

From the book *Mount Analogue,* by René Daumal. Copyright © 1952 by Librairie Gallimard. English translation copyright © 1959 by Vincent Stuart, Ltd. Reprinted by permission of Pantheon Books, a division of Random House, Inc. A new edition is currently available from Overlook Press.

Parabola
Volume: 10.4
The Seven
Deadly Sins

The Human Place

An Interview with Pauline de Dampierre

Parabola's *first opportunity to speak with Pauline de Dampi-erre about the Gurdjieff teaching centered around the theme of wholeness, and we were particularly struck by one idea. We asked her about the words of Gurdjieff: "He can be called a remarkable man who ... knows how to be restrained in the manifestations which proceed from his nature, at the same time conducting himself justly and tolerantly towards the weaknesses of others."*

Her comments about this description intrigued us and led us to explore the question further in relation to our present theme of "The Seven Deadly Sins." We find her insights on this question remarkable in themselves—original, subtle, and clear.

Parabola: *The last time we talked, we spoke of the whole man. How do you feel the whole man relates to the idea of sin?*

Pauline de Dampierre: What interests me is what is at the source of what we call sin. Usually we see sin as a manifestation of a certain intensity, or as an action which is exaggeration, bad, harmful. But what is at the source of that action? Compared to the source, that action is only an excrescence—something that bursts through from an undercurrent which is always acting in human beings.

The undercurrent of tendencies from which these impulses arise is a part of the whole man.

P: *These are the motivating forces?*

PD: Usually these tendencies have a much greater influence on our behavior than we imagine. They are always moving, and they are at the root of what has been called our automatism. If a person were to stop all his outer and inner movements at a given moment in order to see what is acting in him, he would nearly always feel a tendency which has about it something narrow, something heavy, something with a negative aspect that tends to be against, to be egoistic. All that is usually going on unseen. But if he tries to awaken to what is going on in himself, to be sincere, he will be able to witness, in addition to what could be called the "coarse" life in him, another life of another quality—much subtler, much higher, lighter—that is also a part of himself. The contact with this other quality of life helps him to have a quieter presence, a deeper vision. And he feels an urge at that moment to be open to a quality of this sort that would have a force, that would be a center of gravity. He begins to search for a way to serve what he feels would be his real being.

Then he begins to really know that if he lets his attention, his interest, be taken by his automatic tendencies, it deprives him of contact with that other source of life he is searching for. It could be said that there is a continual tendency to sin, in that sense. When these sins are spoken of as deadly, it means that these tendencies—if they are allowed to rule—at every moment deprive the human being of the possibility of turning towards this real life.

P: *When you speak of this undercurrent, do you mean the passive?*

PD: Passive. ... To let oneself be continuously led by these automatic nonconscious tendencies is indeed to be passive. And when a person is passive, the automatic begins to take the initiative, to direct him. When he turns towards something else ...

P: *When he makes a contact between the two?*

PD: Yes, then the undercurrent is able to play its normal role—its very necessary role.

P: *Without a search, is there any sin? Is there responsibility without an aim?*

PD: It is often said that man in his state of illusion about himself is not responsible, and perhaps in that sense it could be said that there is no sin. But to what extent is he absolutely not responsible?

P: *Is he held responsible at some level?*

PD: What we know is that every time we let ourselves go strongly into one of these tendencies, the tendency is strengthened. After a time it becomes very difficult to be free of it. It is in that way I see that one pays for his actions. And what about the harm that has been done to others through us? It is a very serious question. ...

P: *I'm interested in what you say about these tendencies being natural. If they are natural tendencies, always there as an undercurrent, what are they there for? And what is the difference when they are there as an undercurrent and when they are acted out? Do they become sins only when they are expressed?*

PD: One can feel these tendencies as inescapable parts of one's nature which to a certain extent bring data about oneself and the external world. I have to sustain my life. Many demands come to me from external life and I must sustain my outer life with the ego—as I am, I have nothing else. So it is through these tendencies that the ego is informed.

Take anger, for example. With a little vigilance, it is possible at the beginning of a movement of anger to surprise in oneself the sudden, sharp upsurge of an instinctive impulse that tends to immediately reject whatever is irritating us, making us suffer. This impulse is necessary— how could we get along without it? We would be inert: we could let our hand stay in a fire without reacting.

Take envy. There exists a law according to which when two masses of unequal size are near one another, the larger provokes a tension in the smaller. I should add that I know nothing about physics and do not know if this law prevails in that domain. But it is indubitably among the psychic influences that act on us, whether we like it or not. Very probably it is thanks to this law that the child instinctively educates itself, seeking to imitate an older person. He admires him, wants to be like him, wants to draw his attention, and if he doesn't succeed in doing so, he is frightened. For adults, it is exactly the same.

And pride—don't we teach a child to be proud of his successes, of his strength? Lacking this pride, he wouldn't respect himself and wouldn't make himself respected by others.

In a way each one of these tendencies is there to sustain my life at a certain level; they are necessary and healthy. But if I live with them alone, I am an animal. A human being has to stand in between and not allow himself to be taken by these things; not to let them raise opposition and justification. For this he must not let himself identify with them, and this means he must not let them make him forget the one and only thing important for him.

P: *These sins, then, are engines of the ego? They drive the ego?*

PD: I would even say that they are engines of our nature, because we can always find these tendencies acting in us. But if one can see them, one can be informed by them instead of being blindly taken.

You were speaking of the ego. . . . On the portals of certain cathedrals, one can see sculptures representing the vices and, above them, sculptures of the virtues. But between the vices and the virtues, there is something intermediary. And this is not shown. In fact, what remains hidden in the middle is man's wish to be sincere, to try to understand the meaning of his life. But for this, the underlying current must be perceived and respected. Then the virtues take on form on their own. It isn't necessary to seek them directly. They appear.

The rest of the time, it is ego speaking. There is no other alternative.

These virtues do not judge, do not reject, have no violence. They emanate; they radiate. Certain exceptional human beings prove that this is so, and even in someone who is very far from that, the existence of such a possibility can make itself felt.

P: *In a way, it is like saying that only a person who knows fear can be courageous. There is no need of virtue if you don't have vices!*

PD: What is vice? There are many ways to look at the subject—psychologically, analytically, theologically. I have no intention of adding to what has already been said along these lines. I simply want to emphasize one aspect that is rarely brought to light: the role of an inner search in relation to these underlying tendencies. Then the "vices" become simpler. You don't so much think of them as bad, but you feel strongly, painfully, that they are harmful to what you are searching for. They are there and you don't allow them to take too much place. You don't reject them, but you don't let yourself be engulfed by them, either. Through this process, something can be developed in us.

P: *That brings a note of hope—and it bears on our earlier question about why the undercurrent is there.*

PD: What is important is to begin to be able to hold oneself at the source. I heard during my Catholic upbringing that even a saint sinned seven times a day. But I would say that the tendency to sin is at every second.

P: *And it's not one's fault that it is there?*

PD: It is my human place. The power to act is in the body. The wish for evolved being comes from another source. And the two parts must meet. They do not often meet by accident; they meet only when something is acknowledged and held in respect.

P: *These impulses, then, if held at the source, can actually contribute to a continued sense of presence?*

PD: My sense of presence will only be real if I take these impulses into account. I may try to open only to something higher—perhaps it is possible in a posture of meditation, but even then not so easy. But the moment I begin to act these impulses are necessarily there, and must be taken into account.

P: *Unquestionably, they have enormous force. It seems that something else of an equal force needs to be there. One can be aware of one of these impulses for a moment, and suddenly be swallowed by it. And then it is the only thing there.*

PD: I would say that what is needed is not an equal force but another kind of force, more subtle, more active. As in chemistry, one can take a stone and introduce a very active substance and the stone will dissolve. Well, the wish to be can be very active.

In fact it is not possible to experience an opening toward more freedom without obedience toward something higher. A human being has no other possibility. He may think he can be free, but he is either obedient in submitting to this higher, or a slave. But when he submits willingly, he may receive something of such a high quality that he will no longer be attracted to what enslaves him. Every time we are attracted, we think we find life in that attraction. We think we affirm ourselves. But at the moment of submitting to this finer force, we feel life of such another kind that we are no longer tempted.

There is a very strong relation between the action of these tendencies and a certain automatism of the body. Of course, we all know how easily tempted we are by physical satisfactions—resting, moving about, food, sexual attraction. But what I'm speaking of is much more hidden, insidious, almost beyond uprooting by ordinary means. It's a question of a certain "coarseness" inscribed in the body by everything that we have experienced, by the way in which we have allowed ourselves to be led along by these impulses. The body is accustomed to this heavy functioning even if outwardly it seems extremely light and free. The very texture of the body favors these impulses and is reinforced by them. It's a vicious circle. When there is an opening to something higher, the body quietens, and begins to be impregnated with something more subtle. It finds a kind of inner behavior much more in accordance with this opening. And in that way these tendencies begin not to have such a strong action on the person.

P: *What is the place of feeling, here? Does feeling have no action at all? Is this a struggle only between the head and body?*

PD: It is said that we have almost no contact with real feeling. Our emotions are very egoistic. There is no love in them. They always turn me to something other than what is there. When we feel emotions, there is a vibration so quick and tempting that it is difficult to resist. We always think it is our feeling, but it is not our feeling—it is our emotionality. If you observe yourself at that moment, you will recognize that that emotion is not yourself. You have no liberty; you are absolutely engulfed. Yet there is this mysterious power in the human being—to turn also towards something else in himself that may be very weak, nearly inaudible, but of another quality that he respects more. One could say that real feeling appears at those rare moments when what is happening in the individual is of such quality that his only wish is to be able to remain there, and to serve it as best he can. It is only then that he has a positive feeling of the moment, with no wish to be somewhere else.

P: *There seems to be a sense in which the impulses of envy, avarice, and so on seem to have to do with the future or the past—with images of something that I want and fear that I will not be able to have. I am taken out of the present moment by wanting to insure something for the future. Do you think that these impulses are based on fear?*

PD: In our usual state, we have nothing real in us to rely on, so it is necessary for us to create projections and ideas, to have desires of all kinds. We have no aim that would feed our presence. Every real search is about that—to find a place in oneself we could serve, where being could grow and play its role. Then it gives sense to life. When it appears, true relationship begins among the parts of the individual. He sees better, he is clearer at that moment, he is no longer afraid of living. Even outwardly, something is more balanced. Without that, there is never an aim which brings me into contact with the sense of my destiny. But at the moment, no matter how briefly, I see that I am in contact with the aim that I've sought. I know what to place my confidence in.

P: *We are almost forced, then, to imagine some kind of reality for ourselves, because we are not in touch with a true reality. We have to create some sort of world to live in.*

PD: I would say that we haven't been taught that we could be open to the growth of a reality in us. It is a great discovery to touch something real and tangible in us—it is the goal of all the traditions, to help the individual toward what is real in him.

P: *There is very little in our society that lends support to a search of this kind. Why should anyone believe you when you say that something more is possible for human beings?*

PD: These ideas seem quite alien, it's true. Today, however, several great currents of spiritual search are trying to give them new reality. For my part, I would say that one of the most remarkable aspects of Gurdjieff's thought is that it allows us to start from what we are—from our mortal sins, one might say, or more simply from our predominant faults. It casts a vigorous, surprising light of truth on our multiple weaknesses, our prison. And it shows us how to listen to another voice, enter into contact with another reality.

How to be touched? One can be deeply touched by contact with someone who has begun to develop this in himself. Or special events can happen in life—a great happiness, a great sorrow, an impression of nature, of sacred art of the past—that can give an extraordinary feeling of much more life in us, much finer, much broader, as if the horizon were opening.

It gives us a taste that life should always be like that. It doesn't happen often and it comes through events outside of us. But the longing for it is always there. For we are speaking of a human need—the need that makes us alive.

To feel it is to feel that it is true and must be searched for.

A real search is a preparation for an opening to the taste of that life. Gaining knowledge of everything that opposes it is the first step on the path. And it is a great adventure …

Parabola
Volume: 16.3
Craft

BIRTH OF A SCULPTURE

An Interview with Henri Tracol

Henri Tracol's, article "Why Sleepest Thou, O Lord?" gave its title to an anthology of his essays and interviews published in France in 1983 under the title Pourquoi dors-tu Seigneur? *The following is a transcript, translated from that book, of his answers to the questions of a journalist, broadcast December 7, 1981, by the France-Culture network, on Pierre Descargues' program "Le Monde au singulier."*

Henri Tracol: In order to avoid any misunderstanding, let me say that I am not a professional sculptor: I haven't studied at any school of fine arts or even taken part in workshops; at most, I've received some enlightening advice from sculptor friends who have encouraged me to follow what I might well describe as a kind of calling.

Certainly I have the greatest respect for the *craft*, for its rules, its standards, its requirements—its tools, equipment, etc.—and of course above all for the material, for the substance itself, which is no way being violated, destroyed or reduced to nothing, but on the contrary, is being called to life, its own life.

What does this still, silent block of stone wish to say? It is as if it were waiting for me to find its true form through myself. And when I am asked this question, another question is bound to echo in me: I ask myself what "I" wish to say, what is the meaning of my presence

•

on earth, what meaning can I discover in this unknown presence, in this unknown that I am.

Question: *Then we could say that art is self-knowledge—and also that self-knowledge is an art?*

HT: Without a doubt. It is an art which has its own laws, laws which cannot be broken. But I am systematically anti-systematic: I am always careful not to fall into the trap of "thinking I understand" just because I have had a glimmering of certain ideas which are quite plausible but which have not been part of my experience.

To be precise, I believe the most important thing here is to *enter* into the experience, to feel that one is the material on which all sorts of relatively independent forces are acting. What allows me to be in a certain way the sculptor of myself, or at least to cooperate with the forces that shape me? If I don't do that, I am letting these forces operate and make whatever they wish of me. Nevertheless something in me is called on: as a human being, I am invited to take part in my own formation. And perhaps it is that which more and more strengthens my interest in self-knowledge through the experience of art—not an intellectual interest but one that is much more profound and comes from a deeper source.

Q: *How would you relate this very self-knowledge, this immersion in the experience that you just spoke of, with what is called the theory of knowledge? How is the way to be found?*

HT: How is the way to be found? Perhaps a whole lifetime would not be enough for that. But it is possible to search, to search honestly. We are led astray by images of what we thought we understood from reading books and listening to "experts." Whether or not I am working on a sculpture, I need to feel that I am directly concerned, that again and again I give myself to the task as directly as possible. I try to make myself available in such a way that I can be conscious of the forces that pass through me, in order to understand better their direction and orientation, and adapt myself better to them; to try to become a good instrument—and a conscious one.

Here the mystery reappears: how can I be a conscious instrument of the forces which pass through me and define me? How can I be a workman in this work which is in process, at the same time *knowing it*, with the beginning of autonomy, with something which truly obliges me to try to see what corresponds best with what my real self calls me to be?

There is a sentence from Elie Faure which has haunted me since my adolescence, that echoes what I have just tried to say: "The only man who adds to the spiritual wealth of humanity is the one who has the force to become what he is."

Parabola
Volume: 21.3
Peace

Unfolding

William Segal

Watching quietly, anticipating nothing, I am open to what is here, now. I look at myself reading these words. I read slowly. I see the way I am sitting. I sense my body, the arising and the movement of thoughts, of feelings—the way my breath comes and goes. I am the witness and the witnessing, passively watching and actively being watched.

I see that there can be a further letting go, a beginning relationship to an unchanging inner stillness. Like a white sheet of paper that retains its nature, I remain receptive but unstained, quietly in touch with what is taking place, attention wholly in the moment. Is there help in a stop? In an unfolding to a fresh time/space? Is there a way to be without doing?

Listening to the silence which is present in the stillness I become aware of a new web of relationships, of a unity bringing the body/mind structure to another threshold. I sense that there is another Reality that can be served. Again, a stop.

Will the fragility of my attention survive the experience of turning this page?

From William Segal, *The Structure of Man* (Sunderland, Mass.: Green River Press, 1987). Reprinted by permission of the author.

•

Parabola
Volume: 30.3
Body and Soul

Intentional Blending

G. I. Gurdjieff

Every man, if he is just an ordinary man, that is, one who has never consciously "worked on himself," has two worlds; and if he has worked on himself, and has become a, so to say, "candidate for another life," he has even three worlds.

In spite of the fact that everyone, without exception, will certainly think that I have gone completely mad when they read the above statement, I shall nevertheless go on to develop the logical consequences of this ultra-extravagant notion.

If you really want to know the truth, I will tell you how matters stand, and why I pronounced such an absurdity.

First of all, it must be said that in the outpourings of various occultists and other will-less parasites, when they discuss spiritual questions, not everything is entirely wrong.

What they call the "soul" does really exist, but not everybody necessarily has one.

A soul is not born with man and can neither unfold nor take form in him so long as his body is not fully developed.

It is a luxury that can only appear and attain completion in the period of "responsible age," that is to say, in a man's maturity.

The soul, like the physical body, is also matter—only, it consists of "finer" matter.

The matter from which the soul is formed and from which it later nourishes and perfects itself is, in general, elaborated during the processes that take place between the two essential forces upon which the entire Universe is founded.

The matter in which the soul is coated can be produced exclusively by the action of these two forces, which are called "good" and "evil" by ancient science, or "affirmation" and "negation," while contemporary science calls them "attraction" and "repulsion."

In the common presence of a man, these two forces have their source in two of the totalities of general psychic functioning, which have already been mentioned.

One of them coincides with that function whose factors proceed from the results of impressions received from outside, and the other appears as a function whose factors issue chiefly from the results of the specific functioning of the organs, as determined by heredity.

In the common presence of a man, as in everything in the Universe, sometimes one and sometimes the other of these totalities of functioning can serve as the source of one of the forces required for the process of which we are speaking.

For this process, it is not important to know which of the two forces is affirmative and which is negative; what matters is that when one affirms, the other denies.

The full realization and precise determination in man of that totality of functioning whose factors are constituted from impressions coming from outside is called the "outer world" of man.

And the full realization of the other totality, whose factors have arisen from automatically flowing "experiences" and from reflexes of the organism—notably of those organs whose specific character is transmitted by heredity—is called the "inner world" of man.

In relation to these two worlds, man appears in reality to be merely a slave, because his various perceptions and manifestations cannot be other than conformable to the quality and nature of the factors making up these totalities.

He is obliged, in relation to his outer world as well as his inner world, to manifest himself in accordance with the orders received from any given factor of one or the other totality.

He cannot have his own initiative; he is not free to want or not to want, but is obliged to carry out passively this or that "result" proceeding from other outer or inner results.

Such a man, that is to say, a man who is related to only two worlds, can never do anything; on the contrary, everything is done through him. In everything, he is but the blind instrument of the caprices of his outer and inner worlds.

The highest esoteric science calls such a man "a man in quotation marks"; in other words he is named a man and at the same time he is not a man.

He is not a man such as he should be, because his perceptions and his manifestations do not flow according to his own initiative but take place either under the influence of accidental causes or in accordance with functioning that conforms to the laws of the two worlds.

In the case of "a man in quotation marks," the "I" is missing and what takes its place and "fills its role" is the factor of initiative proceeding from that one of the two above-mentioned totalities in which the center of gravity of his general state is located.

The "I" in a real man represents that totality of the functioning of his general psyche whose factors have their origin in the results of contemplation, or simply in the contact between the first two totalities, that is, between the factors of his inner world and of his outer world.

The totality of the manifestations of this third function of the general psyche of man also represents a world in itself, but in this case it is the third world of man.

And thus, this third world of man is, strictly speaking, as the ancient sciences understood, the real "inner world of man" as opposed to the real "outer world."

I shall call this third definite totality of functioning in the general psyche of man by the same name it was given in the distant past, that is: "the world of man."

According to this terminology, the general psyche of man in its definitive form is considered to be the result of conformity to these three independent worlds.

The first is the outer world—in other words, everything existing outside him, both what he can see and feel as well as what is invisible and intangible for him.

The second is the inner world—in other words, all the automatic processes of his nature and the mechanical repercussions of these processes.

The third world is his own world, depending neither upon his "outer world" nor upon his "inner world"; that is to say, it is independent of the caprices of the processes that flow in him as well as of the imperfections in these processes that bring them about.

A man who does not possess his own world can never do anything from his own initiative: all his actions "are done" in him.

Only he can have his own initiative for perceptions and manifestations in whose common presence there has been formed, in an independent and intentional manner, the totality of factors necessary for the functioning of this third world.

Thus it is quite obvious that the whole secret of human existence lies in the difference in the formation of the factors that are necessary for these three relatively independent functions of the general psyche of man.

And this difference consists solely in that the factors of the first two totalities are formed by themselves, in conformity to laws, as a result of chance causes not depending on them, while the factors of the third totality are formed exclusively by an intentional blending of the functions of the first two.

And it is indeed in this sense that one must understand the saying, common to all the old religious teachings, that "man receives all his possibilities from On High."

Parabola
Volume: 9.1
Hierarchy

THE FIRST INITIATION

G. I. Gurdjieff

The following is a translation of words recorded by G. I. Gurdjieff's pupils during a meeting in Paris on December 16, 1941. Printed by permission of Triangle Editions.

You will see that in life you receive exactly what you give. Your life is the mirror of what you are. It is in your image. You are passive, blind, demanding. You take all, you accept all, without feeling any obligation. Your attitude toward the world and toward life is the attitude of one who has the right to make demands and to take; who has no need to pay or earn. You believe that all things are your due, simply because it is you! All your blindness is there! None of this strikes your attention. And yet this is what in you keeps one world separate from another world.

You have no measure with which to measure your-selves. You live exclusively according to "I like" or "I don't like"; you have no appreciation except for yourself. You recognize nothing above you—theoretically, logically, per-haps, but actually no. That is why you are demanding and continue to believe that everything is cheap and that you have enough in your pocket to buy everything you like. You recognize nothing above you, either outside yourself or inside. That is why, I repeat, you have no measure and live passively according to your likes and dislikes.

Yes, your "appreciation of yourself" blinds you! It is the biggest obstacle to a new life. You must be able to get over this obstacle, this threshold, before going further. This test divides men into two kinds: the "wheat" and the "chaff." No matter how intelligent, how gifted, how brilliant a man may be, if he does not change his appreciation of himself, there will be no hope for an inner development, for a work toward self-knowledge, for a true becoming. He will remain such as he is all his life. The first requirement, the first condition, the first test for one who wishes to work on himself is to change his appreciation of himself. He must not imagine, not simply believe or think, but see things in himself which he has never seen before, see them actually. His appreciation will never be able to change as long as he sees nothing in himself. And in order to see, he must *learn* to see: this is the first initiation of man into self-knowledge.

First of all, he has to know what he must look at. When he knows, he must make efforts, keep his attention, look constantly with persistence. Only through maintaining his attention, and not forgetting to look, one day, perhaps, he will be able to see. If he sees one time he can see a second time, and if that continues he will no longer be able not to see. This is the state to be looked for, it is the aim of our observation; it is from there that the true wish will be born, the irresistible wish to become: from cold we shall become warm, vibrant; we shall by touched by our reality.

Today we have nothing but the illusion of what we are. We think too highly of ourselves. We do not respect ourselves. In order to respect myself, I have to recognize a part in myself which is above the other parts, and my attitude toward this part should bear witness to the respect that I have for it. In this way I shall respect myself. And my relations with others will be governed by the same respect.

You must understand that all the other measures—talent, education, culture, genius—are changing measures, measures of detail. The only exact measure, the only unchanging, objective real measure is the measure of inner vision. *I see—I see myself*—by this, you have measured. With one higher real part, you have measured another lower part, also real. And this measure, defining by itself the role of each part, will lead you to respect for yourself.

But you will see that it is not easy. And it is not cheap. You must pay dearly. For bad payers, lazy people, parasites, no hope. You must pay, pay a lot, and pay immediately, pay in advance. Pay with yourself. By sincere, conscientious, disinterested efforts. The more you are prepared to pay without economizing, without cheating, without any falsification, the more you will receive. And from that time on you will become acquainted with your nature. And you will see all the tricks, all the dishonesties that your nature resorts to in order to avoid paying hard cash. Because you have to pay with your ready-made theories, with your rooted convictions, with your prejudices, your conventions, your "I like" and "I don't like." Without bargaining, honestly, without pretending. Trying "sincerely" to see as you offer your counterfeit money.

Try for a moment to accept the idea that you are not what you believe yourself to be, that you overestimate yourself, in fact that you lie to yourself. That you always lie to yourself, every moment, all day, all your life. That this lying rules you to such an extent that you cannot control it any more. You are the prey of lying. You lie, everywhere. Your relations with others—lies. The upbringing you give, the conventions—lies. Your teaching—lies. Your theories, your art—lies. Your social life, your family life—lies. And what you think of yourself—lies also.

But you never stop yourself in what you are doing or in what you are saying, because you believe in yourself. You must stop inwardly and observe. Observe without preconceptions, accepting for a time this idea of lying. And if you observe in this way, paying with yourself, without self-pity, giving up all your supposed riches for a moment of reality, perhaps you will suddenly see something you have never before seen in yourself until this day. You will see that you are different from what you think you are. You will see that you are two. One who is not, but takes the place and plays the role of the other. And one who is, yet so weak, so insubstantial, that he no sooner appears than he immediately disappears. He cannot endure lies. The least lie makes him faint away. He does not struggle, he does not resist, he is defeated in advance. Learn to look until you have seen the difference between your two natures, until you have seen the lies, the deception in yourself. When you have seen your two natures, that day, in yourself, the truth will be born.

•

CHAPTER FIVE

ONLY HE WILL BE CALLED AND WILL BECOME THE SON OF GOD WHO ACQUIRES IN HIMSELF CONSCIENCE

—Beelzebub's Tales to His Grandson

Parabola
Volume: 22.3
Conscience and
Consciousness

THERE ARE TWO RIVERS

G. I. Gurdjieff

Question: There are two rivers—how can a drop go from the first to the second?

Answer: It must buy a ticket. It is necessary to realize that only he can cross who has some real possibility of changing. This possibility depends on desire, strong wish of a very special kind, wishing with the essence, not with the personality. You must understand that it is very difficult to be sincere with yourself, and a man is very much afraid of seeing the truth.

Sincerity is a function of conscience. Every man has a conscience—it is a property of normal human beings. But owing to civilization this function has become crusted over and has ceased to work, except in special circumstances where the associations are very strong. Then, it functions for a little time and disappears again. Such moments are due to strong shock, great sorrow, or insult. At these times conscience unites personality and essence, which otherwise are altogether separate.

•

Parabola
Volume: 8.1
Guilt

THE SEARCH FOR LUCIDITY

An interview with Michel de Salzmann

Dr. Michel de Salzmann was concerned, as he said in a talk given in California in 1975, with both psychotherapy and the sacred. "Generally speaking I would call them both schools of self knowledge," he said. Both "originated from the need to answer our central existential question, 'Who am I?'" But he goes on to say that "though they answer the same need, it is important that they not be confused, especially if we realize they are operating on two different levels."

Parabola: *There have been big changes in our ideas about human nature during this century, and notably in the concept of guilt. How would you approach that?*

Michel de Salzmann: Of course the idea of change refers us also, implicitly, to something that does not change. The concept of guilt carries various insights and connotations that certainly need to be sorted out.

I think one should start by acknowledging that throughout history, guilt is, above all rooted in, the actual fact of law transgression. It is of central importance to start with that approach, since law embodies the conceptions and principles that regulate the life and the meaning of a society and, in a way, has made us what we are.

In traditional societies, law is considered to originate from above and its violation means profanation; that is, it

•

impedes the circulation of the sacred within the body of the community. Of course we don't need to point out the atrocities which, today, the degradation and imperialistic application of such a perspective have led to. In contrast, for the "primitive" mind the indivisible community works essentially as a medium between the sacred and the individual, and any fault or alienation is seen as a cellular symptom of a social disease which requires specific readjustment of the group in order to restore its fundamental function. The individual in this "primitive" society is supported by—and integrated into—an all-embracing network of significations.

P: *This seems far from our personal guilt feelings.*

MS: Yes, indeed. In such a perspective guilt is much more objectified. Our modern mind has originated from, or at least been decisively conditioned by, the split between the spiritual and the temporal, which has induced dualistic and therefore materialistic attitudes; and now it finds itself plunged into a fragmented world where it feels alone and overwhelmed by the challenge of putting all the pieces together. Individualism and its related sense of freedom is the very heavy tribute we have to pay for this fragmentation, since the individual becomes at the same time overburdened with responsibility. Existentialism, for instance, is a heart-rending echo of this situation and centers the human problem precisely around freedom, choice, responsibility, consciousness, and anxiety.

The problem of guilt, as I see it, has progressively shifted from a factual approach to a subjective problem relating, perhaps too much, to the inner "economy" of the individual. Today, guilt is much more related to what we *think* is reprehensible than to what *is* in fact reprehensible, if you see what I mean.

P: *Do you regret that?*

MS: There is no use regretting it. We have to deal with our situation as it is. The point is to try to understand it in order to be able to move towards what appears more real. Just a few minutes ago, for instance, my hastily expressed shortcut through history was so abrupt that I realize it has not conveyed properly what I had in mind, and will inevitably be misleading; yet it is done. I am factually and objectively "guilty," but I may try to do better now. I am probably too modern to follow the example of Vatel, a celebrated cook in the time of Louis the XIVth, who killed himself because of an unsuccessful sauce, or that of the samurai, who, in the event of a serious failure, would consider hara-kiri. We should understand, however, the point of view that made it so important in older days not to "lose face." This face is not "personal" in the restricted sense we usually give this word; it is the actual function or role through which an individual is led, through serving something, to find his significance, his share, his relation to the world he belongs to.

We cannot understand ourselves outside our relation to something. And we desperately need to find our true relation toward things outside and inside ourselves, to find order and justice through discovering reality. This happens when we are aware of ourselves here and now, aware of actual "functioning." The great significance of Watergate, quite beyond the political scene, is that it reminds us that the function is, in a way, prior to the individual; it is really what creates him. And here we should not despise the alarm signal that guilt feelings represent, since they help us remember there is something greater than our ego-centered world.

P: *We have to come to that. But is it not the psychological view today that guilt is an unnecessary burden, something to be gotten rid of?*

MS: Yes, this has to do with another perspective, equally worthy, but applying to the laws that regulate our subjective experience and functioning.

Biologically, and still more psychologically, each individual has his own specificity. There are of course basic constants in our structural organization, but the numerous elements of this structure and their interactions have great individual variations both from the quantitative and qualitative point of view. The sum of our hereditary and acquired equipment gives each of us certain aptitudes and limitations, a certain type, a certain character, and a behavior that distinguishes us from others.

There are people who apparently don't seem to feel guilt, and others in whom it reaches a highly pathological level. One must not forget that it is the study of extreme cases, including neuroses and psychoses, which made it possible for psychoanalysis to elaborate its explanatory system of the functioning of the so-called normal man. And thanks to psychoanalysis, we are much more capable today of understanding the extent to which feelings of guilt can be destructive. We all know that self-accusation can engender such a deprecation of ourselves that we feel ourselves completely annihilated, emptied, inhibited even in our most elementary functions, without appetite, without desire, as if having forfeited the right to existence. For must of us, no accusation coming from the outside could ever have the devastating power of self-accusation. It is only in the little child that similar stresses can be observed, linked to fear and dependence with regard to the almighty adult. In guilt we relive this very same situation; we regress to an infantile state in which we feel ourselves powerless in front of a dominating and punitive inner "agency."

P: *How does this appear? Where does this "agency" come from?*

MS: An extensive treatise would be needed to give an account of the psychoanalytic theory. I can only simplify to the extreme certain fundamental notions.

To answer your question, psychoanalysis shows that the child, through the action of complex mechanisms such as introjection and identification, incorporates and assimilates in himself an aspect or an attribute of another person, and thus transforms himself partially or totally in accordance with this model. By interiorization of parental demands and prohibitions, which are reinforced as time goes on by social and cultural influences, there is formed an agency of the child's personality—or psychic apparatus—that Freud called the super-ego. Its role is that of a judge or a censor as regards the ego, which is another agency of the psychic apparatus that appeared earlier and from which the super-ego has, as it were, differentiated and split off. In the classical theory, the super-ego is the heir to the Oedipus complex. Other theories suggest that it may already appear in pre-Oedipal stages and even much more precociously.

According to psychoanalysis, functions such as conscience, self-observation, and, to a large extent, the formation of ideals are functions of the super-ego. The important thing to realize is that our ideas or presentations and our "affects" are diversely loaded with a certain psychic energy, which can convert itself into various forms. This energy of "cathexis" which, free or bound, is involved in the different psychic processes, comes forth from internal sources called drives. All drives themselves emanate from a primary reservoir of psychic energy called the id. The id is the first agency of the psychic apparatus, out of which are genetically differentiated the ego and super-ego. These two come into conflict with the id, because it obliges them, as it were, to work continuously according to their respective requirements, at transforming an energetic push of which the libidinal or sexual energy is an essential part.

So all processes within the psychic apparatus are thus regulated by the dynamic and intersystemic relations between its three principal agencies; id, ego, and super-ego. The ego, which poses as the mediator in charge of the interests of the whole person, has in reality a very limited autonomy, since it is dependent upon the demands of the id, the imperatives of the super-ego and the requirements of outer reality. Guilt results from the tension, sometimes very acute, between the super-ego and the ego, under the pressure of aggressiveness and infantile sexual desires.

I needn't say any more about this conception which has put its imprint so deeply on psychology. I should only emphasize that each of the psychoanalytical concepts can become clear (in its complexity) only when it is considered in relation to the other concepts, and according to a specific perspective which reflects one of the following definite points of view: topographic, dynamic, or economic.

P: *Where is the anxiety linked to guilt supposed to come from?*

MS: Guilt would remain a simple problem if it were always appropriate to the situation, as it often is or seems to be in normal behavior. Everybody could easily understand that I may have a painful perception of having betrayed my ideals or some explicit moral law. But it becomes more complicated when the reason invoked seems inadequate, if not totally absurd, as is often the case in neuroses and psychoses. Moreover, the problem will appear insoluble when there seems to be no reason at all for guilt, when it presents itself as a diffuse feeling of unworthiness with no reference to a precise action or motivation. Freud's great achievement was to shed light on that enigma through demonstrating the fact of repression and the various mechanisms related to the unconscious. I am using the term "unconscious" here more as an adjective than as the designation for an independent or "topical" system; it qualifies the id and partly the ego and super-ego. One can often observe in delinquents that a sense of guilt does not follow the misdemeanor but precedes it, constituting somehow its deep motive; as though the youngster found relief in finding a justification, a real object for his guilt feelings. Likewise in neurotic behavior, guilt appears as an unconscious system of motivation which leads to and explains all kinds of sufferings that the subject inflicts on himself in a more or less spectacular and symbolic form. Failure-behavior is, for instance, an illustration of this compulsion to self-punishment. The psychoanalytic view is that all guilt problems originate from the Oedipus complex, and that pathological or behavioral types are characterized by a specific position in relation to this basic triangle. If not resolved in a satisfactory way it continues to manifest its pathogenic action. Anxiety is mainly related to the threats of castration—including all its symbolic equivalents—which have from the beginning motivated repression.

P: *It seems that the classical psychoanalytical perspective is losing ground today, especially in the United States. Are there new trends that tend to cover it up or move away from it?*

MS: Is it true that even though it contains broader intuitions which we did not speak about, such as Eros and Thanatos, one does not get an "oceanic" impression from it but rather that of wading in a closed pool. It has a taste of prison. One can understand that some of Freud's direct disciples like Jung felt the need to open the doors in order to enlarge the perspective and situate the problem beyond the limits of individual and cultural consciousness.

According to Jung, there is a collective consciousness, beyond our individual memory, representing an immense potential from which we can draw force and meaning. The unconscious for Jung is not a residue of consciousness (as it is, in part, according to the psychoanalytic theory of repression) but the matrix of consciousness. The "self" in his perspective is the center of the total psyche—including the unconscious and consciousness—and from it emerges the ego, which becomes the center of a developing consciousness. Through consciousness there is actualized a continuing process of maturation, of "individuation"—making possible both differentiation (or uniqueness) of the person and recognition of its fundamental collective make-up—when the ego is aware of a purpose of its own that is embedded in the unconscious. If the ego is properly aware of the values and messages that are sent to it by this "Great Mother," which is the unconscious—notably through dreams but also by various other means—it can realize a powerful and meaningful creativity. Absence of communication, discordance between self and ego, will inevitably create indicative symptoms, which it is important to respect and listen to for a readjustment to inner harmony. Guilt is therefore a symptom related to ego betrayal of self values. Recognized as such, it may further the individuation process—together with the help of meditation and other daily spiritual practice—and can lead to seeing one's place in the universe and to taking part in a larger accomplishment.

Likewise, existential thinkers and analysts criticize psychoanalysis for neglecting ontology and the problems of conscience and self-consciousness. Guilt, when close to anxiety, has to be acknowledged, accepted, and "practiced" in order to fill the gap between "where we are now" and "where we want to be," without indulging in daydreaming. When not appropriate to the situation, anxiety is neurotic and leads to psychosomatic symptoms because of repression. When it is not appropriate to a threat and does not involve repression but active attitudes and awareness, its very tension becomes a source of creativity.

I think one might say that there is a unanimous agreement in psychology today that the real pathogenic factor in our conflicts is repression, however it is conceived of. This also means that the only breakthrough is consciousness. And consciousness leads to reparation, which is universally recognized as the unique specific medicine for guilt feelings.

P: *How do you reconcile psychoanalytical views and views of a spiritual order, such as those you seem to have?*

MS: They are concerned, in my opinion, with different levels. Psychoanalysis, as I approach it, is above all an access to autonomy, and to adulthood, as well as an authentic and difficult test of truth, all the more justified since "only the truth sets us free."

As in any other field of research, psychoanalysis elaborates working hypotheses, many of which prove to be, in practice, extremely helpful. There is a level of lower functioning, unconscious and mechanical, where we are indisputably conditioned by factors that psychoanalysis has very clearly defined. Furthermore, it introduces, in terms of energy, a dynamic (in the sense of conflicting forces) approach to psychic processes; and this, to me, is the most interesting aspect of the revolution in ideas that it represents.

I should mention, however, that highly developed conceptions of the transformation of energy, especially of sexual energy, have always existed in traditional teachings, such as Tantrism—to mention only this one. Freud, in contradistinction to Jung, was not favorably disposed to making a real study of them. But even Jung himself didn't seem to establish there a difference of levels. It seems to me his system does not open to transcendence.

Doubtless it is difficult, when one steps into a system, to see anything except what the system shows you, to avoid its specific blindness. But it is possible, in my opinion, without falling into syncretism, to carry on work of a psychoanalytical nature without adhering to the general doctrine. It is possible to center the work—as, moreover, Freud insisted toward the end—not on interpretation, but primarily on awareness in depth of resistances and on objectifying them, in order to help the ego free itself within its essential function, that of lucidity. It remains for it then to assume its role before many great mysteries, which place guilt in another perspective as a stimulating factor for larger and higher responsibility. And this responsible choice cannot be reduced to a sort of obligatory, civilized retreat into sublimation; it arises from listening to the echo within ourselves of a definite call to be.

P: *From this more conscious level, are there steps that might be taken to enable the ego to accept or refuse the judgment of the super-ego, and thus escape from unconscious guilt?*

MS: Well, of course, first of all we should use our ability to test reality—our ability not to confuse what we actually perceive with what we represent to ourselves. In observing our life more closely, we must certainly be struck by how far from objective we are and how much we interpret and react according to our fantasies, emotional reactions, or conditioning.

This, by the way, shows the importance of sound education. We should not only teach principles but let them be practically tested and experienced. Guilt is closely related to ignorance of what reality is. Let us not forget that law transgression, for instance, may have beneficial aspects: it awakens us to a better understanding of real order. The original meaning of "carnival" was the intentional, temporary turning upside-down of everything, the throwing out of all values, in order to refresh and clarify the inward and outward need for order. Of course, there must be proper indications for such a medicine; in an orderless life, "carnival" just brings more disorder.

The law reminds us that guilt is inseparable from responsibility—that is, from the existence of an alternative, of a choice. We are thus led to the problem of free will, of freedom. But none of this could exist without consciousness. One might say that consciousness is the key to freedom—freedom to see the choice, to start with. But this key is much more rarely used than we think. Most of the time there is no real consciousness of what takes place in us. We take for consciousness what really is simply perception, instead of the result of a confrontation of our situation with all that constitutes our make-up. Most of the time we follow what we passively call "the better choice," essentially in order to not to be misjudged by others. We have inherited a system of values with which we identify ourselves, but I think we should try to make use of it more actively, try somehow to deserve it, see whether we can really make it ours and not simply remain slaves of it. In other words, I think it is important to develop clearly an idea, an ego-ideal which is felt as independent from the super-ego. This ideal might be lucidity.

P: *You touch here something very important, that in our times it seems essential to clarify. In some people, especially those of older generations, the betrayal of their super-ego immediately engenders guilt feelings. In other people there is no guilt, not even that of a delinquent; there is instead a sort of notion of natural freedom without constraint. This idea is obviously reflected in today's society where authority is flouted and values are overthrown. One attempts to turn towards an ideal distant from the super-ego but it nevertheless remains marked by it: it is a way of escape from conformist guilt, but one is recaptured by another form of recognized opinion, which is not lucidity.*

MS: I quite agree. Lucidity is a very high objective. One must first become aware of all the pulls to which the ego is submitted—we have talked about that—and then of the various unconscious defense mechanisms which it has elaborated to protect itself against what it does not want to see. This is particularly difficult to grasp. Other obstacles are raised by the power of suggestion, the tendencies inherent in our character, our various habits, the mechanisms of projection and identification, etc. A great inner tranquility is needed to estimate, understand, taste in a direct, experiential way the instability of the ego. Psychoanalytical experience helps toward that, and so do relaxation techniques when well oriented.

It is a progressive work, going through stages. Trying to succeed immediately in obtaining results is an additional obstacle. As one goes on, one learns to keep in touch with difficulties, to see them in order to get free from them.

In fact, the ego is our attention. It needs to be free and pure. Only through our errors, our gropings, the many traps that threaten our attention, can we discover the way to interiority. All authentic spiritual ways lead to that. But the way is very long. To become conformable to one's essential nature is the most anti-conformist work that can be conceived. It needs total freedom of attention. Meditation and a wide range of exercises are necessary. But fortunately, through what in Christianity is called "grace," light is given, orientation comes, a call is heard. Doubtless, it needs a great quietness, emptiness, transparency to let this influence work upon us. But it is far from being a passive state; it is an action that requires ultimate awareness from the whole being.

P: *You have spoken of grace. It is a word which does not suggest any image, any form, any structure.*

MS: Yes, and analogically, pure attention is beyond word, form, image, and thought—I mean our usual thought. It is often referred to as a living light. When it acts, duality merges into oneness. There is no more room for guilt then. Guilt—or to use a better word, conscious remorse—is nevertheless of dynamic help to put ourselves into question, and recall us to the need of being present, of being purely attentive.

P: *Could we say that the idea of guilt could become indeed a very healthy and powerful catalyst, if we didn't stick to its usual superficial image? If it is taken as a real mystery that has to be explored, like the idea that it originates with the fall of man; if we accept it as a provocation to live a mystery, a research, then this confused feeling becomes a dynamic support in the search for lucidity, especially if we accept not to succeed and continue constantly to reexplore the mystery. The great danger is to accept that without questioning it; it would then lose its power.*

MS: Yes, but we must admit there are degrees, levels, in any learning process. The mystery issues into the infinite, which by definition cannot be defined. But guilt at first refers to idols, to objects of the mind; and spiritual evolution may involve passing from one idol to another until you are able to live the mystery fully. You necessarily start in duality until you reach a point where there is no observer and no observed. Idol dependency is, I think, related to our dependency upon the big world of associations. All our psychic life is governed by the associative process, of which we may nevertheless become conscious. It is terribly difficult to escape this dense dynamic network, but still it is possible to become free from it, thanks to other laws operating in watchfulness.

P: *Among intellectuals and scientists, the acceptance of idols of course raises guilt feelings—as if they were afraid of regressing to some barbarian state and want to make a stand against everything that could appear spiritual.*

MS: I quite share this resistance towards whatever is believed without experimenting and experiencing. Science may be an idol as well. For me, real spirituality is as rigorous as science. They should not contradict but complement each other in order to find what is beyond and animates them both. This attitude seems to gain more and more ground among researchers. André Malraux, one of our great writers, who under de Gaulle's government was appointed Minister of Culture, even ventured these prophetic words: "The twenty-first century will be religious or it will not be at all!"

P: *Would you think there is more guilt in individuals and in society now than in our parents' or grandparents' time?*

MS: Yes, at first sight it seems paradoxical—probably because of our rooted belief in the idea of evolution and progress, and because there has indeed been amazing progress made from many points of view—but I would nevertheless say there is more guilt today.

We also feel powerless in the face of all the problems on a planetary scale with which we are now confronted daily by the media. Sociological and ecological dangers, as well as technology's threats of destruction, mobilize anxiety and our latent guilt feelings all the more because we do not see clearly what can be done, and what is being done doesn't make us feel more secure. I imagine the dreams of present state leaders would be informative with respect to your question. As never before, both the individual and society are confronted with the inescapable necessity to call forth all their potentials to solve the world's vital, overwhelming problems.

We are going through a crisis of civilization where older values are severely shaken and new values not yet settled. We are not supported any more by a system of clearly accepted principles, giving meaning to all aspects and events of our daily life. In our modern society life has been progressively de-ritualized, de-sacralized. Such institutions as marriage, family, state, etc., have lost their structuring function. Pragmatic and economic points of view have discarded the old holistic conceptions of the world. And man is not only an animal: his make-up is such that meaning is of higher importance to him than food or sex. Totally deprived of meaning, he falls into guilt and depression. This essential need for meaning, which rationalism does not answer satisfactorily, is reflected, I think, in the present blossoming of new religions and sects.

Lack of true meaning, that is, of sound relation to what exists around us, makes us feel lonely and ego-centered. Egoism and separatedness are, I think, deep motives for guilt.

Parabola
Volume: 30.1
Awakening

Becoming Aware of Genuine Being-Duty

G. I. Gurdjieff

When the captain had gone, Beelzebub glanced at his grandson and, noticing his unusual state, asked with concern and a shade of anxiety:

"What is the matter, my dear boy? What are you thinking about so deeply?"

Looking up at his grandfather with eyes full of sorrow, Hassein said thoughtfully: "I don't know what is the matter with me, dear Grandfather, but your talk with the captain has brought me to some exceedingly melancholy thoughts. Things I never thought of before are now a-thinking in me.

"Thanks to your talk, it has gradually become clear to my consciousness that in the Universe of our Endlessness things have not always been as I now see and imagine them.

"Formerly I should never have allowed myself to imagine, even if the thought had come to me by association, that this ship we are flying on, for instance, has not always been just as it is now.

"Only now have I come to understand clearly that everything we have and use today, all the contemporary amenities and everything necessary for our comfort and welfare, did not always exist, nor did they make their appearance so easily.

•

"It seems that in the past certain beings must have labored hard and suffered very much for all this, and endured a great deal that perhaps they could have spared themselves. They labored and suffered solely that we might have these advantages today and use them for our welfare.

"And all this, consciously, they did for us—beings quite unknown and entirely indifferent to them.

"And now not only do we not thank them, but we do not even know anything about them, and take it all as a matter of course, and neither ponder this question nor trouble ourselves in the slightest about it.

"I, for instance, have already existed so many years in the Universe, yet the thought has never entered my head that perhaps there was a time when everything I see and have did not exist, and that everything was not born with me like my nose.

"And so, my dear and kind Grandfather, since your conversation with the captain has gradually made me aware of all this with the whole of my presence, the need has arisen in me to make clear to my Reason why I personally have these advantages, and what obligations I am under on their account.

"It is just because of this that there now arises in me a 'process of remorse.'"

Having said this, Hassein bowed his head and became silent.

Looking at him affectionately, Beelzebub began to speak as follows:

"I advise you, my dear Hassein, not to put such questions to yourself yet. Be patient. Only when you reach the corresponding period of your existence for becoming aware of such essence-questions, and reflect actively upon them, will you understand what you must do in return.

"At your age, you are not yet obliged to pay for your existence.

"This present period of your life is not given you for paying for your existence, but for preparing yourself for the future—for the obligations becoming to a responsible three-brained being.

"So in the meantime, exist as you exist. Only do not forget one thing: at your age, it is indispensable that every day when the sun rises, while watching the reflection of its splendor, you bring about a contact between your consciousness and the various unconscious parts of your common presence. Trying to make this state last; think and convince the unconscious parts—as if they were conscious—that if they hinder your general functioning in the process of ordinary existence, then in the period of your responsible age they will not only be unable to enjoy the good that is proper to them, but also your whole presence, of which they are a part, will not be capable of becoming a good servant of our Common Endless Creator, and will thus be unable to pay honorably for your arising and existence.

"I repeat once more, dear boy, try in the meantime not to think of these questions: at your age it is still too early to think about them.

"Everything in its proper time!

"Now ask me whatever you wish, and I will tell you. As the captain has not yet returned, he must be occupied with his duties and will not be coming back for quite a while."

Parabola
Volume: 14.4
Triad

THE HORSE, THE CARRIAGE, AND THE DRIVER

G. I. Gurdjieff

Maybe you remember it being said that man is like a rig consisting of passenger, driver, horse and carriage. Except there can be no question of the passenger, for he is not there, so we can only speak of the driver. Our mind is the driver. ...

Inside us we have a horse; it obeys orders from outside. And our mind is too weak to do anything inside. Even if the mind gives the order to stop, nothing will stop inside.

We educate nothing but our mind. We know how to behave with such and such. "Goodbye." "How do you do?" But it is only the driver who knows this. Sitting on his box he has read about it. But the horse has no education whatever. It has not even been taught the alphabet, it knows no languages, it never went to school. The horse was also capable of being taught, but we forgot all about it. ... And so it grew up a neglected orphan. It only knows two words: right and left.

What I said about inner change refers only to the need of change in the horse. If the horse changes, we can change externally. If the horse does not change, everything will remain the same, no matter how long we study.

It is easy to decide to change sitting quietly in your room. But as soon as you meet someone, the horse kicks. Inside us we have a horse.

•

The horse must change.

If anyone thinks that self-study will help and he will be able to change, he is greatly mistaken. Even if he reads all the books, studies for a hundred years, masters all knowledge, all mysteries—nothing will come of it.

Because all this knowledge will belong to the driver. And he, even if he knows, cannot drag the cart without the horse—it is too heavy.

First of all you must realize that you are not you. Be sure of that, believe me. You are the horse, and if you wish to start working, the horse must be taught a language in which you can talk to it, tell it what you know and prove to it the necessity of, say, changing its disposition. If you succeed in this, then, with your help, the horse too will begin to learn.

But change is possible only inside.

As to the cart, its existence was completely forgotten. Yet it is also a part, and an important part, of the team. It has its own life, which is the basis of our life. It has its own psychology. It also thinks, is hungry, has desires, takes part in the common work. It too should have been educated, sent to school, but neither the parents nor anyone else cared. Only the driver was taught. He knows languages, knows where such and such a street is. But he cannot drive there alone.

Originally our cart was built for an ordinary town; all the mechanical parts were designed to suit the road. The cart has many small wheels. The idea was that the unevennesses of the road would distribute the lubricating oil evenly and thus oil them. But all this was calculated for a certain town where the roads are not too smooth. Now the town has changed, but the make of the cart has remained the same. It was made to cart luggage, but now it carries passengers. And it always drives along one and the same street, the "Broadway." Some parts got rusty from long disuse. If, at times, it needs to drive along a different street, it seldom escapes a breakdown and a more or less serious overhaul afterwards. Badly or well, it can still work on the "Broadway," but for another street it must first be altered. ...

Question: *Why was the horse not educated?*

Answer: The grandfather and grandmother gradually forgot, and all the relatives forgot. Education needs time, needs suffering; life becomes less peaceful. At first they did not educate it through laziness, and later they forgot altogether.

Here again, the law of three works. Between the positive and the negative principles there must be friction, suffering. Suffering leads to the third principle. It is a hundred times easier to be passive so that suffering and result happen outside and not inside you. Inner result is achieved when everything takes place inside you.

Sometimes we are active, at other times we are passive. For one hour we are active, for another hour passive.

When we are active we are being spent, when we are passive we rest. But when everything is inside you, you cannot rest, the law acts always. Even if you do not suffer, you are not quiet.

Every man dislikes suffering, every man wants to be quiet. Every man chooses what is easiest, least disturbing, tries not to think too much. Little by little our grandfather and grandmother rested more and more. The first day, five minutes of rest; the next day, ten minutes; and so on. A moment came when half of the time was spent on rest. And the law is such that if one thing increases by a unit, another thing decreases by a unit. Where there is more it is added, where there is less it is reduced. Gradually your grandfather and grandmother forgot about educating the horse. And now no one remembers any more.

Question: *How to begin inner change?*

Answer: You should begin to teach the horse a new language, prepare it for the desire to change.

The cart and the horse are connected. The horse and the driver are also connected by the reins. The horse knows two words—right and left. At times the driver cannot give orders to the horse because our reins have the capacity now to thicken, now to become more thin. They are not made of leather. When our reins become more thin, the driver cannot control the horse. The horse knows only the language of the reins. No matter how much the driver shouts, "Please, right," the horse does not budge. If he pulls, it understands. Perhaps the horse knows some language but not the one the driver knows. ...

We must understand the difference between a casual passenger and the master of the cart. "I" is the master, if we have an "I." If we have not, there is always someone sitting in the cart and giving orders to the driver. Between the passenger and the driver there is a substance which allows the driver to hear. Whether these substances are there or not depends on many accidental things. It may be absent. If the substance has accumulated, the passenger can give orders to the driver, but the driver cannot order the horse, and so on. At times you can, at others you cannot; it depends on the amount of substance there is. Tomorrow you can, today you cannot. This substance is the result of many things.

One of these substances is formed when we suffer. We suffer whenever we are not mechanically quiet. There are different kinds of suffering. For instance, I want to tell you something, but I feel it is best to say nothing. One side wants to tell, the other wants to keep silent. The struggle produces a substance....

Question: *Conflict of two desires leads to suffering. Yet some suffering leads to a madhouse.*

Answer: Suffering can be of different kinds. To begin with, we shall divide it into two kinds. First, unconscious; second, conscious.

The first kind bears no results. For instance, you suffer from hunger because you have no money to buy bread. If you have some bread and don't eat it and suffer, it is better.

If you suffer with one center, either thinking or feeling, you get to a lunatic asylum.

Suffering must be harmonious. There must be correspondence between the fine and the coarse. Otherwise something may break.

Parabola
Volume: 12.2
Addiction

THE CENTER OF OUR NEED

An Interview with Pauline de Dampierre

*Pauline de Dampierre was a familiar figure to readers of
Parabola. She was featured in interviews in the issue on
"Wholeness" (10:1) and also in "The Seven Deadly Sins"
(10:4). It was a privilege to speak with her again on the
theme, "Addiction." Her penetrating thought, informed by
many years of involvement in the teaching of G. I. Gurdjieff,
both expands and refines the meaning of addiction.*
—Lorraine Kisly

Pauline de Dampierre: The first thing I'd like to know is
what you mean by addiction.

Parabola: *We started thinking about addiction with the
observation that individuals, relationships, organizations of
all kinds, appear to become fixed in repetitive patterns. We
seem to want to hold on, to stay in the same place. Meanwhile,
life is always moving. So this issue is about the fatal human
tendency to become fixed, to be attached to what was, to repeat
what has been, and to not want to move. We first thought
of calling the issue "Habit," but this term did not convey the
quality of actively clinging to something. We are interested in
rigidity in all of its forms—intellectual addictions and emotional ones as well as physical.*

PD: You remember the last time we spoke we talked about sin? Today I think about addiction as an addiction to virtue, the opposite aspect. The things you have just spoken of, the ambition, the greed, do not always come consciously from the psyche of people. So where does this come from, the element of compulsion that appears even in respect to the good? We don't really know what is acting in us at a given moment. We begin to do something with a certain intention, and without our knowing it, one or another aspect of us takes over.

Many different motivations are at play within us depending on what part is acting, what I would call a center of functioning. Let's take something obviously good—the wish to give oneself entirely to what one is doing. What could be better? For instance, a woman has to maintain her home. She has to sweep, and do other chores, and she decides to do it at her best. It puts her body in motion. According to the more or less harmonized way she is in the body, she can have a feeling of being balanced. Much of the time, however, there may be a part of her that objects to what she is doing and a certain frenzy comes into her activity. After a while, that frenzy is leading her without her knowing it; even when later she goes shopping, for instance, this same frenzy is going on. And it will also be felt by anyone she meets. She feels exhausted, she wishes to be somewhere else. She had wanted to give herself entirely to what she was doing, but one part of her has taken over the rest. And this one part has taken a great place.

P: *You are speaking of something that goes beyond momentum?* Frenzy *is a very strong word.*

PD: It is a tense momentum. There must be momentum, or it would not be possible to go from one action to another. But there can be harmonious momentum. I walk; I am relaxed. I take a step, and from the impulse of the step, as I am very relaxed, I'm led in an easy way to the next step. In this way, momentum is acting as it should. Certain nomads in the desert are said to be able to go on walking in this way for sixty miles without having to stop. Usually, we interrupt this momentum—we don't let it go smoothly—we move too abruptly so that it becomes a momentum of tension. The reason I would say it has the quality of frenzy is because it is not harmonious. Something emotional becomes invested in the physical action and takes over. And this is going on even when the action I'm doing is in itself beneficial.

P: *What do you mean by* harmony? *How could the body be in a nonaddictive state?*

PD: In addiction you have the sense of something rigid, something narrow. You would never say of an animal, for instance, that it is addicted to hunting, even if hunting plays a central part in its life. One feels that the animal acts as a harmonious whole. We can sense a lack of harmony in ourselves and in others when nervous tensions exist to the point where it's even impossible for the body to move freely.

And as human persons we are not only the body; we also have wishes, thoughts, etc. And in order to support our life, to care fully for what we are doing, we need to have an impression of well-being. We need the support of the body as something in which we feel well. Otherwise, our attention is partly taken by uneasiness. But it is not only the state of the body that may initiate the division. Maybe we are angry with someone, anxious about something. The woman who wants her house in order may perhaps feel in a hurry because she has many other things to do. She begins to do something towards her aim, and a strain comes into it—a useless strain. When this happens she is divided and has the impression of not really living; the whole is not being supported. It creates a state that persists for a long time. The state continues into other activities, so that one finds oneself feeling pushed, walking tensely, feeling irritable, hurried. So it is in that sense that we could say we are not harmonious.

P: *It seems what you are speaking of can begin in any one part of ourselves. Say someone is fanatical—about an idea, a cause, a religion. What does it mean to be a fanatic?*

PD: There are many parts to the human being, and when he's not balanced, even when he cares for something, he's not able to be entirely filled by the love he has for it. He is taken—with the same strength, if not more—by the hatred of what is opposite to it. He has an idea; and he has a love for this idea. But in himself he is also filled with hate of what is opposite to this idea, or at the very least, he can't help being dogmatic.

That feeling limits something in him—it limits a part of himself that could have a sensitivity and a broader mind. Initially the feeling in itself is good. We must be devoted to what we do. If we don't have that devotion, we won't be able to go as far as we need to go to accomplish what we wish. But it is very difficult to be devoted without being blind. The frenzy of the body can come in as well as the hatred. Again we become fixed—by something that initially was good.

P: *Addiction to virtue, as you say.*

PD: And what is the work of the mind? It is to be open to what really is—for example, what does it mean that something is good? There are many consequences to everything we do. We are part of a whole, and there are many aspects. And it is not always immediately obvious what the good is. Let's say I have a child. I want him to behave in a certain way, because I think it is bad if he doesn't behave in that way. Now, I am here with him, and I see he is going to make a mistake, and I want to prevent him from making that mistake. What is important? Is it that he does not make the mistake? Or that something in him arises so that he can be aware of what he is doing? That something coming from his own will can appear and begin to lead him? Am I able—in front of the difficulty, even the danger to the child—am I able to be open to that question?

So you see it's very difficult to have the mind, the body, and the feeling together. I may be very intelligent, I may have a very clever mind, and at the same time I may be lazy. I sit in my armchair, and I explain to everyone what should be done. But I won't get up from my armchair to help someone who is doing something in the room, because I am lazy. So there are many ways of being addicted.

P: *So addiction is a passive state, and as long as I am passive I will be addicted?*

PD: We all have had experiences of a nonpassive state—perhaps after a shock or after a great effort or a deep impression of nature. Why do some people like to climb mountains? There comes a moment when they feel that everything is in accordance. The body has worked and worked and is absolutely relaxed; it feels free and light. The air is light, and the impressions are light, and there is a sense of reaching a part of oneself that one seldom reaches, where there is that vividness. That kind of harmony is something very special. Afterwards one has the memory of it and will perhaps decide to go on and on climbing mountains. But will that help me to have that freedom in my ordinary life? That is much more important than climbing mountains. Will it help me in the midst of the responsibilities in my life, in society? Probably not.

P: *Being addicted is the same thing as being identified?*

PD: It's quite true. In the mind there is a virtue, a real virtue to which we very seldom give a place: It is the ability to be open to a question. This virtue is calm, broad, and steady, and it is ready to welcome any truth that can appear. There are so many sides in life, but we always want to come to a conclusion in our minds—to say "it should be like that." We say it should be like that, and again something closes.

P: *There seems to be a real compulsion to be certain.*

PD: And yet the whole of my mind is there to see, to be in contact with all sorts of impressions of what is real. It is not so easy. As soon as I stop being able to be open like that, I am identified with a part of myself that comes again to be fixed on an idea. We can't prevent that. It is one thing or the other. Of course, we need to have certain things fixed in us. We have to rely on decisions that we have made at a moment when we have considered a situation. These ideas that come to us are like signposts; without them we couldn't take the simplest action. An inner sensitivity could prevent us from believing too much in the absolute value of those ideas. We don't listen to it. An inner pressure is always acting in us, projecting us into one or another aspect of ourselves. Only an opening to a much more central and essential question enables us to become conscious of that, and gives us the strength to resist this inner pressure.

P: *As you were speaking about fanaticism, I was reminded of what happens to isolated tribes when they come in contact with modern culture, and when their beliefs are eroded thereby. What happens to them is what is happening to us now. Violence increases, alcoholism develops, their social structures disintegrate. It seems that we are all members of that kind of tribe today. It has many negative results, but it seems also that something more is being asked of us than has been asked before. We no longer seem to be able to simply rely on one set of beliefs. Is it a time when more is demanded? We certainly cannot afford the kind of fanaticism we now see in ourselves and all around us.*

PD: Yes, we can't afford it, but something else must be felt. The need to believe is a limitation in ourselves, but we are limited. It's not so much belief that is the problem if we are also open to the need for another quality and for more unity—then the belief will be just part of us, something very calm that will help us. If a more conscious search does not begin in us, we really won't be able to prevent those habitual tendencies from taking over. Something more subtle is needed, something created by the search of more conscious people for a spiritual opening. That opening to the need for a higher quality of life is necessary, because without that help a person will never be united within himself. Many traditions and texts speak of that opening as the greatest treasure in the world, very difficult to find, very difficult to keep. It has mostly been forgotten.

P: *It seems to be the first thing that is lost sight of. Christ, Buddha, the founders of each of the traditions, all point to it. And then as soon as they are gone, their followers begin to cling to a fixed form. One of the key conditions of this state of being open seems to be a feeling of uncertainty, of something not known. This is what is so difficult.*

PD: Because from the start there must be a help, there must be the beginning of a perception of something else. If that doesn't appear, we will begin to construct a philosophical system based on the certainty that we can't be certain. So it doesn't lead anywhere. There must be the gift of that certain light, that sensitivity to that higher quality.

P: *In looking at myself, I feel that in any kind of addiction there is an element of avoidance. I am trying to avoid something by going very strongly into something else—into one part or another part.*

PD: Because there is in us a very strong impulse of life that wants to go toward what is attractive to us at the moment. When I am blind, I am obliged to be identified in the way I am. I need to feel myself, to affirm myself, and I have no inner standpoint. But I am a human being, and I want to go to life. So it's quite true I avoid something. We always avoid something. We are partial.

P: *And feeling partial, we intensify the feeling of partiality.*

PD: Yes, why does it increase? It is because the idea I have is emphasized by something emotional. It's a part of our automatism. When that harmony is not there, every function takes a place that is not its real place. When the mind is not open to real thinking, it is led by the emotions. If I have an idea connected with an emotion, it is very difficult to accept that there could be another idea. Why will I give up an idea that I like to accept another that I don't like? There is no reason. We can't imagine how strong our attachment to ideas is, what turmoil is produced in us when we hear that our speech is not true—that it is lies. It is lies, because no word can convey more than what we are living of it at the present moment. Even the word *God.* Maybe a simple need to quieten, to come back to ourselves, will convey more of that word, even without saying it, even without knowing that it exists. If I could face the possibility of the action of the truth—in itself, not of my ideas—then I would be able to put my idea in question.

P: *We can be addicted to even the highest things. I remember that Simone Weil once said that all passions produce prodigies. She said that a gambler is capable of watching and fasting for days and that we must not love God the way a gambler loves his game.*

PD: When there is a need to be open to something higher, a sensitivity to the state in which one is begins to develop. It is very important. It is a part of consciousness that is not developed in our civilization. It has nothing to do with the belief that something is bad, that I shouldn't be that way, but it is a sensitivity to a coarseness in us. Simone Weil in another place spoke of gravity and grace. This coarseness is related to a certain state of the body, a certain agitation of feeling, a tenseness of the mind. The wish for openness is brought about by the awareness of all that. It is part of what is truthful in that wish—the awareness that we are not in a state that corresponds to what we wish for. After a while that awareness is very important in life, because we cannot be open in a meditative state all day long. Life requires us to be active. But one can stay open to the awareness that there is something coarse in oneself. And then one begins not to be like a gambler.

I would come back to what I said in our talk about the sins. You remember the two statues in the cathedral representing virtue and vice and the need to stay between the two? You have to stay in between.

P: *Certain traditions seem to encourage one-sidedness—they might even declare that we need to be addicted to God. Is there a danger there? We may be completely open and completely surrendering at one moment, and then at the next moment, we have another motive.*

PD: I always feel uneasy responding to specific questions about other ways, questions that others could answer much better. But it seems to me that everything depends on how the surrendering is approached. If people are called to give themselves entirely, with a very open body, with absolutely no wish on the body's part to go its own way with impatience and tensions, absolutely surrendering to that love, with the mind very alert to see the exact moment when the submitting is no longer there, then a great deal might be possible.

P: *The danger comes when something is forced?*

PD: We must be very modest and know that we are able to understand every idea only partially. But I would say that today there is a "way of understanding" that corresponds to a wish to know what is true, and that wish could be more at the center of our need. We can feel a necessity for harmony in ourselves that comes from the discovery—our own discovery—of *not* being in harmony. We have a real need to develop a sensitivity to what is finer and deeper. It is a real, living energy, and what does it require from us to be in contact with it? I think that is at the center of what a real search is.

P: *Gurdjieff says to repeat, repeat, repeat. Repetition seems to create intensity—mechanical repetition creates intensity and conscious repetition also.*

PD: In the repetition of the litany, for example, even if one is able to say a single word with that need, something new can appear.

I have been speaking of nonaddiction, but at the end there must be addiction to nonaddiction. It means that one should be able to accept the inevitability of being addicted, and also the reality that it is possible not to be addicted. Then if we take the example of the litany, where the words are there as a support for my mind and to which the feeling has the possibility of corresponding, I may realize at some time that I am totally unable to focus—that I am distracted, that my mind is tense, or that I no longer care. If for one second I recognize that all of this activity coming from my functioning is absolutely incapable of achieving anything, the place is made in me ready to receive.

P: *Is this what a state of nonaddiction would mean?*

PD: Yes, but we have to exercise in life also. There is a simple way in life just through casual observations of being too much addicted to something—I'm addicted to my tensions, and I notice them. I'm addicted to my emotions—I begin to brood, and I can recognize a certain activity of my energy when I am emotional. There is a certain vibration we can recognize that begins to create agitation. We can begin to feel it burning and sense that the body does not feel well. We are too much addicted to all the ideas that are in our heads; we can also sense this. We are always addicted unconsciously to that inner pressure. When we discover this, we are led back to ourselves, and all of this uprising of useless energy begins to fall away. It comes by itself, because there is in us a natural tendency to balance when the need is felt, just as when the body, if it is falling, has a natural tendency to right itself.

P: *It is natural and yet rare.*

PD: Because, as with every natural tendency, there is also the opposite.

P: *Why is it so difficult if it is natural?*

PD: Why is it so difficult? The first thing is to discover that it really is so—to feel how strong is one's slavery and how much we lose of our life at any moment. Certain teachings coming from ancient traditions can explain to us: the idea of the Fall, of illusion; the idea that human beings are on earth to be related to higher spiritual energies as well as those of their own earthly natures. They were born for that, called to that, and in doing so, called to the life of their true being. And when this happens to be felt, such an urge to find an issue arises that the real question is no longer "why?" but "how?"!

It is very striking to see that when people begin to open to this need, even the simplest contact they have with something finer in themselves, they very naturally feel a sense of duty towards it—nobody needs to tell them. It is very intimate. So something is there, even though it is not at all developed in our civilization. It has been forgotten long ago.

P: *But the need is still there?*

PD: Of course. Why wouldn't it be?

Parabola
Volume: 11.3
Sadness

I Am Dead Because
I Lack Desire

René Daumal

I am dead because I lack desire;
I lack desire because I think I possess;
I think I possess because I do not try to give.
In trying to give, you see that you have nothing;
Seeing you have nothing, you try to give of yourself;
Trying to give of yourself, you see that you are nothing;
Seeing you are nothing, you desire to become;
In desiring to become, you begin to live.

René Daumal, *Mount Analogue* (New York: Pantheon Books, 1960).

Parabola
Volume: 8.3
Words of Power

Learning to Pray

P. D. Ouspensky

One must learn to pray, just as one must learn everything else. Whoever knows how to pray and is able to concentrate in the proper way, his prayer can give results. But it must be understood that there are different prayers and that their results are different. This is known even from ordinary divine service. But when we speak of prayer or of the results of prayer we always imply only one kind of prayer—petition, or we think that petition can be united with all other kinds of prayers. This of course is not true. Most prayers have nothing in common with petitions. I speak of ancient prayers; many of them are much older than Christianity. These prayers are, so to speak, *recapitulations*; by repeating them aloud or to himself a man endeavors to experience what is in them, their whole content, with his mind and his feeling.

In Christian worship there are very many prayers … where it is necessary to reflect upon each word. But they lose all sense and all meaning when they are repeated or sung mechanically.

Take the ordinary *God have mercy upon me!* What does it mean? A man is appealing to God. He should think a little, he should make a comparison and ask himself what God is and what he is. Then he is asking God to have *mercy* upon him. But for this God must first of all *think of him, take notice of him*. But is it worth while taking notice of him? What is there in him that is worth thinking about? And who is to think about him? God himself. You see, all these thoughts and yet many others should pass through his mind when he utters this simple prayer. *And then it is precisely these thoughts which could do for him what he asks God to do.* But what can he be thinking of and what result can a prayer give if he merely repeats like a parrot: "God have mercy! God have mercy! God have mercy!" You know yourself that this can give no result whatever.

Excerpt from *In Search of the Miraculous: Fragments of an Unknown Teaching*, by P. D. Ouspensky. Copyright © 1949 and renewed 1977 by Tatiana Nagro. Reprinted by permission of Harcourt, Inc.

Parabola
Volume: 21.4
Play and Work

A Child's Ground
of Discovery

An Interview with Margaret Flinsch

*Margaret Flinsch, a longtime student of G. I. Gurdjieff and
sister of D. M. Dooling, the founder of Parabola, has explored
many different approaches to the education of the young. She
founded one of the first nursery schools in America in the
1920s and more recently established the Blue Rock School of
West Nyack, New York, where children's natural intelligence
is allowed to guide their learning and their questions are
encouraged. In this way, the children come to live their own
knowledge while continuing to search for an understanding
of the world within and without.*
*I brought my questions on play and work as I visited her
home in White Plains, New York, one warm summer day.*
—David Appelbaum

Parabola: *How do you understand play in human life?*

Margaret Flinsch: I think of play first and foremost as
children's play. Children's play is their approach to understanding what's there. In contrast, adults' play is an attempt
to retreat from effort. Yet a lot of effort goes into play for
both children and adults. Children's play uncovers their
world. There are certain things children are obliged to do,
but in play—where there is no obligation—they come to

•

something new and fresh. Play is a trying out—experimenting. It's not a joke. Children don't play for fun. They play for real, and adults don't understand that: they laugh at what children do. To children, play is very serious. As a child, I remember that we couldn't wait to get out of school to go home and take on our roles of knights, ladies, dragons, whatever we were on the weekends. For children, play is real and work is often meaningless obligation. Yet when given the role of carrying something out there is no opposition. Children like to work hard and well, when it makes sense to them. It's the question of how to find the right balance between the joy of execution and the satisfaction from the result.

P: *Is the need to play inborn?*

MF: Play is basic. There's no "getting there" in play. It's all in the circumstances one is involved in.

P: *How is the sense of play supported?*

MF: Playing along. Joining in. Dropping off that sense of compulsion. Play is always of the moment, what calls one at that very moment. Certain people drop everything when it's a moment of play, and then they're accused of being irresponsible. Though work is needed, life couldn't go on without play.

P: *What happens when a child's play is thwarted or blocked?*

MF: Children are rechanneled into a kind of rationality. They accept that one thing has to follow another thing. But often when they are engaged in constructing an aspect of who they are, some grown-up tells them, "You have to come now and get your hands washed for supper." The way children are interrupted in their play by adults is brutal. Maybe it has to be, but it seems as though more understanding of where they are in their play is needed. Play is the vehicle of their growth. Play is exploration, a growing process. At a later point they need to conform to the structures of time. In play, there's no time. Once, working with a group of children, we were engaged in a project and decided that we wouldn't keep track of time, and would just go on doing whatever we were doing. It was a very serious work: we were building things. It was the first occasion in which a child came and asked me if she could go to bed. [*Laughter*]

P: *Is the use of the attention different in play and work?*

MF: It's a mistake to make too big a division between the two. We seem to be defining work only as the carrying out of what has to be done according to outer necessity. But working is working *at something*, applying energy to a specific task. Given the need for this task to be carried out, that energy has to be brought to it over and over and over again. In other words, there's a required repetition. If something is new to a child, he or she can continue to do it over and over and over again in play. Work is in play. Work is not separate from play. If we divide the two the mistake comes there.

P: *When it comes to inner work, does our division of work from play create difficulties for us?*

MF: The way you put the question, it's difficult for me to understand how to look at it. Attention is the real link between play and work. Play is a kind of movement around itself, attention to itself. In contrast, work goes in a direction, a way. The two movements belong together. To someone who has forbidden himself or herself to play by falling into a routine of obligation, play suddenly comes as an interruption. The attention is usually caught by one movement or the other. We have no free attention. Either my attention is riveted on the computer, the cleaning job, or driving the car, or it's available for appreciation of what's around me and my own life. When one is near a person who encompasses both moments, one feels that this person is very alive. In simple people, one feels that they are immediately available in a way that overcomplicated, mental, modern people, like us, are not. Playfulness and a readiness to work go together.

We're conditioned to be regulated and to fit in with an existing outer world. Small children are free of that routine. They're in touch with a vitality that we don't feel. When children go to school, long before they're ready to relinquish this immediacy, we set forth prohibitions. Energy is no longer available for exploratory experience. Look at what we do today: we're putting first-graders in front of computers. By introducing

290 A CHILD'S GROUND OF DISCOVERY

a mechanical outer stimulus, we close off the channel to their inventiveness. It thwarts the wish to discover a real world for themselves. We're killing this wish in children. It's frightening to imagine what's going to happen to the human race. That's why, for instance, in a school like The Blue Rock School, the teachers are struggling to allow play for children and not to squash it.

P: *Is it possible for an adult to find his or her way back to that self-contained movement of energy?*

MF: Not through games and sport, or "vacations of relaxation." I can more easily say what I think is not possible! Children and adults are both helped by shocks, when in a moment one is disarmed from the usual conditioned response. At that moment, one is a little freer and more open to what is. The freedom is an avenue to play.

P: *Is play connected to resourcefulness? I mean, being available to what there is in the moment?*

MF: It's more recklessness than resourcefulness. Resourcefulness comes when one finds unexpected consequences of recklessness. Children are completely reckless. They'll climb a tree or get on the roof of a house, and the agonized adult below is afraid that they will fall. I have a great belief in the human wish to be who one is and to affirm it. Children have this until they give in to being afraid. If we could interfere less with that wish and support it more, maybe a sense of self could begin to grow.

P: *One speaks also about playing a role in the theater or in life. Is this at the core of playing?*

MF: It is. I don't let on that secretly I am what I tell myself I am. This begins very early on. It can have a bad side in that my image of myself becomes me and colors my whole life. The roles that children have are infinitely more real to them than the fact that they have a name. Secretly, they know perfectly well that they're not the name, but something else. That other identity has a whole life. When taken to an extreme, it can become a terrible illness. Autistic children retire into their own world, which is completely real for them. But all children have an inner world more real than the outer. When I was only four, I was trained to pray at night. I said my prayers at my mother's knee, but I soon felt that I had to have private prayers. So I told her that I would keep on with these prayers with her, but would also have my private prayers.

P: *So there's a kind of secret in play, isn't there?*

MF: Absolutely, absolutely.

P: *And I seem to get in trouble when I lose that secret.*

MF: Yes.

P: *And nobody else can really tell me that secret again.*

MF: No. The secret is something that somehow needs to be guarded inside, maintained, kept alive.

P: *I suppose that a child learns to guard the secret too, at a certain point, if he or she survives as a child.*

MF: The children who are able to maintain it will be infinitely better workers, because they work with life.

P: *And work, for the child?*

MF: Children love "working," which is not the same thing as "work." Work can be donkey work, terrible, mechanical work, but "working" is how I engage myself. This engagement can be very alive, if my own wish to do well is maintained in it. When that's lost, then I'm swallowed. When the loss begins early with children, it is very frightening to see. The effect is in the attention, which becomes so dispersed that they no longer can concentrate.

P: *What about attention deficit disorders?*

MF: These terms, like "attentions deficit disorder" or "hyperactivity," didn't exist fifty years ago. When television came in, they came in. Television is mild in comparison to the Nintendo games and other new "inventions" that we succumb to with an unquestioning attitude. We seem to be completely paralyzed in our minds. We never ask why. What has happened to the human mind?

P: *What is a "good teacher" in your opinion?*

MF: A teacher who wishes to learn how to be much more alert to different signals in a child. In modern public schooling the size of the class is one reason that prohibits that attentiveness in teaching, because no human being can be aware of so many children at once. The system is quantitative, and therefore becomes a factory rather than a school.

P: *And the teachers who teach adults about play?*

MF: Who teaches adults about play? [*Laughs*] Play leaves open how it's going to come out. If a person is in a situation in which he or she already sees where it has to go and what they have to do, everything is geared toward that end. If I work directly toward that result, I miss the opportunities as I go along. There can be no play. If a teacher recognizes that the situation is a learning situation, they're more exploratory in trying to find their way. There is an approach that allows a child all of a sudden to say, "Ah, I've got it!" Then there's an extraordinary joy shared between the child and the teacher.

P: *Does playing have to do with the facing of an openness?*

MF: Facing an unknown outcome. There are people who play games either to win or to play. You hear arguments from people who haven't won and who are very angry about it. Others will say, "It's just a game." Children use the word "fun" a lot. When they work tremendously hard, they say, "That was such fun." I remember one time when we had to get a lot of coal moved to a cellar. With a cart and wheelbarrows, some small boys were transporting the coal. Everybody was very black. And after lunch someone suggested that we should stop, and there was a great outcry. "No! We want to go on until it's finished." Now was that play or work?

P: *It was fun.*

MF: It was fun, growing up and being like adults without being an adult. Being like an adult, I work as hard as an adult. When given a light thing to carry, obviously I'm being treated as a child. But if I'm given a big, heavy box and told, "You can do that," I do it and feel wonderful afterwards. I've worked very hard. If a child wishes to bring all his energy to carry out something, he gains a sense of being himself. He knows that he is a human being.

Perhaps the greatest trouble with our lives is that we forget. We don't remember how we were even a week ago. You can be certain we don't remember how we were when we were younger. Our memories of childhood are tremendously sparse. We would have answers to all these questions if we had a better memory.

Parabola
Volume: 4.4
Storytelling and
Education

ON BECOMING A REAL MAN

G. I. Gurdjieff

I also very well remember that on another occasion the father dean said:

"In order that at responsible age a man may be a real man and not a parasite, his education must without fail be based on the following ten principles.

"From early childhood there should be instilled in the child:

> *Belief in receiving punishment for disobedience.*
> *Hope of receiving reward only for merit.*
> *Love of God—but indifference to the saints.*
> *Remorse of conscience for the ill-treatment of animals.*
> *Fear of grieving parents and teachers.*
> *Fearlessness towards devils, snakes and mice.*
> *Joy in being content merely with what one has.*
> *Sorrow at the loss of the goodwill of others.*
> *Patient endurance of pain and hunger.*
> *The striving early to earn one's bread."*

•

Parabola
Volume: 16.2
The Hunter

Remembering

P. L. Travers

A Hebrew myth, a potent element in the annals of the bees, tells us that when a child is born an angel takes it under his wing and recites the Torah to it. Having done that he puts his forefinger on the infant lip and says one word, "Forget!"

Clearly, every tradition has a similar angel, for where is the human creature who lacks that indentation of the upper lip, that little valley of flesh where the same word has been so ineffaceably impressed? And, indeed, of necessity. For how, without forgetting, can remembering arise? And remembering leads to search.

Maybe it needs another angel, though this time leaving no manifest mark, to set us on our way. Angels, anyway, thread through our lives, invisible presences, energies, messengers, bringers of dreams not the hodge-podge of daily events—but those rare dreams of portent and revelation that can change the course of our lives. There are angels who walk beside us as Raphael walked with Tobias, pilgrim angels who carry bowls, not for begging at doors but to hold to our lips from time to time to refresh us with a taste of that emptiness which in their land is fullness. Such a draught—even the brush of an angel wing—can bring one to oneself, and thus to remembering; for without remembering we dream our life away and arrive at the end of it to find that there has been nobody there, the initiatory touch truly forgotten and never woken from. The way has been in us but we have not been on the way.

I cannot recall the time when I was not searching for a nameless unknown. Something Else, I called it as a child, and as that it is still known to me. The longing for it affected me most strongly at sundown, and I would weep, not allowing the grown ups to comfort me, tenderly or testily, with assurances that the sun would surely rise in the morning. I knew that. But this unknown was clearly connected with it and seemed to depart with the sun.

As I grew, I learned to contain my sorrow, indeed—except at moments when an angel passed—entirely to forget it. Daily life needs its full share of the human creature's two natures—the mind its inventions and imaginings, the heart its orchestra of feelings (oh, the drumbeats, the clarinets, the trombones!), flesh and blood and their various feastings, in order to have the material to question and to know. Was it not this share that the Prodigal Son—and most of us are Prodigal Sons—set out with his portion to seek? And after, again like most of us, spending it—the revellings and the consequent sufferings—he came at last to himself. Having forgotten, he had to remember, reminded, perhaps, by a passing angel, and he knew he had to return home.

The parable does not tell us much more. But can we suppose that he spent the rest of his life making merry and feeding on fatted calves? Would he not, after such an awakening, such a realization of his own unworth and at length such a welcome home, feel the need to search within for his essential self? Prodigal in all things, would he not submit himself to the fire of self-question, pursue the reparation of the past through the process of metanoia, and with this new energy stirring in him, apply himself to working in the patriarchal fields along with his elder brother who, significantly, had never left them?

There is much to be said for that elder brother who is so often maligned. Clearly, having been told to forget he had very soon remembered that what he was searching for was to be found nowhere but at the father's side.

Most of us have to go far before we find what is nearer than the neck vein, but the very distance draws one closer. For myself, Something Else no longer sets with the sun. Rather, the sun goes down in myself and I am lost in the twilight. O Forgetting, sustain my

Remembering! Stay my feet, angels, upon the way, so that the seeker becomes the sought, and I, too, may be spied from afar as someone comes running to meet me. ...

Parabola
Volume: 16.1
Money

Payment

P. D. Ouspensky

Many people were very indignant at the demand for payment, for money. In this connection it was very characteristic that those who were indignant were not those who could pay only with difficulty, but people of means for whom the sum demanded was a mere trifle.

Those who could not pay or who could pay very little always understood that they could not count upon getting something for nothing, and that G.'s work, his journeys to Petersburg, and the time that he and others gave to the work cost money. Only those who had money did not understand and did not want to understand this.

"Does this mean that we must pay to enter the Kingdom of Heaven?" they said. "People do not pay nor is money asked for such things. Christ said to his disciples: 'Take neither purse nor scrip,' and you want a thousand roubles. A very good business could be made of it. Suppose that you had a hundred members. This would already make a hundred thousand, and if there were two hundred, three hundred? Three hundred thousand a year is very good money."

G. always smiled when I told him about talks like this.

"Take neither purse nor scrip! And need not a railway ticket be taken either? The hotel paid? You see how much falsehood and hypocrisy there is here. No, even if we needed no money at all it would still be necessary to keep this payment. It rids us at once of many useless people. Nothing shows up people so much as their attitude towards money. They are ready to waste as much as you like on their own personal fantasies but they have no valuation whatever of another person's labor. I must work for them and give them gratis everything that they vouchsafe to take from me. 'How is it possible to *trade in knowledge*? *This* ought to be free.' It is precisely for this reason that the demand for this payment is necessary. Some people will never pass this barrier. And if they do not pass this one, it means that they will never pass another. Besides, there are other considerations. Afterwards you will see."

The other considerations were very simple ones. Many people indeed could not pay. And although in principle G. put the question very strictly, in practice he never refused anybody on the grounds that they had no money. And it was found out later that he even supported many of his pupils. The people who paid a thousand roubles paid not only for themselves but for others.

Parabola
Volume: 13.1
The Creative
Response

THE TRANSMISSION OF CONTENT

An Interview with Paul Reynard

Paul Reynard was born in Lyon. His training in painting began there and continued in Paris, where he worked with Fernand Léger. In 1968 he moved to New York where he maintained a studio, taught at the School of Visual Arts, and had a number of one-man shows.

Our interview with him reveals that both the man and his work embody the central possibility of an artist in our time.

—Lorraine Kisly

Parabola: *We were originally going to call this issue "The Creative Process," but we ultimately felt "The Creative Response" was closer to what was really interesting. A work of art is not something created out of oneself in isolation so much as a response to something much larger. Do you agree?*

Paul Reynard: It depends on what you mean by "response." It seems to me there is a deep necessity in man to express himself. But exactly what does it mean to express myself? To express what of myself? It seems to me that all arts respond to the same need, the need to express something which I could never discover in any ordinary way, something that needs to be sought for, that doesn't come by itself. In painting, in writing, the work very seldom just comes out. It has to be reworked, approached again and again, even if one starts with a very precise idea. Each time it is a repetition of the same attempt to find this possibility, which is usually a hidden possibility. So it is something very personal which at the same time has a larger dimension, too. When a work succeeds in speaking to many others, obviously both are there.

P: *A difficulty for me in the course of this issue is that there is only one Creator—everything has been given, is being given at every moment, the creative process is going on on a scale vastly bigger than the human level. What are we really speaking of when we speak of human creativity?*

PR: You carry something when you are born. Some people are going to enrich and develop this; for others it is there, but does not emerge. And there are many degrees and variations. In someone like Rimbaud, by the age of nineteen he seems to have exhausted everything. For others, like Titiano, perhaps his best years were the last. Through the years he built up something very fine. Some people have possibilities which are not exhausted in a lifetime—for others it is finished in two years.

But let's come back to what you said about "creation" and human creativity. Creativity today is a very "in" word. There are "creativity" workshops everywhere, and the word has lost much of its meaning. Nevertheless, a different quality of energy may sometimes appear within a human being, and if expressed may give birth to a work of art bearing some reality. The recognition of this quality of energy within an individual may lead us to the understanding of what could be called the sacred. Right now there is a tremendous movement in America toward a new dimension of life that all of our material progress does not bring. It seems there is a hunger for something else, a need for another way of living.

P: *How is it possible to discriminate between good work and work which is not so good?*

PR: By the force, the quality of energy which is contained in the form and expressed by it.

P: *Is struggle an element that helps bring force to a work? There needs to be a state of very alert and active receptivity in order to work as an artist, and at the same time it seems that there is an opposite movement needed in order to express that. Is there a contradiction here? Is it in the change from one to the other that the struggle comes in?*

PR: It seems to me that, on the contrary, it is very close. It is only at the moment that you are open that something is expressed. It is a rather mysterious process, because you can work and work for a long time and not find what you want. You come to a point where you seem to have exhausted all the possible means for this work, all the thought you have, all the emotion, in other words, you are finished. There's no more to say—you are like a fruit that has been squeezed. And this moment is very important. It's the moment when you may open. All the necessary elements are present without any order. You are even at the point where you are ready to destroy what you have done. It is nevertheless a very precious moment, because it is then when something new may emerge, something which was in you but which you didn't know, you didn't see. And that is the real moment of expression.

When I'm no longer trying to do something, I begin to feel I am led, as if my brush was just following a definite path. I am just following something which I merely initiated. At that point I am open to something which I was unable to express before, when I wanted to direct it. And strangely enough the best moment, and the best result, is when I am here in front of the painting, and the hand is so to speak free. I am not imposing. At the same time it is me who paints. But it is as if I were following a kind of secret indication. I am no longer fighting. The struggle has taken place before this moment, when I was at the point of giving up. And if at that point I'm open enough, then something occurs, something completely new, something which seems to be true, something true in relation to what was within myself at that very moment.

P: *And yet one must begin with an intention?*

PR: It depends on the person. As for me, I cannot start without an intention. I think that any great work of art carries an intention you can feel. You can feel it without being able to express it in words.

P: *You once made a distinction between the content of a painting and the object. We don't normally think of still lifes as sacred objects, and yet their content can touch us very deeply.*

PR: Yes, and it is obvious too that there exist paintings of religious subjects which are merely illustration, and don't bear in them anything of the sacred.

P: *Last summer I saw in a museum a torso of a bodhisattva. It stopped me in my tracks. It has since occurred to me that this art was created to remind us of something. Looking at it I remembered things I hadn't felt for a long time. What is the artist today doing? Is he or she also trying to remind us of something?*

PR: Whatever his field of expression, I think an artist must be revolutionary. Content is always revolutionary because it is always putting in question what has been said before. For example, planets orbit the sun, follow the same ellipse, and yet it is never the same ellipse. In their revolutions they never follow the same path. To be conservative is to always follow the same path in a movement which becomes completely automatic. There's no more life. Sacred art is always revolutionary. The piece of art you mentioned was very old, and it still had that revolutionary power—it brings about a new interrogation.

P: *The questions have to be asked again and again because we become dulled to the old answers?*

PR: Yes.

P: *But they are the same questions?*

PR: Fundamentally, yes. It seems to me that there's a need in all men and women to discover new territory. And here is where what we call culture and what we could call society are opposed. It's as true in science as it is in art. Someone discovers a new approach, a new avenue, and immediately a resistance arises against it. "How can you do that?" society says. "Up to now we have lived in a certain way, thought in a certain way, felt in a certain way. Suddenly you are bringing something different. Why? Why are you going against the existing order?" It is not that the forms lose their meaning but that we forget the sense of their existence, which is the expression of a meaning.

It seems to me that people go to museums, or to concerts, in response to their own need for discovery, and there they respond to the discovery of someone else. If you are really open in seeing something you have never seen before, or listening to something you have never heard before, then you are very close to understanding what is meant by creation. You will find yourself in the same movement by which the work has been produced.

P: *What you say about the artist as a revolutionary connects with the question of the human role in the creative process. Why is this revolution needed?*

PR: The world completely changes, but the forms remain. Therefore we are compelled to find new forms of expression corresponding to our own time. We need new questions to be able to respond to the old ones.

P: *Can you say anything about how to look at art, at a painting?*

PR: If art is revolutionary, it has to bring new sounds, new ideas, new images. And to be receptive to that, the spectator needs to make a certain effort, an effort similar to the effort the artist put into what he did.

P: *The Russian poet Sinyavsky said that all art is a meeting place. What does that mean to you?*

PR: I don't know if what I'm going to say is what you'd like me to say. For example, sometimes in doing a painting I find myself struggling, covering it up and beginning again. One part begins to be what I want, but it's not balanced with the other parts. So I begin to work with the other parts which become better than the first, and the first one has to be destroyed. All this. And then comes the time when it is finished. In spite of my uncertainty, suddenly there is a kind of satisfaction. So there is the meeting of this suffering felt when doing the work and satisfaction at the same time. That's a good moment.

P: *It also points to the possibility of a new ground. You said before that there is a need in all men and women to discover new territory.*

PR: Yes, there is a need to explore.

P: *Inner territory?*

PR: Yes, and outer territory. There is also a great deal of unconscious material which needs to come to the surface.

P: *You have spoken of a force which is carried on through generations which needs to be recognized in art.*

PR: There are forces, unknown forces, which may be called God if you wish. But you can also say, the unknown. For instance, I live, but I am the son of my parents, they were the children of their parents, and so on. There is a kind of energy which has been sustained, kept alive through ages. And something of that needs to be expressed in art: a kind of force that contains within itself both material and spiritual forces at the same time, something perennial.

New discoveries in science, even some of the greatest ones, don't act on us for very long and can even seem absurd to later generations. But a great poem, or great music, say, retains its force. We don't paint today the way the Gothic artists expressed themselves. But something has remained which is absolutely independent of the form and the language of expression, and speaks to us as it spoke to the people at that time.

Why is that? How to understand? The Egyptian culture, for instance, was based on the sacred. And the point was not so much to create beautiful works of art but to serve, and perhaps to hand down to future generations a better understanding of something which is out of our grasp today. People looking at it feel that it is beautiful, but it doesn't mean very much intellectually. Still, we are touched by something which is much deeper. Our feeling is touched in a very mysterious way. It is a transmission of what we call the content, and at the same time it depends on the expression of the form.

P: *The material form embodies the content which is not material?*

PR: I think a work of art is the embodiment of the artist through his mind, certainly, but also through his feeling, through his body, at the same time. Perhaps it is more obvious in modern times—you can see a work which is interesting, but almost completely mental, and so it vanishes. I think that what constitutes the genius of an artist such as Picasso is that you can perceive his intelligence, you feel the tremor of the emotional content, and sense the physical element also very much.

P: *A distinction has been made between symbolic images, which link worlds, and diabolic images, which separate worlds.*

PR: Yes, and we need both of them. There is a tendency to divide things too much, for example between what is sacred and what is not sacred. There are many degrees between the two. A small simple pot made by an American Indian can be more sacred than a large new church such as Notre Dame de Montmartre in Paris.

P: *Many people do not feel the need for art in their lives. What is it that art does for a culture?*

PR: Nothing—except for those who feel that something is missing. And everyone has the possibility of finding his own art, which can be the art of living. We need to find our own sound, to be this sound, to discover it.

P: *One does have the sense that every moment contains the potential to be responded to in a creative way.*

PR: Henry Miller once said that one day art will disappear and only the artist will remain. The sacred has to do with life, with the art of life. What you see in Japanese Zen is a good example of that. There is no special honor given to painting or flower arranging or other things. They are simply ways to understand how you can make a certain order out of your life, really find a certain order to understand better why you are on this earth.

P: *How would you characterize your own direction?*

PR: I am interested in studying light, not from any physical point of view. I rather dream to understand how a painting could emanate light in such a way that it could evoke silence.

•

CHAPTER SIX

It is in My Essence That I May Be Reunited with the One Who Sees. There, I Would Be at the Source of Something Unique and Stable, at the Source of That Which Does Not Change

—Jeanne de Salzmann

Parabola
Volume: 14.1
Disciples and
Discipline

THE STAIRWAY

P. D. Ouspensky

Once there was a meeting with a large number of people who had not been at our meetings before. One of them asked: "From what does the way start?" The person who asked the question had not heard G.'s description of the four ways and he used the word "way" in the usual religious-mystical sense.

"The chief difficulty in understanding the idea of the way," said G. "consists in the fact that people usually think that the *way* (he emphasized this word) starts on the same level on which life is going. This is quite wrong. The way begins on another, much higher, level. This is exactly what people usually do not understand. The beginning of the way is thought to be easier or simpler than it is in reality. I will try to explain this in the following way.

"Man lives in life *under the law of accident* and under two kinds of influences again governed by accident.

"The first kind are influences created *in life itself* or by life itself. Influences of race, nation, country, climate, family, education, society, profession, manners and customs, wealth, poverty, current ideas, and so on. The second kind are influences created *outside this life*, influences of the inner circle, or esoteric influences—influences, that is, created under different laws, although also on the earth. These influences differ from the former, first of all in being *conscious* in their origin. This means that they have been created consciously by conscious men for a definite purpose. Influences of this kind are usually embodied in the form of religious systems and teachings, philosophical doctrines, works of art, and so on.

"They are let out into life for a definite purpose, and become mixed with influences of the first kind. But it must be borne in mind that these influences are conscious only in their origin. Coming into the general vortex of life they fall under the general law of accident and begin to act *mechanically*, that is, they may act on a certain definite man or may not act; they may reach him or they may not. In undergoing change and distortion in life through transmission and interpretation, influences of the second kind are transformed into influences of the first kind, that is, they become, as it were, merged into the influences of the first kind.

"If we think about this, we shall see that it is not difficult for us to distinguish influences created in life from influences whose source lies outside life. To enumerate them, to make up a catalogue of the one and the other, is impossible. It is necessary to *understand*; and the whole thing depends upon this understanding. We have spoken about the beginning of the way. The beginning of the way depends precisely upon this understanding or upon the capacity for discriminating between the two kinds of influences. Of course, their distribution is unequal. One man receives more of the influences whose source lies outside life, another less; a third is almost isolated from them. But this cannot be helped. This is already fate. Speaking in general and taking normal life under normal conditions and a normal man, conditions are more or less the same for everybody, that is, to put it more correctly, difficulties are equal for everybody. The difficulty lies in separating the two kinds of influences. If a man in receiving them does not separate them, that is, does not see or does not feel their difference, their action upon him also is not separated, that is, they act in the same way, on the same level, and produce the same results. But if a man in receiving these influences begins to discriminate between them and puts on one side those which are not created in life itself, then gradually discrimination becomes easier and after a certain time a man can no longer confuse them with the ordinary influences of life.

"The results of the influences whose source lies outside life collect together within him, he *remembers* them together, *feels* them together. They begin to form within him a certain whole. He does not give a clear account to himself as to what, how, and why, or if he does give an account to himself, then he explains it wrongly. But the point is not in this, but in the fact that the results of these influences collect together within him and after a certain time they form within him a kind of *magnetic center*, which begins to attract to itself kindred influences, and in this manner it grows. If the magnetic center receives sufficient nourishment, and if there is no strong resistance on the part of the other sides of a man's personality which are the results of influences created in life, the magnetic center begins to influence a man's orientation, obliging him to turn round and even to move in a certain direction. When the magnetic center attains sufficient force and development, a man already understands the idea of the way and he begins to look for the way. The search for the way may take many years and may lead to nothing. This depends upon conditions, upon circumstances, upon the power and the direction of inner tendencies which are not concerned with this search and which may divert a man at the very moment when the possibility of finding the way appears.

"If the magnetic center works rightly and if a man really searches, or even if he does not search actively yet feels rightly, he may meet *another man* who knows the way and who is connected directly or through other people with a center existing outside the law of accident, from which proceed the ideas which created the magnetic center.

"Here again there are many possibilities. But this will be spoken of later on. For the moment let us imagine that he has met a man who really knows the way and is ready to help him. The influence of this man upon him goes through his magnetic center. And then, *at this point*, the man frees himself from the law of accident. This is what must be understood. The influence of the man who knows the way upon the first man is a special kind of influence, differing from the former two, first of all in being a *direct* influence and secondly in being a *conscious* influence. Influences of the second kind, which create magnetic center, are conscious in their origin but afterwards they are thrown into the general vortex of life, are intermixed with influences created in life itself, and are equally subject to the law of accident. Influences of the third kind can never be subject to the law of accident; they are themselves outside the law of accident and their action also is outside the law of accident. Influences of the second kind can proceed through books, through philosophical systems, through rituals. Influences of the third kind can proceed only from one person to another, directly, by means of oral transmission.

"The moment when the man who is looking for the way meets a man who knows the way it is called the *first threshold* or the *first step*. From this first threshold the *stairway* begins. Between 'life' and the 'way' lies the 'stairway.' Only by passing along this 'stairway' can a man enter the 'way.' In addition, the man ascends this stairway with the help of the man who is his guide; he cannot go up the stairway by himself. The *way* begins only where the *stairway* ends, that is, after the *last threshold* on the stairway, on a level much higher than the ordinary level of life.

"Therefore it is impossible to answer the question, *from what does the way start?* The way starts with something that is not in life at all, and therefore it is impossible to say from what. Sometimes it is said: in ascending the stairway a man is not sure of anything, he may doubt everything: his own powers, whether what he is doing is right, *the guide*, his knowledge and his powers. At the same time, what he attains is very unstable; even if he ascended fairly high on the stairway, he may fall down at any moment and have to begin again from the beginning. But when he has passed the last threshold and enters the way, all this changes. First of all, all doubts he may have about his guide disappear and at the same time the guide becomes far less necessary to him than before. In many respects he may even be independent and know where he is going. Secondly, he can no longer lose so easily the results of his work and he cannot find himself again in ordinary life. Even if he leaves the way, he will be unable to return where he started from.

"This is almost all that can be said in general about the 'stairway' and about the 'way,' because there are different ways. We have spoken of this before. And, for instance, on the fourth way there are special conditions which cannot be on the other ways. Thus the conditions for ascending the stairway on the fourth way are that a man cannot ascend to a higher step until he places another man upon his own step. The other, in his turn, must put in his place a third man in order to ascend higher. Thus, the higher a man ascends the more he depends upon those who are following him. If they stop he also stops. Such situations as this may also occur on the way. A man may attain something, for instance, some special powers, and may later on sacrifice these powers in order to raise other people to his level. If the people with whom he is working ascend to his level, he will receive back all that he has sacrificed. But if they do not ascend, he may lose it altogether.

"There are also various possibilities as regards the teacher's situation in relation to the esoteric center, namely, he may know more or he may know less about the esoteric center, he may know exactly where this center is and how knowledge and help was or is received from it; or he may know nothing of this and may only know the man from whom he himself received his knowledge. In most cases people start precisely from the point that they know only one step higher than themselves. And only in proportion to their own development do they begin to see further and to recognize where what they know came from.

"The results of the work of a man who takes on himself the role of teacher do not depend on whether or not he knows exactly the origin of what he teaches, but very much depends on whether or not his ideas come *in actual fact* from the esoteric center and whether he himself understands and can distinguish *esoteric ideas*, that is, ideas of objective knowledge, from subjective, scientific, and philosophical ideas."

Parabola
Volume: 7.3
Ceremonies

Esoteric Christianity

P. D. Ouspensky

"Generally speaking we know very little about Christianity and the form of Christian worship; we know nothing
at all of the history and origin of a number of things.
For instance, the church, the temple in which gather the
faithful and in which services are carried out according
to special rites; where was this taken from? Many people
do not think about this at all. Many people think that
the outward form of worship, the rites, the singing of
canticles, and so on, were invented by the fathers of the
church. Others think that this outward form has been
taken partly from pagan religions and partly from the
Hebrews. But all of it is untrue. The question of the origin
of the Christian church, that is, of the Christian temple,
is much more interesting than we think. To begin with,
the church and worship in the form which they took in
the first centuries of Christianity could not have been
borrowed from paganism because there was nothing like
it either in the Greek or Roman cults or in Judaism. The
Jewish synagogue, the Jewish temple, Greek and Roman
temples of various gods, were something quite different
from the Christian church which made its appearance in
the first and second centuries. The Christian church is—a
school concerning which people have forgotten that it is a
school. Imagine a school where the teachers give lectures
and perform explanatory demonstrations; and where the

pupils or simply the people who come to the school take these lectures and demonstrations for ceremonies, or rites, or 'sacraments,' i.e., magic. This would approximate to the Christian church of our times.

"The Christian church, the Christian form of worship, was not invented by the fathers of the church. It was all taken in a ready-made form from Egypt, only not from the Egypt that we know but from one which we do not know. This Egypt was in the same place as the other but it existed much earlier. Only small bits of it survived in historical times, and these bits have been preserved in secret and so well that we do not even know where they have been preserved.

"It will seem strange to many people when I say that this prehistoric Egypt was Christian many thousands of years before the birth of Christ, that is to say, that its religion was composed of the same principles and ideas that constitute true Christianity. Special schools existed in this pre-historic Egypt which were called 'schools of repetition.' In these schools a public repetition was given on definite days, and in some schools perhaps even every day, of the entire course in a condensed form of the sciences that could be learned at these schools. Sometimes this repetition lasted a week or a month. Thanks to these repetitions people who had passed through this course did not lose their connection with the school and retained in their memory all they had learned. Sometimes they came from very far away simply in order to listen to the repetition and went away feeling their connection with the school. There were special days of the year when the repetitions were particularly complete, when they were carried out with particular solemnity—and these days themselves possessed a symbolical meaning.

"These 'schools of repetition' were taken as a model for Christian churches—the form of worship in Christian churches almost entirely represents the course of repetition of the science dealing with the uni-verse and man. Individual prayers, hymns, responses, all had their own meaning in this repetition as well as holidays and all religious symbols, though their meaning has been forgotten long ago."

Continuing, Gurdjieff quoted some very interesting examples of the explanations of various parts of orthodox liturgy.

The idea was that, beginning with the first words, the liturgy so to speak goes through the process of creation, recording all its stages and transitions. His explanations differed very greatly from the usual theological and even from mystical interpretations. And the principal difference was that he did away with a great many allegories. I mean to say that it became obvious from his explanations that we take many things for allegories in which there is no allegory whatever and which ought to be understood much more simply and psychologically.

"Every ceremony or rite has a value if it is performed without alteration," he said. "A ceremony is a book in which a great deal is written. Anyone who understands can read it. One rite often contains more than a hundred books."

"A grain of truth in an unaltered form is sometimes found in pseudo-esoteric movements, in church religions, in occult and theosophical schools. It may be preserved in their writings, their rituals, their traditions, their conceptions of the hierarchy, their dogmas, and their rules.

"Esoteric schools, that is, *not pseudo-esoteric schools*, which perhaps exist in some countries of the East, are difficult to find because they exist there in the guise of ordinary monasteries and temples. Tibetan monasteries are usually built in the form of four concentric circles or four concentric courts divided by high walls. Indian temples, especially those in Southern India, are built on the same plan but in the form of squares, one contained within the other. Worshipers usually have access to the first outer court, and sometimes, as an exception, persons of another religion and Europeans; access to the second court is for people of a certain caste only or for those having special permission; access to the third court is only for persons belonging to the temple; and access to the fourth is only for Brahmins and priests. Organizations of this kind which, with minor variations, are everywhere in existence, enable esoteric schools to exist without being recognized. Out of dozens of monasteries one is a school. But how is it to be recognized? If you get inside it you will only be inside the first court; to the second court only pupils have access. But this you do not know, you are told they belong to a special caste. As regards the third and fourth courts you cannot even know anything about them. And you can, in fact, observe the same order in all temples and until you are told you cannot distinguish an esoteric temple or monastery from an ordinary one.

"The idea of initiation, which reaches us through pseudo-esoteric systems, is also transmitted to us in a completely wrong form. The legends concerning the outward rites of initiation have been created out of the scraps of information we possess in regard to the ancient Mysteries. The Mysteries represented a special kind of way in which, side by side with a difficult and prolonged period of study, theatrical representations of a special kind were given which depicted in allegorical forms the whole path of the evolution of man and the world.

"Transitions from one level of being to another were marked by ceremonies of presentation of a special kind, that is, initiation. But a change of being cannot be brought about by any rites. Rites can only mark an accomplished transition. And it is only in pseudo-esoteric systems in which there is nothing else except these rites, that they begin to attribute to the rites an independent meaning. It is supposed that a rite, in being transformed into a sacrament, transmits or communicates certain forces to the initiate. This again relates to the psychology of an imitation way. There is not, nor can there be, any outward initiation. In reality only self-initiation, self-presentation exist. Systems and schools can indicate methods and ways, but no system or school whatever can do for a man the work that he must do himself. Inner growth, a change of being, depend entirely upon the work which a man must do on himself."

Parabola
Volume: 15.3
Liberation

LIBERATION LEADS
TO LIBERATION

An Early Talk of G. I. Gurdjieff

Liberation leads to liberation. These are the first words of truth—not truth in quotation marks but truth in the real meaning of the word; truth which is not merely theoretical, not simply a word, but truth that can be realized in practice. The meaning behind these words may be explained as follows:

By liberation is meant the liberation which is the aim of all schools, all religions, at all times.

This liberation can indeed be very great. All men desire it and strive after it. But it cannot be attained without the first liberation, a lesser liberation. The great liberation is liberation from influences outside us. The lesser liberation is liberation from influences within us.

At first, for beginners, this lesser liberation appears to be very great, for a beginner depends very little on external influences. Only a man who has already become free of inner influences falls under external influences.

Inner influences prevent a man from falling under external influences. Maybe it is for the best. Inner influences and inner slavery come from many varied sources and many independent factors—independent in that sometimes it is one thing and sometimes another, for we have many enemies.

There are so many of these enemies that life would not be long enough to struggle with each of them and free ourselves from each one separately. So we must find a method, a line of work, which will enable us simultaneously to destroy the greatest possible number of enemies within us from which these influences come.

I said that we have many independent enemies, but the chief and most active are vanity and self-love. One teaching even calls them representatives and messengers of the devil himself.

For some reason they are also called Mrs. Vanity and Mr. Self-Love.

As I have said, there are many enemies. I have mentioned only these two as the most fundamental. At the moment it is hard to enumerate them all. It would be difficult to work on each of them directly and specifically, and it would take too much time since there are so many. So we have to deal with them indirectly in order to free ourselves from several at once.

These representatives of the devil stand unceasingly at the threshold which separates us from the outside, and prevent not only good but also bad influences from entering. Thus they have a good side as well as a bad side.

For a man who wishes to discriminate among the influences he receives, it is an advantage to have these watchmen. But if a man wishes all influences to enter, no matter what they may be—for it is impossible to select only the good ones—he must liberate himself as much as possible, and finally altogether, from these watchmen, whom some consider undesirable.

For this there are many methods, and a great number of means. Personally I would advise you to try freeing yourselves and to do so without unnecessary theorizing, by simple reasoning, active reasoning, with yourselves.

Through active reasoning this is possible, but if anyone does not succeed, if he fails to do so by this method, there are no other means for what is to follow.

Take, for instance, self-love, which occupies half of our time and our life. If someone, or something, has wounded our self-love from outside, then, not only at that moment but for a long time afterwards, its momentum closes all the doors and therefore shuts out life.

When I am connected with outside, I live. If I live only inside myself, it is not life: but everybody lives thus. When I examine myself, I connect myself with the outside.

For instance, now I sit here. M. is here and also K. We live together. M. called me a fool—I am offended. K. gave me a scornful look—I am offended. I consider, I am hurt and shall not calm down and come to myself for a long time.

All people are so affected, all have similar experiences the whole time. One experience subsides, but no sooner has it subsided than another of the same nature starts. Our machine is so arranged that there are no separate places where different things can be experienced simultaneously.

We have only one place for our psychic experiences. And so if this place is occupied with such experiences as these, there can be no question of our having the experiences we desire. And if certain attainments or liberations are supposed to bring us to certain experiences, they will not do so if things remain as they are.

M. called me a fool. Why should I be offended? Such things do not hurt me, so I don't take offense—not because I have no self-love; maybe I have more self-love than anyone here. Maybe it is this very self-love that does not let me be offended.

I think, I reason in a way exactly the reverse of the usual way. He called me a fool. Must he necessarily be wise? He himself may be a fool or a lunatic. One cannot demand wisdom from a child. I cannot expect wisdom from him. His reasoning was foolish. Either someone has said something to him about me, or he has formed his own foolish opinion that I am a fool—so much the worse for him. I know that I am not a fool, so it does not offend me. If a fool has called me a fool, I am not affected inside.

But if in a given instance I was a fool and am called a fool, I am not hurt, because my task is not to be a fool; I assume this to be everyone's aim. So he reminds me, helps me to realize that I am a fool and acted foolishly. I shall think about it and perhaps not act foolishly next time.

So in either case I am not hurt.

K. gave me a scornful look. It does not offend me. On the contrary, I feel sorry for him because of the dirty look he gave me. For a dirty look must have a reason behind it. Can he have such a reason?

I know myself. I can judge from my knowledge of myself. He gave me a dirty look. Possibly someone had told him something that made him form a bad opinion of me. I am sorry for him because he is so much a slave that he looks at me through other people's eyes. This proves that he is not. He is a slave and so he cannot hurt me.

I say all this as an example of reasoning.

Actually, the secret and the cause of all such things lies in the fact that we do not possess ourselves nor do we possess genuine self-love. Self-love is a great thing. If we consider self-love, as we generally understand it, as reprehensible, then it follows that true self-love—which, unfortunately, we do not possess—is desirable and necessary.

Self-love is a sign of a high opinion of oneself. If a man has this self-love it proves what he is.

As we have said earlier, self-love is a representative of the devil; it is our chief enemy, the main brake to our aspirations and our achievements. Self-love is the principal weapon of the representative of hell.

But self-love is an attribute of the soul. By self-love one can discern the spirit. Self-love indicates and proves that a given man is a particle of heaven. Self-love is I—I is God. Therefore it is desirable to have self-love.

Self-love is hell, and self-love is heaven. These two, bearing the same name, are outwardly alike, but totally different and opposite to one another in essence. But if we look superficially, we can go on looking throughout our whole life without ever distinguishing the one from the other.

There exists a saying: "He who has self-love is halfway to freedom." Yet, among those sitting here, everyone is full to overflowing with self-love. And in spite of the fact that we are full to the brim with self-love, we have not yet attained one tiny bit of freedom. Our aim must be to have self-love. If we have self-love, by this very fact we shall become free of many enemies in us. We can even become free of these principal ones—Mr. Self-Love and Mrs. Vanity.

How to distinguish between one kind of self-love and another? We have said that on the surface it is very difficult. This is so even when we look at others; when we look at ourselves it is still more difficult.

Thank God we, who are sitting here, are safe from confusing the one with the other. We are lucky! Genuine self-love is totally absent, so there is nothing to confuse.

In the beginning of the lecture I used the words "active reasoning."

Active reasoning is learned by practice; it should be practiced long and in many varied ways.

Parabola
Volume: 23.3
Fear

FEAR AND THE EGO

Michel de Salzmann

Question: Is fear a property of the ego-consciousness?

Answer: Of course in a human being fear is mainly related to the problem of the image of oneself, to the identification with this image and the phantasms of its being threatened. In animals images, memory, or associations also exist, but fear is not anticipatory, it does not exist out of an immediate realistic context. There are many aspects to that question. We are governed by our associations, much more so than we think. Fear-related associations differ greatly with people. It is instructive, for instance, from a very simple practical point of view, to see these differences between us. Some people are more free or courageous with their minds. They don't fear to have some strange ideas, or even hallucinations. Some others will be more courageous as far as their body engagement is concerned but are not able to face internal conflicts. Fear is a fundamental problem. Very large. Maybe the basic fear is *not to be*. So it is only when you die, when you die to yourself, that you are delivered from fear, because then you discover the realm of being.

From *On the Way to Self-Knowledge*, edited by Jacob Needleman and Dennis Lewis (New York: Alfred A. Knopf, 1976), p. 79.

•

Parabola
Volume: 4.2
Sacred Dance

A Film and a Legend

An Interview with Peter Brook

Peter Brook: When preparing the film of *Meetings with Remarkable Men*, many people asked: How is it possible, in a form as documentary as the cinema, to show people in a certain state of inner development, masters, or people on the way to becoming masters, unless you are doing it with the real people? And it seemed that maybe this would be impossible. In fact at the same time, a big commercial company got in touch with me and said, "We are interested in making a film on the life of Gurdjieff. Would you like to direct it as well?" They knew, of course, that we were just starting to prepare this film, so when I said, "No, thank you," they said, "Why not?" I told them, "Well, for a very simple reason. In *Meetings with Remarkable Men* we are showing someone at a very young age, taking the first steps to being something. And I think that it is not impossible that we could find actors who could hoist themselves to that level. But you want to make a film where you have to show Gurdjieff as an accomplished being, and this is something you can't ask an actor to express." An actor can only take things that are in himself and amplify them; so an actor who is only slightly jealous in his nature can turn into a roaring madman in *Othello*, if he is a little introspective or melancholy he can become much more so, or if he is fairly jolly he can become outrageously comic. But an actor can't acquire the genuine

•

look in the eyes that goes with a completely accomplished human being. In the film of the life of Muhammad they tried to get out of it by sticking him behind the camera! There are *no* good films showing the most highly developed men. A Renaissance painter could picture Christ—maybe an icon painter more so—but if you are photographing an actor, you are up against it. Either you show him, and it is not satisfactory, or you pretend he is out of sight, and it is not satisfactory; so the best thing is to say it can't be done. Our task was on another level, which was to show remarkable men. Actors who have no interest in a spiritual way couldn't by any set of techniques and rehearsals develop a semblance of this, because the spark isn't there; but actors—and there are a great many of them—who in their own lives are concerned, who are searching or who have even the half-articulate potentiality of searching, can amplify that through the normal, legitimate process of rehearsal and performance to the point where they become *temporarily* what they would like to be, provided it is for a limited duration. An actor who has within him the possibilities of being a remarkable man can't by two or three months of rehearsals turn into one and sustain it for a year or a month; but he can sustain it for the time a given shot may take in a film; and it isn't a lie. It would be a lie if he went off the film set and started an esoteric group! But it can be true as long as he is there in front of a camera recognizing that this moment is between the director saying, "Action," and the director saying "Cut," which is often a matter of seconds, and trying again, and maybe spending a whole day going uphill toward that and just reaching it once, for a moment or two. That is possible. And it happens through the same laws of compression, just for that compressed time, in that compressed space, with that compression of gesture. Yes, that is possible; and at that moment—I am right back to where we started—two worlds meet. At that moment he is *there* with what he has to offer, which is his everyday person, which isn't concealing; he is what he is. And yet for a tiny space of time he becomes the meeting point with something else which expresses itself through him.

Parabola: *This compression that you speak of seems difficult sometimes to make believable. There were some very rapid transitions in the film; was there an intention behind that? There were some that seemed to me abrupt, almost disturbing. Things can't go that fast—as in the incident about Soloviev, for instance, which of course gets much fuller treatment in the book. I even wondered what significance Soloviev had in the film, and why he wasn't just omitted, like some other characters who appear in the book.*

PB: I feel that the film is a story—a not totally truthful story, somewhat oriental, sometimes accurate, sometimes not, sometimes in and sometimes out of life, like a legend. It is told like a legend in the remote past, for a purpose: which is to follow in a certain order the search of the searcher who is the central character. The entire film has been constructed around that one essential thread; and this is quite different in structure from the book. The searcher begins to search and as he goes on, his search changes color, changes register, changes tone, but it always goes forward until it reaches a certain intensity. So the film is a direct expression, for the person watching it, of a growing search; the sense of the growing search and the changing taste of it is what the film is there to show.

What the film is *not* trying to show is the biography of G. I. Gurdjieff. It isn't trying to show social conditions and life in that part of the world at the turn of the century. Nor is it trying to do what the book does, which is to bring to life a lot of criss-cross relationships between fairly evolved people, like some of the characters in the book who were left out of the film as well as those like Yelov and Vitvitskaia, who were much more developed in the book. Because while that elaborate criss-cross structure belongs very well to the book's weight and length, we decided quite definitely that in the film all the other people, all the descriptions and events, were to be shown only in relation to following Gurdjieff's story. So, for instance, the story of Soloviev is in relation to something one never wants to lose sight of, which is that the central figure is Gurdjieff, going in a certain direction—he is the searcher that we are following. It is very much related to what we were talking about earlier: his search takes place within life, so one must never lose contact for too long with a life that includes street fights and railway engines and soldiers shooting and fierce dogs, yet none of those can become too important either. There is always a proportion, and the search must always be there, more important than anything else.

In the book—and I hope in the film—there is something about the search that is very clear and easy to believe, and something that is totally mysterious. The book is made up, like a legend, of incredible coincidences, which I feel exist to remind one constantly of the mystery of what actually is going on. One can try to grasp the currents that are running behind all this, but eventually they are mysterious. For instance, in the film you see the prince mysteriously whisked away at a crucial moment by his meeting with the Tamil (and this isn't the way it happened in the book, but it makes the same point). Suddenly out of nowhere comes a man who changes the whole destiny of the prince, and he disappears. Then you see Gurdjieff totally lost. At that moment, also from nowhere, through hearing a shout in the street, there is a new person in his life—Soloviev. He is no longer alone, he is involved in something, and in the next second something quite different comes into his life; a moment ago he was going to Bokhara and suddenly he is caught up in an expedition into the Gobi desert. Looked at as plausible coincidences, none of them hold up. But from the point of view of legend and fairy story—yes!

Actually we are asking the audience to allow itself to be carried by the process, half-real, half-legendary, of one man's search; because though on the outward level these events don't fit together, actually on another level there is something that is quietly pursuing its way through the line of the central character. That is what the film is constructed around.

One sees one thing in particular in relation to the young people that Gurdjieff is with: one by one they fall by the way. Gurdjieff has to accept this and go on without them. He gets other companions; they meet in the desert and something goes wrong—Soloviev's death—and they break up again. Soloviev, it seems to me, has a very clear function, which is to show how a man with tragically limited possibilities still had a search, and no sooner had this man found something that could help him when life comes in on its most ordinary level, which none of us is ever free from—he dies by accident, like being knocked down by a truck. Pogossian falls away because of his passionate identification with his life's interest. Yelov has his life in the bazaar, and we don't know what will happen to Vitvitskaia. Soloviev perhaps could have been a close comrade for years and years; you can see there was something in the man that touched Gurdjieff, and though he was a drunk and mixed up in fights and so on, he responds to Gurdjieff, and Gurdjieff says, "I will help you." But Soloviev is killed; there is no explanation. Gurdjieff is standing by his tomb, with no comment.

Then, Gurdjieff gets another close person, a much older man, Skridlov, who in a way is the third character in the story and who stops when he finds his place with Father Giovanni. So Gurdjieff goes on again by himself.

In that sense you have to let the film wash over you to follow the central process. If you ask yourself about logical reasons for transitions, that sets up a difficulty that I don't think is there otherwise.

P: *There is certainly some process that goes on while you are watching it; you find yourself affected by it, without knowing it was happening. I think almost everyone must experience that.*

PB: Talking with a lot of people who have seen the film, one is constantly finding that testimony; someone saying, "I suspended my normal reactions, and I don't see how to talk about what I got. I received something very strong." But of course there are some cases of people whose developed reflexes are so powerful that they are registering at every second what they are *not* with, and that prevents them from entering into what is there.

P: *I heard one man say: "But they are just ordinary people, they aren't remarkable men!"*

PB: The strange thing is that one takes for granted that the remarkable men are all those with chapter headings in the book; but in the film, Father Giovanni, who hasn't a chapter heading, and the dervishes, and the Tamil, are clearly some of the remarkable men that he meets. There is a chain that goes through the story, beginning with the father who brings something very important to the formation of the young boy. Then the movements, the dance exercises you see in the monastery, you might say actually fill the role of "a remarkable man"; not any one dancer individually, of course; but that group of people, doing those movements in the way they have learned, at that moment, present an open illustration, for anyone who wants to look at it, of what it means to be in touch with another level. Again, only for a few seconds, but it isn't a fake. One is actually showing something, which you can only show if it is true. We don't say anywhere in the film what a "remarkable man" is; there is a very striking formulation in Gurdjieff's book, which we didn't include because we didn't want to be in the least didactic. The people doing the movements are simple human beings searching for something remarkable and consequently enabling the onlooker to understand what "remarkable" could mean. Between two of the dance exercises the prince says, "If the dancer can keep in balance these two energies, then he has a force that nothing else can give." You can say that is the exact explanation of what is a remarkable man. And it is an *if*.

P: *What can you tell us about these Movements? People must be very struck by them, I should think.*

PB: When we were filming, they made a great impression on the people working with us and they asked very simple questions. The people doing them of course are not actors but pupils who have been studying for a number of years, some of whom were taught directly by Gurdjieff, others by the person who received the Movements directly from him, who was Mme. de Salzmann. One of the things that encouraged me to make the film in the first place was that, owing to Mme. de Salzmann's wish and readiness to participate in the whole film, I saw a possibility that I don't think anything else could give, which was to make a film about a certain tradition and, when it actually came to the crunch, being able to show something genuine. In almost any religious film, you come to a monastery or you show a ritual, like that of early Christians meeting in a grotto—and the ceremony has to be invented. By whom? By someone with no qualifications. It has to come from the fantasy of an artist. That is why it has always seemed to me impossible to do this sort of thing in the ordinary way, because to show a monastery that doesn't belong to a known order and that no one has ever seen, could only be based on the invention of an art director or choreographer and this could only lead one into *Lost Horizons*. But here we had someone who was prepared to make available to the public glimpses of the real thing. So that although reconstructing a monastery in a studio meant plaster walls and backcloths, the critically important point is that what the people did was for real. The film clearly was trying to avoid any kind of verbal formulation: What did he find? What was it all about? But we wanted to give a taste of it so the film could make sense, and go toward a climax which neither cheated nor begged the question.

It should be quite clear that what we are showing in the film is not a series of ceremonies and rituals. You arrive at a monastery and you expect to see the sort of ritual you might see with the dervishes at Konya. But the head of the monastery says: "Go to the courtyard and you will see people doing certain *exercises*." An exercise is very different from a ritual, because it means that as a beginner you do an exercise to learn.

Parabola: *Certainly the impression I had was that this was work—these were people working and learning. There was a contrast between that moment and another earlier in the film, in the workshop with Gurdjieff and his friends with all their young, ardent enthusiasm, and he says suddenly in a fury, "You're working in the dark!" Here in the monastery is the same intensity, but one feels that here also is knowledge, here is light: they aren't working in the dark. He had found a source of knowledge where work could go on, and an order. The dances didn't seem to be ceremonies; they were all going on at once, each group was working quietly by itself, paying no attention to any other. So it certainly gave the impression of students working.*

PB: He found an order in every sense of the word—an order, and a place of work. That is why it was of great importance to the film to show the head of the monastery as a man of humor but of real severity. There is no sentimental, religious, "Give up life and settle down here and everything will be lovely"; on the contrary, now he has come to a place of work.

P: *And eventually he will have to leave it and do it himself.*

PB: And in this way two worlds unite.

Parabola
Volume: 15.2
Attention

THE FORCE OF ATTENTION

William Segal

Attention is the quintessential medium to reveal man's dormant energies to himself. Whenever one witnesses the state of the body, the interplay of thought and feeling, there is an intimation, however slight, of another current of energy. Through the simple act of attending, one initiates a new alignment of forces.

Maintenance of a conscious attention is not easy. The movement, the obligations of day-to-day existence, completely distract. With no base of operations, no home in one's organism, the attention serves random thoughts, feelings, and appetites which conflict and tyrannize each other.

Sensation of parts or the whole of the body can anchor the attention, provide it with a kind of habitat. The structure, becoming more sensitive, helps to unify attention, so it is less liable to veer into mental channels that consume its power. In turn, perceptions and sensations are quickened, insights are multiplied.

Opening to the force of attention evokes a sense of wholeness and equilibrium. One can glimpse a possibility of a state of awareness immeasurably superior to that of the reactive mechanism, an awareness which transcends one's automatic subject/object mode of response.

Freely flowing, the concentrative, transforming effect of conscious attention brings the disparate tempos of the centers to a relatively balanced relationship. Thought, feeling, and sensing are equilibrated under this vibrant, harmonizing influence.

Attention is an independent force which will not be manipulated by one's parts. Cleared of all internal noise, conscious attention is an instrument which vibrates like a crystal at its own frequency. It is free to receive the signals broadcast at each moment from a creative universe in communication with all creatures.

However, the attention is not "mine." In a moment of its presence, one knows that it does not originate entirely with oneself. Its source surrounded by mystery, attention communicates energies of a quality the mind cannot represent. One needs to be at the service of conscious attention; one prepares for its advent through active stillness.

In quiet, tension-free moments, man's structure is open to energy flows which are ordinarily blocked. In turn, these energies blend with previously received materials, to serve the higher in a wordless, nameless exchange.

Attention is not only mediating; it is transmitting. Giving and receiving, God speaks to man. Receiving and giving, man speaks to God. Just as man's structure needs to be vivified by the infusion of finer vibrations, those very same vibrations require the mixing of coarse material for their maintenance. Without the upward transmission of energies through the intermediary of conscious attention, the universe would give in to entropy.

In man, the smallest deformation of a balanced attention closes down this two-way communication. Alone, the mind cannot maintain it. A relaxed body, too, is needed.

Midway between micro- and macrocosmos, man has his part to play. Returning to the body is a gesture of opening to the attention which, beckoned, is ready to serve its cosmological function.

From William Segal, *The Structure of Man* (Brattleboro, Vermont: Green River Press, Stillgate Publishers, 1987).

Parabola
Volume: 13.3
Questions

SOMETHING ELSE

P. L. Travers

What is it? I have been asking myself that question all my life, ever since I became aware that after the long aureate day the sun inevitably goes away to the West. And with that going down of the sun would arise the lonely, aching, nostalgic longing that never failed to assail me.

"There must be Something Else!" I would say, not aloud, not to any authoritative ear, for the tongue belonging to that ear, no matter how benignant, would never, I knew, speak the adequate word.

It was not more of what I had that I looked for, being filled full of what was given and what I myself imagined and fashioned. No. It was something totally other, another kind of world, perhaps, another way of being. The word "transcendent" might have fitted my need, could I have understood it. As it was, a knowing beyond my knowing evoked the equivocal question that neither expected nor asked for an answer. I knew it was something that had to be borne—or endured—not verbally responded to.

Whitman, comforting a child, came within distance of it in "On the Beach at Night":

> *Something there is,*
> *I give thee the first suggestion, the*
> *   problem, the indirection,*

Something that will endure longer even
  than lustrous Jupiter,
Longer than sun or any revolving satellite
Or the radiant sisters, the Pleiades. ...

He had the grace not to say more, not to arrogate to himself the role of guru. And the child who was weeping because a cloud had covered the stars—a mere temporary phenomenon—would doubtless have dried her eyes and found solace in that "first suggestion."

But when I grew to my full height and discovered—as who does not?—that life was not expressly designed to fulfill my personal dreams and desires, and that death, on the other hand, was expressly designed to put an end to them, I knew that for me "the problem and the indirection" would be the fateful way-showers.

For as I pursued the business of living, the revelries, the moments of tedium, the seekings and findings, I still sustained within myself—though there were times when it slept and dreamed—that homesickness of my childhood. And aways—again!—at sunset. This moment of the day, I found, has its own peculiar vibration, an invisible hand plucking the strings of an invisible harp.

Sometimes I would hush the question as one does a wakeful child. Let me be! Lullaby. Let me listen to the mermaids singing and the mermen blowing their conches! But rarely would it be denied.

And now, after all the agonies and exultations (our friends, as the poet Yeats calls them); the enigmas and dimensions of love which, if they do not include those of Something Else, the word is merely mocked; the long dailiness of existence ("Many the burials, many the days and nights passing away"), still, at the going down of the sun on a planet that is itself declining, I am assailed incessantly by that "dart of lovely longing."[1] And still I find no demand for an answer. There are, in any case, only questions. The Word alone, not words, would suffice. But who would speak that and what would hear?

And yet, and yet, unspoken, is it not somehow soundlessly heard? *Purusha* has need of *Prakriti* in order to manifest itself and soul has need of flesh to be its witness. Thus the body, that essential alchemical vessel in which, through the affinity of its functions, the question must first have arisen, begins to receive—oh, visitations, unwonted physical impressions, parables, as it were, of the senses, that wordlessly convey their meaning to essence, mind, and heart.

This is not at all to suggest that the Something Else is now comprehended, safely possessed, tucked away into the understanding like a jewel in a box. That would be to misprize both question and questioner, making of them a trifling matter, a game or riddle to be solved.

Far from it. What was once is now and always. It is possible to long as ardently for what one has as for something one has not. But, little by little, those voiceless parables make known the significance of my question.

They remind me of the fairy-tale theme, familiar to every mythology, of the hero who sets bravely out to find some desirable object—or person, or state of mind—and, after many vicissitudes, returns empty-handed and desolate only to find that what he sought had always been in his own home.

So it is with my Something Else. What I had envisaged as being beyond the utmost stars is nowhere else but here. My longing has been a homeward journey. *Here* has drawn forth emanations from *There* that reveal the Something Else as my own, my inward treasure, call me to find my place in the world and what it is I must serve, and bid me, as the bee never ceases to gather pollen, not to cease from mental fight.

The problem and the indirection have indeed been accurate wayshowers. Through them I have come to understand that the finding is hidden in the seeking; sky covers earth with its mantle; moon is reflected in every fishpond; and the astral sun that sets and rises is mirrored in another sun that neither rises nor sets and is to be found a finger's length below the human heart. It, too, has vibrations. Thus cosmos ferments in the crucible. Purusha leavens Prakriti.

This is not merely my story. It belongs to everyone. The whistling man going past my door could tell it as well as I. Perhaps better. His look of serenity suggests that he knows where the kingdom of Heaven is and that to discover it needs no great odyssey.

I have not been so skilled a geographer.

Note:

1 *The Cloud of Unknowing.*

Parabola
Volume: 30.3
Body and Soul

THE TRUE HUMAN BODY

Interview with Jacob Needleman

For over half a century Jacob Needleman has confronted the central questions of our era in light of the vision that lies at the root of the world's great spiritual traditions.
    Parabola *recently sat down with him to discuss the nature of consciousness and its relationship to the body. Amid the current talk of "consciousness studies," Needleman returns us to the heart of the matter: Should the mind and body be understood as two aspects of one thing, or as two distinct realities? And what does this question mean for our sense of ourselves?*
    —Mitch Horowitz

Parabola: *A recent* New York Times *op-ed piece advanced the idea, by now at least forty years old but just becoming "common knowledge," that consciousness is a secondary result of chemical processes in the brain. Despite recent scientific alternatives, this reductionist view of human life is still what is presented to us.*

Jacob Needleman: Yes, the current prevailing view is of the universe as inorganic, non-purposeful, non-meaningful, and mechanical. Everything just happens, working by principles of what is called efficient causality. There's no sense that there is Mind at all in the universe—it's just matter, in the modern sense of the word. But if matter is non-purposeful,

•

non-intelligent, and without intentionality, how could it be that something qualitatively different from matter arises out of matter?

In this view of the universe, that which is dead is considered the real and that which is living needs to be explained. How can something alive and purposeful emerge in a universe that is fundamentally dead? In the ancient world, by contrast, reality was understood to be fundamentally alive, while death was the problem to be explained.

In an ordinary sense, it's a puzzle how things can change qualitatively. To have a quality emerge from something that doesn't already contain it is like stirring a bucket of white paint and having it turn red. No matter how much you stir the paint, you aren't going to get red. So, if life had appeared out of non-life, which is what seems to be, life must have already been present in some sense of the term. But that's unacceptable in the modern conventional view, or in what you might call scientism. And scientism is not science. Scientism is an unwarranted extrapolation of scientific method, making the method into a worldview and an exclusivist canon of all-knowing. In its framework, life becomes a problem to be explained by reducing it to non-life or non-living functions.

Now, if life is a problem in a world that is non-living, how much more of a problem is mind? Mind comes out of life. And there is also the question of higher states of mind. On the one hand, there is a view of the universe that is totally leveled and reductionistic. On the other, a view of a universe of levels, purpose, intelligence, mind, and meaning, all the way up to what is called God, in some traditions, or the Absolute, or Brahman, or the Void.

P: *How would you define consciousness?*

JN: I wouldn't. Nobody can, unless they reduce it to something that is non-conscious. What we can say has been said by greater minds than ours: you know it when you have it. If I say that consciousness is awareness, that is simply explaining one unknown by another. Calling something you don't understand by another name doesn't do anything. But we know, more or less, when we wake from sleep, that we are awake. We know what it means to be aware of something. But there's no definition. Look it up in the dictionary. You'll find just another synonym. So I think what people mean by consciousness is the ordinary experience that we're having now speaking to one another, looking at each other. When we begin speaking about not only altered states of consciousness but of higher states of consciousness, then there is even less possibility of a clear definition.

P: *There's a popular literature in what we might call consciousness studies, which views consciousness as an independent phenomenon. Many of its theorists and writers seem determined to avoid language that sounds theistic or religious, so today we hear of quantum fields, whereas in the 19th century a term like Oversoul might have been used. By trying to conform to the customary language of science, is something lost?*

JN: Let's take the Oversoul, using it in Emerson's sense. Of course he was reflecting a timeless idea of Hinduism, in a way Buddhism, in a way all of the great spiritual traditions of the world. The Oversoul is a deeply moral, intentional intelligence penetrating all the interstices of reality, the whole universe. And it enters equally into human life when a human being actualizes the possibility of intentionally accessing that action of the Oversoul in his or her own individual self. So, the Oversoul is that in us which really perceives, acts, and wills, according to the good, the overall beneficence of the universe.

What is called the quantum field, however is usually understood as a totally non-intentional, non-conscious field of forces. It is a region in which certain events are taking place involving material entities or electronic entities or nuclear subatomic entities. It's called a field because it's not a thing that you can point to but rather a region, maybe even a region of mathematical space, in which events can and do happen. Now, could we make a bridge between that and the Oversoul? Does this region, does this field, care for human beings? Does the quantum field love? Does it allow you to will the good for your neighbor? It's quite a stretch to try to claim that. But if you say yes, if you say the quantum field does have those qualities, you've simply defined the quantum field as the Oversoul.

P: *The scientific method usually seeks results that can be replicated, and the inner experience of consciousness is not repeatable on those terms.*

JN: In a certain sense such experiences *are* repeatable. Let's take a great modern empirical thinker, David Hume, who shook the world by arguing that all we have in our so-called self are impressions of passing thoughts, emotions, sensations, and perceptions. When I look at the theater of my mind, I see only such impressions one after the other. I have no actual experience of an enduring self. Therefore, he concluded, the belief in the self as an entity subsisting throughout my life is unwarranted.

Hume looked into his mind. But how did he look into his mind? What does it mean to look into yourself? How do you do that? Does everybody understand what that means in the same way? If Hume had had the luck to be near a Zen teacher, unlikely in Scotland at that time, the teacher might have said: "Very good work, David, but you've just begun. Let me show you how to go further. We've worked at this for hundreds and hundreds of years and I'm going to show you a way to do it that can produce even more interesting observations. Sit in this way, hold your hands like this, close your eyes, and follow what I say and just try to work."

In any case, there is a long history of an empiricism that looks into the mind—in Buddhism, in Hinduism, in Sufism, in Christian contemplative tradition, and in the Kabbala. To those who say deep inner experiences can't be scientifically repeated, one can reply that, well, perhaps they can't be induced in a laboratory—although more and more we can measure corresponding neurophysiological phenomena. However, over the centuries, the great spiritual teachings of the world have shown that it is very possible for individuals to come repeatedly to such experiences under precise inner conditions.

The kind of knowledge that can be verified in the scientific sense does not presuppose higher states of consciousness in the investigator. He or she simply has to have a certain ordinary level of sanity, training, and education. But deep inner knowledge, self-knowledge, involves a certain willingness to put one's whole mind, one's whole self, in question. It's a different movement of knowing. It's an inward movement—not the same as with the other sort of knowledge, which is a movement out, that is, a knowledge based on sense perceptions and organized by the logical mind and by mental concepts such as those offered by scientific theory. So in the spiritual traditions there is an interior empiricism, whereas science in general is based on external empiricism.

P: *There are influential educators who tell their students and the media that the time is near when we'll be able to create a computer with what they call consciousness.*

JN: When you think of some of the dogma and some of the metaphysical balloons and some of the fairytales that are pernicious in what we know of religion, you begin to respect that scientific thinkers might want to free us from all that. I'm glad they've done that clean-up job. But it may be just another illusion to assume that in order to know something one must reduce it to elements that submit to scientific analysis.

When we begin to take seriously the idea of higher states of consciousness, this changes everything. This is perhaps the most revolutionary idea of our time: a higher state of consciousness is not a mode, not an alternative state but a higher state. Our waking state is to our sleep as a higher state is to our waking state. Just as we can know things in our waking state that we can't know in our dreaming state, we can know things in a higher state that we can't know in our waking state.

There is what Charles Tart has called state-specific knowledge. We modern men and women are infinitely more capable cognitively in our waking state than when we are asleep in bed. A higher state of consciousness also brings with it its own state-specific knowledge. We can know things in a higher state of consciousness that we cannot even imagine in our ordinary state—no matter how brilliant we are.

It's a revolutionary idea that almost all of our knowledge is state-dependent. As soon as you have sustained access to another state of consciousness, you realize you have an instrument of knowing that is not otherwise available. It casts a new light on what science knows. Not that things are disproved, but that the data and discoveries of modern science can be organized differently and become evidence of a higher level of truth. But this can't be communicated to someone who has not only never experienced a higher state but who also refuses to believe *a priori* that such a state really exists.

P: *Several years ago a colleague of mine said that in the spiritual search, or in the search for consciousness, the body is everything. Do you agree with that?*

JN: What the body is for is the question. Our ordinary mind has a relatively superficial relationship to the body. The body goes along digesting food, regulating instinctive functions, and doing things of unbelievable complexity. Our puny little mind is not directing any of that, obviously. We can sometimes tell the body what to do with a whip, but there's a kind of violence in that. Most of the time the body is going its own way. The body is stronger in that sense.

In meditation you can see that the body really wants to obey something higher. But there's no real authority that the body can respect or even understand most of the time. We all discover in the West, when beginning to try to meditate, that the body resists. It fidgets, it wants to move, tries to tell us that something bad is going to happen if we don't move our leg, and so on. But if the meditator goes on trying to keep the body quite still, the body relaxes a bit; it just doesn't go very far and doesn't last very long.

In one sense, everything's in the body, but in another sense, no. There may be little or no relationship among the fundamental elements that live in the body. Take, for example, a marriage in which two people are fighting each other; they sleep in different rooms. Yet, it's all within the marriage. So to say it's all in the body doesn't say much yet.

I'm trying to point to something experiential. Sooner or later, the body begins to feel respect for that within it which is gently saying to it, don't move, remain still. The body begins to like that. It begins to understand that there's something else within it that it never knew about. In the West, in our contemporary world—I'm not talking about other cultures—the body is accustomed to getting what it wants, or to rebelling inwardly, and waiting for the time to get it in some other way, or resisting, or getting itself cut off.

If the body works in a spiritual discipline, sooner or later it begins to recognize another authority, and it wants to obey that authority: "At last, somebody I can obey. How I have wished for that!" It joyously begins to recognize a master. And that's the beginning of the idea that "everything is in the body." Because then the body itself is suffused by the mind in a way that it isn't usually. Not by thoughts, but by another quality of attention which we haven't spoken about.

There are many images and symbols in the wisdom traditions that show us the human body irradiated by a finer energy, a vibrant sensation, a body full of light. That's the true human body, and everything may very well be in that body. But that's not the body that's going out and smoking cigars and stuffing its face. In fact, our body is more like a place where evolution needs to proceed. It needs to be transformed.

P: *What is the body for? If, as some teachings suggest, the soul is already perfect, if it comes from a perfect reality and it's going to a perfect reality, what is incarnation for?*

JN: The mind can ask questions that the mind alone cannot answer. There are certain questions that are answered only by a state of being, which then can be reflected in words. That's not an evasion, but we have to bear in mind that the only really good questions are those unanswerable questions, and they're the ones that require another state of being in order to really have the answer to them. Woe to us if we stop asking them; but how to ask such questions? What is the body for? Perhaps you could say that it's to be an instrument in the search, to be part of our search.

There's something about the body that's absolutely essential to the development of man's possibilities, of why we are on earth. If we are on earth for a reason, for a purpose, then the body must be there to serve that purpose. It's sort of a backward way of putting it, but there's an idea that God's love, God's creation, God's purpose, requires man—a being who is able intentionally to allow the purposes of the higher to go toward the world of matter and life. And of course if a human being can allow that, he can also not allow that. If we weren't able to block it we wouldn't be able to allow it.

Here we are faced with the age-old drama of human freedom. Man is free, which means there's a certain freedom that makes it possible to become what we are meant to be. To me, it has to do with the possible freedom of our attention, which is perhaps the only really free element in human beings. Such as we are, the possibility of human freedom exists in the attention, and that can carry an influence down into our bodies and into the life of the earth. We become instruments of God. And in the process we become truly human.

P: *Is consciousness given, or is it something that we have to earn?*

JN: It's both. Supposedly it's St. Augustine who said that God provides the wind but man must raise the sails. So consciousness is grace, in a way; it is given. Therefore you don't have to earn it, but the work consists in raising the sail, or preparing the body, if you like, preparing this being to receive the gift that is always being offered. And all the great mystics' teachings are telling us that it's there, it's waiting, it's calling, it's closer than your jugular vein, it's constantly knocking, saying let me in, let me in, and all you have to do is open the door. But that's no mean feat, to open the door. So, it's work. The work is preparing to receive the gift, and that's a struggle.

P: *As this discussion is occurring, everyone is following the case in Florida of a comatose woman and the battle over removing her feeding tube. Can consciousness still be present in such a person?*

JN: [*long silence*] I really don't know that. I don't know. My experience in ethics committees and ethical situations, however, is that when you visit the situation yourself, and use your eyes and ears and heart, and get to know everything you can, your intuitions awaken on the spot. Ninety-five percent of the time the dilemma answers itself. An ethical problem that is intractable in the abstract is often not intractable in the concrete. You *know*. You see a patient, you see the family, and you see what's going on all around the situation. When you are there, once you meditate and reflect on it, it usually answers itself.

P: *Is that why we can't define consciousness in the abstract? It can only be understood through direct experience when it is actively present in oneself?*

JN: That's right. And what light does that throw on these apparently intractable ethical dilemmas? You need the development of an ethical intuition, which is called "conscience." And consciousness without conscience is an abstraction. Consciousness in its ultimate sense is a moral force, not just an intellectual or cognitive one. Reality is suffused with a value component. It's not "value-free." A lot of Western thought ignores Plato—for whom the highest reality is called the Good—and claims instead that fundamentally things either are or are not, and are value-free.

But the element of value is an objective fact. An idea that came into modern Western thought and was highlighted in the scientific revolution in modern Western thought is that it is only "primary" qualities that are measurable and therefore real. Secondary qualities represent only the interaction between the observer and the observed, and tertiary qualities exist only in the observer—in that sense they are not "real." In this view, the *Mona Lisa* is nothing but pigments on canvas in a frame, weighing sixty pounds, or whatever it is. That it is also an intriguing, mystical, beautiful image is not part of the painting, it's only my reaction to the painting. The *Mona Lisa* is just pigments on canvas—that's what it really is in this view—and it only becomes beautiful when someone reacts to it. But the view that I'm speaking of asserts that the *Mona Lisa* is intrinsically beautiful, and that this value is part of its objective reality.

We are surrounded by an assumption that "everything is relative," that Mozart and a Coca-Cola jingle are just music, the value of each depends only on taste: you happen to like Mozart; I happen to like Coca-Cola jingles. Who's to say? And I say, *I'm* to say. Listen to Mozart, learn what Mozart's doing. If I listen to an Indian *raga* and I've never heard it before, I don't know what it is; it's boring. But when somebody can help me understand what's going on, then when I listen to this music, something actually takes place in me. So, it's the same with the universe. The universe is like the *Mona Lisa*. We hear, "It's just atoms and molecules, buddy." But, no, the universe, like *Mona Lisa*, requires the observer—and with the possibility that he brings, the possibility of attention and even of higher states at a certain level, only then can we begin to understand how large the truth really is.

Parabola
Volume: 17.4
Power and Energy

FOOD FOR TRANSFORMATION

P. D. Ouspensky

Ouspensky's recollection of a talk by G. I. Gurdjieff.

G. at once went further.

"We want to 'do,' but" (he began the next lecture) "in everything we do we are tied and limited by the amount of energy produced by our organism. Every function, every state, every action, every thought, every emotion, requires a certain definite energy, a certain definite substance.

"We come to the conclusion that we must 'remember ourselves.' But we can 'remember ourselves' only if we have in us the energy for 'self-remembering.' We can study something, understand or feel something, only if we have the energy for understanding, feeling, or studying.

"What then is a man to do when he begins to realize that he has not enough energy to attain the aims he has set before himself?

"The answer to this is that every normal man has quite enough energy to *begin* work on himself. It is only necessary to learn how to save the greater part of the energy we possess for useful work instead of wasting it unproductively.

"Energy is spent chiefly on unnecessary and unpleasant emotions, on the expectation of unpleasant things, possible and impossible, on bad moods, on unnecessary haste, nervousness, irritability, imagination, daydreaming, and so on. Energy is wasted on the wrong work of centers; on unnecessary tension of the muscles out of all proportion to the work produced; on perpetual chatter which absorbs an enormous amount of energy; on the 'interest' continually taken in things happening around us or to other people and having in fact no interest whatever; on the constant waste of the force of 'attention'; and so on, and so on.

"In beginning to struggle with all these habitual sides of his life a man saves an enormous amount of energy, and with the help of this energy he can easily begin the work of self-study and self-perfection.

"Further on, however, the problem becomes more difficult. Having to a certain extent balanced his machine and ascertained for himself that it produces much more energy than he expected, a man nevertheless comes to the conclusion that this energy is not enough and that, if he wishes to continue his work, he must increase the amount of energy produced.

"The study of the working of the human organism shows this to be quite possible.

"The human organism represents a chemical factory planned for the possibility of a very large output. But in the ordinary conditions of life the output of this factory never reaches the full production possible to it, because only a small part of the machinery is used which produces only the quantity of material necessary to maintain its own existence. Factory work of this kind is obviously uneconomic in the highest degree. The factory actually produces nothing—all its machinery, all its elaborate equipment, actually serve no purpose at all, in that it maintains only with difficulty its own existence.

"The work of the factory consists in transforming one kind of matter into another, namely, the coarser matters, in the cosmic sense, into finer ones. The factory receives, as raw material from the outer world, a number of coarse 'hydrogens' and transforms them into finer hydrogens by means of a whole series of complicated *alchemical* processes. But in the ordinary conditions of life the production by the human factory of the finer 'hydrogens,' in which, from the point of view of the possibility of higher states of consciousness and the work of higher centers, we are particularly interested, is insufficient and they are all wasted on the existence of the factory itself. If we could succeed in bringing the production up to its possible maximum we should then begin to save the fine 'hydrogens.' Then the whole of the body, all the tissues, all the cells, would become saturated with these fine 'hydrogens' which would gradually settle in them, crystallizing in a special way. This crystallization of the fine 'hydrogens' would gradually bring the whole organism onto a higher level, onto a higher plane of being.

"This, however, cannot happen in the ordinary conditions of life, because the 'factory' expends all that it produces.

"All the substances necessary for the maintenance of the life of the organism, for psychic work, for the higher functions of consciousness and the growth of the higher bodies, are produced by the organism from the food which enters it from outside.

"The human organism receives three kinds of food:

1. The ordinary food we eat;
2. The air we breathe;
3. Our impressions.

"It is not difficult to agree that air is a kind of food for the organism. But in what way impressions can be food may appear at first difficult to understand. We must however remember that, with every external impression, whether it takes the form of sound, or vision, or smell, we receive from outside a certain amount of energy, a certain number of vibrations; this energy which enters the organism from outside is food. Moreover, as has been said before, energy cannot be transmitted without matter. If an external impression brings external energy with it into the organism it means that external matter also enters which feeds the organism in the full meaning of the term.

"For its normal existence the organism must receive all three kinds of food, that is, physical food, air, and impressions. The organism cannot exist on one or even two kinds of food, all three are required. But the relation of these foods to one another and their significance for the organism is not the same. The organism can exist for a comparatively long time without a supply of fresh physical food. Cases of starvation are known lasting for over sixty days, when the organism lost none of its vitality and recovered very quickly as soon as it began to take food. Of course starvation of this kind cannot be considered as complete, since in all cases of such artificial starvation people have taken water. Nevertheless, even without water a man can live without food for several days. Without air he can exist only a few minutes, not more than two or three; as a rule a man dies after being four minutes without air. Without impressions a man cannot live a single moment. If the flow of impressions were to be stopped in some way or if the organism were deprived of its capacity for receiving impressions, it would immediately die. The flow of impressions coming to us from outside is like a driving belt communicating motion to us. The principal motor for us is nature, the surrounding world. Nature transmits to us through our impressions the energy by which we live and move and have our being. If the inflow of this energy is arrested, our machine will immediately stop working. Thus, of the three kinds of food the most important for us is impressions, although it stands to reason that a man cannot exist for long on impressions alone. Impressions and air enable a man to exist a little longer. Impressions, air, and physical food enable the organism to live to the end of its normal term of life and to produce the substances necessary not only for the maintenance of life, but also for the creation and growth of higher bodies."

CONTRIBUTOR PROFILES

Henry Barnes is former Chairman of the Board of the Association of Waldorf Schools of North America. He is the author of *A Life for the Spirit: Rudolph Steiner in the Crosscurrents of Our Time* and *Into the Heart's Land: A Century of Rudolph Steiner's Work in North America.*

Peter Brook is director of the International Center of Theater Research in Paris and former director of the Royal Shakespeare Company. His many pioneering theatrical productions include *Marat/Sade, A Midsummer Night's Dream,* and *The Mahabharata.* In collaboration with Jeanne de Salzmann, he directed the film *Meetings with Remarkable Men.*

Pauline de Dampierre (1911-2003) met Gurdjieff in 1942 and later became one of the principal leaders of the work in Paris and one of the closest pupils of Jeanne de Salzmann.

René Daumal (1913-1944), poet, writer and Sanskrit scholar, was one of the founders of the avant-garde journal *Le Grand Jeu.* From 1930 until his death he worked closely with Jeanne de Salzmann and Gurdjieff. Among his celebrated books and essays, *Mount Analogue* stands out as one of the most sensitive evocations of the nature of the Gurdjieff teaching.

Margaret Flinsch, a longtime student of Gurdjieff and a principal leader of the work of the Gurdjieff Foundation in New York, founded one of the first nursery schools in America in the 1920s and more recently established the Blue Rock School of West Nyack, New York.

Christopher Fremantle (1906-1978) was a student of both Ouspensky and Gurdjieff and continued his work with Jeanne de Salzmann in Paris and New York. He led numerous groups in the United States and Mexico and wrote *On Attention,* a practical approach to the spiritual search.

Martha Heyneman is a poet, essayist, and author of *The Breathing Cathedral: Feeling Our Way into a Living Cosmos.* She met the Gurdjieff teaching through Hugh Ripman in 1952 in Washington, D.C.

Mitch Horowitz is a writer and publisher of many years experience with a lifelong interest in man's search for meaning. The editor-in-chief of Tarcher/Penguin in New York, he is completing a book, *Occult America: The Secret History of How Mysticism Conquered America*, to be published by Bantam. At Tarcher/Penguin, Horowitz has published some of today's leading titles in world religion, esoterica, and the metaphysical.

Roger Lipsey is the author of numerous books on art and spirituality, most recently *Angelic Mistakes: The Art of Thomas Merton.*

Jacob Needleman is Professor of Philosophy at San Francisco State University and the author of numerous books, including *The American Soul* and *Why Can't We Be Good?*

Maurice Nicoll (1884-1953) was a practicing psychiatrist and close pupil of C. G. Jung. He met P. D. Ouspensky in 1921 and in 1922 went for a year to work with Gurdjieff at the Prieuré in Fontainebleau, France. From 1931 until his death he conducted groups based on the Gurdjieff ideas and authored several books, including, most notably *The New Man, Living Time* and the five-volume series, *Psychological Commentaries on the Teaching of Gurdjieff and Ouspensky.*

Alfred R. Orage (1873-1934) was editor of *The New Age*, one of the most celebrated and influential journals of literature, politics and the arts of its time in England and also in America. In 1914 he met P. D. Ouspensky, who introduced him to Gurdjieff in 1922. In 1924 Gurdjieff appointed Orage to lead study groups in America.

P. D. Ouspensky (1878-1947) is best known as the author of *In Search of the Miraculous*, the most masterful and influential account of the Gurdjieff teaching written by a pupil. A profound and celebrated spiritual philosopher in his own right, he met Gurdjieff in Moscow

in 1915 and was a close pupil until his separation from Gurdjieff
in the 1920s, after which he led his own groups and community of
inner work, based mainly in England, until his death.

John Pentland (1907-1984) was a student of the Ouspenskys,
Gurdjieff and Jeanne de Salzmann, and was instrumental in spreading
Gurdjieff's teaching throughout the United States. He was President
of the Gurdjieff Foundation of New York from its inception in 1953,
and established the Gurdjieff Foundation of California.

Ravi Ravindra is Professor Emeritus at Dalhousie University, Hali-
fax, Canada, from where he retired as Professor of Physics and of
Comparative Religion. Among his books is *Heart Without Measure:
Gurdjieff Work with Madame de Salzmann.*

Paul Reynard (1927-2005) studied painting in Paris under Fernand
Léger and came to New York in 1968. Working closely with
Jeanne de Salzmann, he was given the responsibility for the sacred
dances known as the Movements in the Gurdjieff Foundation of
New York as well as in the Gurdjieff foundations of California and
Canada. He later became one of the main leaders of the work in
North America.

Laurence Rosenthal is a composer, pianist and conductor whose
work includes musical scores for numerous major motion pictures,
notably *The Miracle Worker* and *Becket.* He composed the score
for the film *Meetings with Remarkable Men*, which included the
arrangement and orchestration of many of the pieces composed by
Gurdjieff and de Hartmann.

Jeanne de Salzmann (1889-1990) was Gurdjieff's chief pupil and
was responsible for transmitting the teachings, including the
Movements and the essential dynamics of all the forms of the
Work, after Gurdjieff's death in 1949. Based in Paris, she brought
the Work to many of the major centers of the Work throughout
the world, especially the Gurdjieff Foundations in Paris, New York
and Caracas, and the Gurdjieff Society in London.

Michel de Salzmann (1923-2001) was trained in medicine, neurology and psychiatry at the University of Paris in the years following World War II. He was one of the most widely respected and influential leaders of the Gurdjieff Work throughout the world and served as President of the Gurdjieff Foundation in Paris for the last several years of his life.

William Segal (1904-2000) was a pupil of P. D. Ouspensky, Gurdjieff, and Jeanne de Salzmann and was also closely associated with the Zen Buddhist tradition and several of its leading teachers and interpreters, including Daisetz Suzuki. His paintings have been exhibited in numerous galleries in New York, Tokyo and Jerusalem, and several collections of his writings have been published, along with a comprehensive collection of articles by and about him, entitled *A Voice at the Borders of Silence.*

Henri Tracol (1909-1997) was a close pupil of Gurdjieff for over ten years. Together with Jeanne de Salzmann he was one of the leading exponents of Gurdjieff's teaching in Paris and throughout the world, and in his later years was President of the Gurdjieff Institute in Paris. *A Taste for Things That Are True*, a collection of his talks and essays, is due to be republished in revised and augmented form by Sandpoint Press, an imprint of Morning Light Press.

P. L. Travers (1899-1996) was the creator of the famous fictional nanny Mary Poppins, of the book of the same name. She met Gurdjieff in Paris in the 1930s and later became one of the senior leaders in the work in London.

Michel Waldberg lives in France, where he is a widely published author, poet and translator. Among his numerous books is *Gurdjieff: An Approach to His Ideas.*

FOR FURTHER READING

Books by Gurdjieff

All and Everything is the inclusive title Gurdjieff gave to the three volumes of his major writings. These volumes are individually titled *Beelzebub's Tales to His Grandson, Meetings with Remarkable Men* and *Life Is Real Only Then, When "I Am"*. Gurdjieff referred to them as the First, Second and Third Series of his writings.

Gurdjieff, G. I. *Beelzebub's Tales to His Grandson*. New York: Harcourt Brace, 1950 and New York: Jeremy P. Tarcher/Penguin, rev. 2006.

Long read and respected and perennially in print, the 1950 edition was edited by A. R. Orage on the basis of a literal English text prepared from Gurdjieff's original Russian and Armenian by pupils at the Institute for the Harmonious Development of Man. This version may become the reader's preference. However, the revised translation, initially published in 1992 and republished with corrections in 2006, should also be read. This edition reflects to some extent the greater ease of expression of the French edition of 1956 and also benefited from direct access to the original Russian text, published in 2000 by Traditional Studies Press (Toronto). Both versions of the book can be trusted.

_____. *Meetings with Remarkable Men*. New York: Dutton, 1963.

_____. *Life Is Real Only Then, When "I Am"*. New York: Dutton, 1982.

_____. *Views from the Real World: Early Talks of Gurdjieff As Recollected by his Pupils*. New York: Dutton, 1973.

Accounts by Direct Pupils

Ouspensky, P. D. *In Search of the Miraculous*. New York: Harcourt Brace, 1949.

This book may be given a special significance in this list of reliable recommended works. Since its first publication in 1949, Ouspensky's *In Search of the Miraculous* has served as the most artful, electrifying and profound account written by a pupil. As noted by Michel de Salzmann in his bibliographic essay contained in this volume, Ouspensky's book retains a remarkable strength and freshness to this day and continues to help readers at all levels of preparation and acquaintance with the Gurdjieff teaching. For many it remains the book of choice for those approaching the teaching for the first time.

de Hartmann, Thomas and Olga. *Our Life with Mr. Gurdjieff*. New York: Cooper Square, 1962.

Several revised and enlarged editions have been published over the years. The most recent and definitive: Sandpoint, ID: Sandpoint Press, an imprint of Morning Light Press, 2008. This book describes the dangerous flight by Gurdjieff and a handful of pupils out of war-torn revolutionary Russia, ending with the establishment of the Prieuré community in France.

Lannes, Henriette. *This Fundamental Quest*. San Francisco: Far West Institute, 2007.

Henriette Lannes was responsible in later years for the study of the Gurdjieff teaching in Lyon (France) and London.

Pentland, John. *Exchanges Within*. New York: Continuum, 1997.

John Pentland was immensely influential in the transmission of the Gurdjieff teaching in America.

de Salzmann, Michel. "Man's Ever New and Eternal Challenge." In *On the Way to Self Knowledge*. New York: Alfred A. Knopf, 1976, pp. 54-83.

_____. "Seeing: The Endless Source of Inner Freedom." *Material for Thought* 14, pp. 12-30. Michel de Salzmann was both a trained psychiatrist and one of the most respected leaders of the work throughout the world.

Segal, William. *A Voice at the Borders of Silence*. New York: The Overlook Press, 2003. William Segal was for many years a leading figure in the development of the Gurdjieff Work in America.

Tracol, Henri. *The Taste for Things That Are True*. Longmead, Shaftesbury, Dorset: Element Books, Ltd., 1994. Henri Tracol was a pupil of Gurdjieff for over ten years and worked as a leader of the work closely alongside Jeanne de Salzmann in the years following Gurdjieff's death.

The following books seem to the editor of the present volume to be among the most honest attempts by pupils of Gurdjieff to depict the personal impact of the man and his way of teaching:

Anderson, Margaret. *The Unknowable Gurdjieff*. New York: Weiser, 1962.

Hands, Rina. *Diary of Madame Egout Pour Sweet*. Aurora, OR: Two Rivers Press, 1991.

Hulme, Kathyrn. *Undiscovered Country*. Boston: Little Brown, 1966.

Nott, C. S. *Teachings of Gurdjieff: The Journal of a Pupil*. London: Routledge & Kegan Paul, 1961.

Peters, Fritz. *Boyhood with Gurdjieff*. Fairfax, CA: Arete Communications, 2005.

Tchekhovitch, Tcheslaw. *Gurdjieff: A Master in Life*. Toronto: Dolmen Meadow Editions, 2006.

Zuber, René. *Who Are You, Monsieur Gurdjieff?* London: Routledge & Kegan Paul, 1980.

Accounts by Other Pupils of the Gurdjieff Work

Ravindra, Ravi. *Heart Without Measure*. Sandpoint, ID: Morning Light Press, 1999. The first published account of the teaching of Jeanne de Salzmann, Gurdjieff's greatest pupil, who was responsible for the work after his death.

Vaysse, Jean. *Toward Awakening*. San Francisco: Far West Undertakings, 1978. Written by a long-time pupil of Jeanne de Salzmann, this concise exposition clarifies much that has seemed obscure in the Gurdjieff teaching.

Also Recommended

Driscoll, J. Walter, and the Gurdjieff Foundation of California. *Gurdjieff: An Annotated Bibliography* (New York: Garland Publishing, 1985).

Guide and Index to Beelzebub's Tales to His Grandson. 2nd ed. Toronto: Traditional Studies Press, 2003.

Gurdjieff International Review: see: www.gurdjieff.org

Material for Thought, journal published occasionally in San Francisco by the Gurdjieff Foundation of California under the imprint of Far West Editions. See: www.farwesteditions.com.

Needleman, Jacob and George Baker, eds. *Gurdjieff: Essays and Reflections on the Man and His Teaching*. New York: Continuum, 2004.

The essay in this volume called "The First Initiation" had been attributed to Jeanne de Salzmann. The article is now attributed to G. I. Gurdjieff.

Music

Recommended Recordings (commercially available):

The Music of Gurdjieff/de Hartmann. Performed by Thomas de Hartmann. 3-CD set. Triangle Records.

In these essential recordings one feels immediately the authority of the composer's interpretation of his own music, although de Hartmann was not always aware that his performances were being recorded. Thus certain pieces contain spontaneous departures from the printed text. The original recordings were made largely on an early, somewhat primitive, wire recorder. Many years later the transfer to LP, and eventually to CD, included an electronic process designed to clarify the sound and eliminate extraneous noises and background hiss. In the course of this improvement, some of the vitality and immediacy of de Hartmann's playing may have been lost. Nevertheless, the authenticity of these recordings make this a definitive historical document and an invaluable reference.

Gurdjieff/de Hartmann Music for the Piano. Vols. 1-4. Perf. Linda Daniel-Spitz, Charles Ketcham, and Laurence Rosenthal. Schott Wergo Music Media.

These performances were recorded by the three editors of the published complete musical works. This edition was produced under the guidance of Mme. Jeanne de Salzmann. A major feature of these four CDs is that they comprise a complete recording of the four volumes of the published music, presented in the same order. Thus it is possible for the listener to follow in sequence the printed scores.

Gurdjieff/de Hartmann. Vols. 1-10. (Various titles: "Meditations," "Music of the Sayyids and Dervishes," "Hymn for Christmas Day," "First Dervish Prayer," "Circles," etc.). Performed by Alain Kremski. Producers, Maria and Michel Bernstein.

Alain Kremski's interpretations are often imaginative and unusual, and always there is great authority in his playing and technique. Although the music for the Gurdjieff Movements is generally not designed to be heard separately from the dances themselves, Kremski has elected to include many examples of de Hartmann's music for the Movements in these collections.

Gurdjieff/de Hartmann. Vols. 1-2. Performed by Laurence Rosenthal. Windemere.

These recent recordings, part of a series still in progress, were made by a composer and pianist with a long association with the Gurdjieff/de Hartmann music. Rosenthal arranged and orchestrated many of these pieces for inclusion in the musical score of Peter Brook's film *Meetings with Remarkable Men*. The CD of the score for the film is available from Citadel Records.

Film

Meetings with Remarkable Men. Directed by Peter Brook. Remar Productions, Inc., 1978.

DVD included with this volume distributed by Morning Light Press, Sandpoint, ID.

Call of the Tradition and Chapter Citations

1 P. D. Ouspensky, *In Search of the Miraculous* (New York: Harcourt Brace, 1949) p. 145.

2 G. I. Gurdjieff, "Aphorism 4," *Views from the Real World* (New York: Dutton, 1973) p. 272.

3 Gurdjieff, *Views,* pp. 57-59.

4 G. I. Gurdjieff, "The First Initiation." Reprinted by permission of Triangle Editions. In Needleman and Baker, eds., *Gurdjieff: Essays and Reflections,* p.6.

5 G. I. Gurdjieff, *All and Everything: Beelzebub's Tales to His Grandson* (New York: Harcourt Brace, 1950), p. 368.

6 "The source of that which does not change ..." de Salzmann, Jeanne, "The Awakening of Thought." In Needleman and Baker, eds., *Gurdjieff: Essays and Reflections,* p. 3.

Photography Credits

Cover Photo: Courtesy of The Gurdjieff Foundation of New York

Spine Photo: © Institut G. I. Gurdjieff

Back Page photo: Screen capture from *Meetings with Remarkable Men.* Dir. Peter Brook. Remar Productions, Inc., 1978.